HENRY VIII'S CHILDREN

As always, to my most precious children, Grayson, Torben, Aelia, and Lachlan

HENRY VIII'S CHILDREN

Legitimate and Illegitimate Sons and Daughters of the Tudor King

Caroline Angus

PEN & SWORD HISTORY

AN IMPRINT OF PEN & SWORD BOOKS LTD.
YORKSHIRE – PHILADELPHIA

First published in Great Britain in 2023 by
PEN AND SWORD HISTORY
An imprint of
Pen & Sword Books Ltd
Yorkshire – Philadelphia

Copyright © Caroline Angus, 2023

ISBN 978 1 39909 586 0

The right of Caroline Angus to be identified as Author of this work has been asserted by her in accordance with the Copyright, Designs and Patents Act 1988.

A CIP catalogue record for this book is available from the British Library.

All rights reserved. No part of this book may be reproduced or transmitted in any form or by any means, electronic or mechanical including photocopying, recording or by any information storage and retrieval system, without permission from the Publisher in writing.

Typeset in Times New Roman 11/13.5 by
SJmagic DESIGN SERVICES, India.
Printed and bound in the UK by CPI Group (UK) Ltd.

Pen & Sword Books Limited incorporates the imprints of Atlas, Archaeology, Aviation, Discovery, Family History, Fiction, History, Maritime, Military, Military Classics, Politics, Select, Transport, True Crime, Air World, Frontline Publishing, Leo Cooper, Remember When, Seaforth Publishing, The Praetorian Press, Wharncliffe Local History, Wharncliffe Transport, Wharncliffe True Crime and White Owl.

For a complete list of Pen & Sword titles please contact
PEN & SWORD BOOKS LIMITED
George House, Units 12 & 13, Beevor Street, Off Pontefract Road,
Barnsley, South Yorkshire, S71 1HN, England
E-mail: enquiries@pen-and-sword.co.uk
Website: www.pen-and-sword.co.uk

Or
PEN AND SWORD BOOKS
1950 Lawrence Rd, Havertown, PA 19083, USA
E-mail: Uspen-and-sword@casematepublishers.com
Website: www.penandswordbooks.com

Contents

Preface		vi
Chapter 1	Two Tudor Princes	1
Chapter 2	Prince Henry, Duke of Cornwall and the Heirs Lost to Fate	9
Chapter 3	An English Princess	19
Chapter 4	A Son at Last	28
Chapter 5	Princess Mary: Queen or Empress?	36
Chapter 6	Henry Fitzroy, Ruler of the North	51
Chapter 7	The Princess of Wales	61
Chapter 8	The Destruction of a Royal Family	75
Chapter 9	A Worldly Jewel Lost	83
Chapter 10	A Reformist Princess	99
Chapter 11	Finally, A Male Heir	121
Chapter 12	Changing Queens, Changing Fortunes	127
Chapter 13	The Education of Heirs and Leaders	140
Chapter 14	A Tudor Born to Rule	155
Chapter 15	The Reputation of a Royal Sister	160
Conclusion	Triumph of the True Queens	169
Epilogue	The Illegitimate Children of Henry VIII	174
Bibliography		193
Illustrations		199
Endnotes		201
Index		219

Preface

King Henry VIII's struggles to have a legitimate son are well known. Henry's paranoid desperation for a son to rule after him gave rise to the largest social upheaval England had faced, outshining anything he achieved in his reign. Henry spared no one in his ever-changing quest. From those close to Henry, to strangers who could only worship the way he approved, the people of England, Wales and Ireland were forever damaged by one man's inability to see his daughter as a leader.

King Henry is noted as a man who would promote from outside his class, bringing in common-born men such as Thomas Wolsey and Thomas Cromwell to rule in his place, but Henry holds one other distinction; he was the king who constantly married for love. While there had been royal love matches in the past, usually with varying degrees of carnage, Henry relentlessly pursued his desires ahead of the needs of his country. No one else could dare make such a reckless choice.

King Henry and Katharine of Aragon were the perfect couple, only to have their close relationship marred by grief and misery. Katharine was the stronger one of the pair, but Henry held all the power. But when the king noticed the unsuspecting Anne Boleyn, their affair gave rise to the destruction of the Catholic Church in England. Henry's infatuation with Anne existed purely on what she could provide him, never what he offered in return. As soon as Anne could not deliver Henry's impossible demand, she was murdered to make space for another woman. Jane Seymour could deliver a son but never really captured her husband's heart. A diplomatic marriage with Anna of Cleves caused chaos at home and abroad as Henry acted like a fool, only to rebound into a love affair with teenager Katheryn Howard, who was beheaded like her Boleyn cousin. Kateryn Parr was roped into something she did not want and was soon forgotten by her husband as he focused only on himself.

Underneath the drama of Henry's marriages and the social upheavals they created, four children, Princess Mary, Henry Fitzroy, Princess Elizabeth and Prince Edward, lived with the consequences of King Henry's desires. All were fit to rule England, and yet, for Henry, they were never enough.

Preface

They had their own lives and stories as they grew up in the shadow of a tyrant they would love and sometimes loathe. Princess Mary was forced to watch her father's obsession with a male heir as her future slipped from her grasp. Henry Fitzroy lived a life of potential and neglect. Princess Elizabeth was a child born of intense love and left to see the misery that romance created. Prince Edward was treated as a prize, a symbol, never a person, a boy crying out for love that would never come. For these four children, as their childhoods stretched into teenage years and then adulthood, the scars of Henry's desperation for a legitimate son would forever leave a mark on their political and romantic decisions.

While King Henry removed the titles of princess from Mary and Elizabeth, this book does not, as a mark of respect to the daughters left in the wake of their father's behaviour. King Henry VIII may have had his precious son, but the Tudor line died because of Henry's behaviour and the decisions his children had to bear.

Chapter 1

Two Tudor Princes

While the pressure to provide a son and heir for the realm had always been an essential task for a royal couple, in 1486, the need would have felt acute for newly crowned Henry VII and his bride Elizabeth of York. Henry Tudor was born with little claim to the English throne in 1457. His father was Edmund Tudor, half-brother to King Henry VI, but the Tudors had a better claim to the French throne through Edmund's mother Catherine of Valois. Henry's mother, Margaret Beaufort had a claim to the English throne; her father was John Beaufort, Duke of Somerset, grandson of John of Gaunt. Gaunt was King Edward III's son, but his illegitimate line of children was excluded from the succession.[1] Heirs born to women like Margaret Beaufort were no threat – no male line of succession, no crown. When Edward IV deposed Henry VI in 1461, the Tudor claim diminished further, and Henry Tudor, who was being raised by his mother (who was only thirteen when her son was born), was placed in a Yorkist household. But a decade later, when battles had decimated both sides of the War of the Roses, fourteen-year-old Henry Tudor was the last man standing with a Lancastrian claim. Nothing but life in exile in Brittany with his uncle Jasper Tudor awaited Henry through his formative years. Fate was often cruel to male heirs, and when Edward IV died and his young sons disappeared, Richard III had to take over, but his son also died young. Henry Tudor was suddenly one of the last alive to claim the English crown. The battle of Bosworth commenced; Henry Tudor won the crown. A male heir now meant everything in the fragile new world of 1485.

Only now would a female heir be helpful. Elizabeth of York, eldest daughter of Edward IV, stepped forward to marry Henry Tudor, and finally, the Lancastrian and Yorkist heirs of Edward III were again united (the couple being third cousins, not close enough cause any issues[2]). Just eight months after the wedding, Queen Elizabeth gave birth to a son, Arthur.[3] The kings and their heirs who came before Henry and Arthur were plagued with disaster; child heirs dying of illness, disappearances, war, fractious uncles, heirs at odds with their fathers, feckless grandsons, promising heirs cut down in their prime, incompetent kings deposed by their sons, the list goes on. If the Tudors, a dynasty started by a French queen falling in love with a Welsh servant, were to rule England, legitimacy on the throne would come through healthy, legitimate, male offspring.

King Henry and Queen Elizabeth understood their task; Henry had come to the crown in battle, and Elizabeth was the eldest child of a crowned king. Prince Arthur was the shining beacon of perfection for a precarious country emerging from endless war. Born in September 1486, Arthur became the Duke of Cornwall at birth, the title of the rightful heir.[4] Children were to 'live among the women', and under nurse Katharine Gibbs,[5] until the age of six or seven, Arthur had a safe and happy upbringing.

In 1489, the year Princess Margaret was born,[6] Arthur became the Prince of Wales and Earl of Chester by right as heir to the throne.[7] By this time, as a three-year-old and a duke, Arthur had his own household, paid for with the revenues he earned from the Cornwall duchy. Arthur was strong and healthy, already had a sister, and several battles had been fought and lost by those ready to take power from his father. In March 1489, Arthur's claim was further legitimised, when King Ferdinand and Queen Isabella of Spain agreed their youngest daughter Katharine would be the future queen of England at Arthur's side. The Treaty of Medina del Campo showed the new Tudor dynasty's place among the elite of Europe.[8] Katharine of Aragon had been born a year before Arthur, and styled as Princess of Wales in her childhood, awaiting the day she would move to England.

While Princess Margaret's birth was fortuitous in 1489, Prince Henry's birth in June 1491 was more welcome, a second son, a spare heir. Yet Henry's birth was not celebrated or championed like Arthur's. Henry was simply a back-up plan, another healthy child born to a happy couple. Henry's birth went entirely unrecorded, save for a note written in Margaret Beaufort's Book of Hours. Prince Henry was born at Greenwich Palace and christened just after his 28 June birth at the Observant Friars beside the palace.[9] Henry was nursed by a woman named Anne Locke, as Queen Elizabeth needed to get on with the business of having another child.[10] While Arthur was being carefully raised in a fine household with the best of everything, Prince Henry does not rate a single mention during his early years. As his sister Princess Elizabeth was born a year after Henry, he was likely raised alongside the new baby and older sister Princess Margaret. They would have lived within the court, and Henry only received a title in April 1493, when he became Constable of Leeds Castle and Lord Warden of the Cinque Ports.[11] By this time, Arthur had become the Keeper of England when his father was away. But in late 1494, Henry gained a new promotion as Lieutenant of Ireland.[12] Deputies were obviously working in

Henry's place, but the role in Ireland was a significant one, and not given to Arthur. This showed Prince Henry did have a place, roles in simpler positions behind Prince Arthur. King Henry had bigger plans for his namesake son, installing him as a Knight of the Bath and Duke of York.[13] The second title was important; routinely given to the second royal heir, the York imposter Perkin Warbeck had already claimed the title without merit. Prince Henry needed to be named the second legitimate heir to the crown and ward off Warbeck's claims he was the true king of England ahead of his 'sister's' husband.

For the investiture, the royal family travelled from their palaces at Richmond and Eltham, and Prince Henry paraded through London on 28 October to a state dinner at Westminster. Young Henry also took part in the ceremony of becoming a Knight of the Bath, where he and thirty other men were installed, where they were bathed as part of a spiritual purification, and ceremonially put to bed before keeping vigil in the chapel, though Henry was likely past his bedtime at that stage. The following morning Henry was reportedly well-behaved as the Duke of Buckingham and Marquess of Dorset placed spurs on his heels while the king dubbed him a knight. Prince Henry himself laid his sword at the altar after the ceremony, again with an adult chaperone, before retiring to his chambers while the other knights took part in the traditional banquet.[14] The young boy needed the rest; the following morning on 1 November, Henry, wearing miniature robes of the Garter, was installed as Duke of York by his father in front of the highest nobles in the country. The role came with an income of 50,000l a year (almost £34,000,000 today). Ceremonial jousting tournaments were held between 9-12 November, attended by the royal couple, Margaret Beaufort, styled as the king's mother, and the royal children, with Princess Margaret giving out prizes.[15] Whether three-year-old Henry could keep his attention on the events is unrecorded, though if the prince acted up, it is unlikely any writer was keen to make a note.

Prince Henry did not gain his own household after becoming a duke, continuing this life in the nursery, still taught by his mother, as evidenced in surviving handwriting showing Elizabeth teaching Henry (and his younger sister) to write. Tragedy struck the royal nursery in September 1495, when Princess Elizabeth died of illness at Eltham Palace, aged three. Queen Elizabeth was newly pregnant at the time, giving birth to Princess Mary six months later. It may have been these upheavals that prompted the royal couple to start preparing their son for his education outside his mother's care. Prince Arthur was already ten years old at Mary's birth, and under the care of Bernard Andre, learning a curriculum organised by

King Henry. In 1497, a similar education was prescribed for Prince Henry, with a tutor named Mr Holt, followed by John Skelton, who would spend the next five years caring for the boy. Henry's topics were the same as Arthur's household, heavy on scripture, including the vulgate Bible, and Roman classics.[16]

By the time Prince Edmund was born in 1499, Henry still did not have his own household, living in the royal nursery despite his age. Records show Henry still spent time with his sisters and infant Prince Edmund, as renowned scholar Desiderius Erasmus visited the royal nursery at Eltham Palace in late 1499. Young Henry asked Erasmus to write him something to keep, causing the scholar to sweat for three days creating something suitable for a prince. But in June 1500, Prince Edmund died while the royal children were together at Hatfield in Herefordshire, where they had moved from Eltham to hide from the plague. The king and queen had sailed for Calais and Prince Arthur was in his own household preparing to meet his Spanish bride. The royal couple returned from their trip to France to find their youngest son had been carried off by illness and buried alongside his infant sister Elizabeth at Westminster.[17] After the plague season eased, this may have been the time Henry, at nine years old, had his own household established within the court, and later documents show Henry's household of 102 men and thirteen women working for the prince.[18] With such a hefty income from the duchy of York, the household could afford the best, and Henry was taught by schoolmaster John Skelton, Giles Duwes was Henry's French teacher, with Thomas Simpson, master-at-arms organising the household. Henry kept busy in his classroom, and Skelton wrote a *Speculum Principis,* a guide to being a king, though, in theory, the prince would never need such a guide. Prince Henry was especially skilled at music, and yet the only teacher for such subjects is listed as 'William', as schoolmaster of pipes. Henry's teachers praised the boy as an exceptional rider, shooter, and tennis player, and yet no record of who helped him with these remains, possibly Thomas Simpson, or the controller of King Henry's household Sir Richard Guildford. With Henry's household running independently of the royal household payments, sadly many of the records have been lost to time.

Prince Henry's first public duty is well-recorded; he was part of the procession when fifteen-year-old Katharine of Aragon married Prince Arthur on 14 November 1501.[19] Henry was only ten years old at the time but was able to play an influential role in the dancing after the wedding, already talented and with a love of pageantry. The boy would have continued living in relative obscurity had Prince Arthur not fallen ill and died on 2 April 1502.[20] Given the five-year age gap and the fact Arthur and Henry never lived in the same household, they were unlikely to have ever been close, nothing like Henry's relationship with his sisters. Losing a sibling was less of a consideration, as suddenly the realm needed another male heir. Prince Henry would have seen the extreme grief of his parents in the loss of their precious, well-rounded, and crafted eldest son.[21] Katharine of Aragon was now a princess without her prince, with their impeccably curated world stolen when Arthur perished at Ludlow Castle in Wales.

Meanwhile, already nearing his eleventh birthday, Henry's future wife would be Marguerite of Angoulême, sister to future King Francis of France.[22] Arthur had created a Spanish alliance through marriage, and Henry was to do the same with France. A Valois alliance was important, but nothing compared to Arthur's alliance with the house of Trastamara. Spanish King Ferdinand of Aragon wanted to keep their alliance with England, and England needed their support. Prince Henry may not have known he had become a bargaining chip, but negotiations for him to marry Princess Katharine began as early as September 1502. Katharine had been prepared to be England's queen as a toddler (despite also being the heir to her father's half of the Spanish throne) and was prepared to marry Prince Henry when the time came, as Katharine was as levelheaded as the adults in the discussion.

But nothing was more important than a male heir to stabilise the Tudor dynasty, and King Henry and Queen Elizabeth needed to have another son, with two of their three boys already buried. Elizabeth became pregnant just a month after Arthur's death, such was the need to steady their country. Life in Prince Henry's household continued as normal while his parents sought to steady the succession, but on 11 February 1503, Queen Elizabeth died of childbirth complications just nine days after the birth of a daughter, Catherine, who also did not survive.[23] Henry had been raised alongside his sisters, and not long out of a household of maternal nurturing. Now his beloved mother was gone, and his father, who had been putting in the challenging work to make Arthur a suitable heir, was profoundly devastated. A portrait portraying Queen Elizabeth's empty throne next to King Henry was created soon after Arthur and Elizabeth's deaths, and it shows young Henry in the far corner hunched over, crying for his mother.[24]

Suddenly, being the second son was not a secure position, for King Henry could now remarry and have more children. While the king had no desire to ever replace his beloved Elizabeth, he was a king without a wife, and subject to rumour and speculation from international cohorts. Alliances beckoned, but King Henry kept the post of queen wide open and should have been preparing his young son to inherit, but this did not happen. Instead, King Henry focused on keeping the Spanish alliance by holding teenage widow Katharine of Aragon in England, signing the treaty for her to marry Prince Henry in late 1503. But by the end of 1503, Henry was still only twelve, and could he rule if his grieving and ever-more reclusive father followed his wife to the grave? King Henry made the decision for those wondering, as on 18 February 1504, Prince Henry became Prince of Wales, Duke of Cornwall and Earl of Chester, the titles of the heir to the throne. It should have been a glorious time, celebrated with jousts and pageants just as Henry's elevation to Duke of York had received ten years earlier. But it did not gain any celebration, just an act in parliament ratifying the changes.[25]

Prince Henry's life continued as it was, though known as the heir-apparent, and living off the lucrative duchy of Cornwall rather than the duchy of York. The only other change was the loss of his sister Princess Margaret, who was forced north to Scotland to marry King James IV at only fourteen years old.[26] At least Henry still had his favourite sister Mary, and his grandmother Margaret Beaufort in his life. Henry's household shifted between the royal palaces at Greenwich, Eltham, Richmond, Windsor and Westminster, an endless cycle of cloistered lifestyles, but this also meant he could spend time with his remaining relatives.

As the second throne in England sat empty, another became available when Katharine of Aragon's mother Queen Isabella of Castile died, leaving her daughter devastated and a long way from her family. Katharine was living in England waiting for Henry to grow up, but the death of her beloved power-wielding mother was a tragic blow. Isabella was a queen in her own right, and her husband King Ferdinand was the ruler of Aragon, the pair combining to rule Spain. Isabella had named Juana, her eldest daughter as heir. Juana and her husband Archduke Philip, son of Holy Roman Emperor Maximilian, took the throne by right, leaving King Ferdinand vulnerable in newly formed Spain. But Juana was not her father's heir; Aragon belonged to Princess Katharine, still stuck in England.[27] If she stayed in London, Ferdinand would be comfortable on his throne. Katharine was still styled as the Princess of Wales, the future queen of England, and rumours of a 29 August 1505 wedding circled far and wide. Ferdinand would do anything to gain control over all of Spain, even offering his daughter Juana as a bride for King Henry VII when her husband Philip suddenly died just after she inherited Castile.[28] But whether Princess Katharine fought for her right to half of the Spanish throne, or stayed in England to be the next queen, depended entirely on the whims of others.

Prince Henry had been living in his private household, continuing his education. Scholar William Hone joined the household in 1504, first to teach Henry and then Princess Mary. The teaching paid off; a letter written to Erasmus by Prince Henry in 1506 was so well-crafted that it was thought to be a forgery.[29] Hone had fought hard to make his student (known throughout his life for hating to write) take more care with his scholarly pursuits. As Prince of Wales, Henry spent his time at court under his father's watch, living a life of a daughter hidden away from the world, whereas Arthur had a wife and Wales to oversee by age fifteen. Even as late as 1508, Henry never saw anyone unless his father allowed him and would never speak to anyone but King Henry.[30] The prince should have been crafted into a future ruler, but instead, he was wrapped up tight and stowed away for fear of disaster.

Prince Henry lived in a state of suspension, just like Katharine of Aragon, except for the fact Katharine also lived in poverty in London. King Ferdinand took the crown of Castile from his daughter Juana, citing her unproven mental problems after widowhood, making himself king of all of Spain, plus Sicily, Sardinia, and Naples. Ferdinand eventually decided to remarry to Germaine de Foix, creating an alliance with the French king.[31] In 1505, in retaliation for this treaty, Prince Henry, only fourteen but old enough to marry, announced he would not marry Katharine of Aragon.[32] It was unlikely Henry ever considered the match due to his age, but this was a convenient way to break the marriage alliance with Ferdinand.

King Henry VII struggled through the final years of his life, desperate to create an England safe and prosperous for his son to inherit but did not allow said heir to exercise any control or responsibility. Margaret Beaufort oversaw much of Prince Henry's education, as the scholars employed came from Cambridge University, often favoured by the king's mother. The king hired a teacher from Spain to allow Henry to learn tennis, hunting, and archery and was spotted at Richmond Palace in 1508 as a talented jouster, though Henry could only be allowed to compete in private against a small group of selected men. But a young man like Prince Henry could not be constrained forever, and he was aware a beautiful, pious, and educated Spanish princess living in poverty could be his bride and queen. For King Henry, the world had stopped after the death of Queen Elizabeth, but the new generation was keen to improve themselves.

The great King Henry VII, the man who brought peace to England, died after succumbing to a lengthy illness on 22 April 1509, just shy of his only son's eighteenth birthday.[33] The king's mother, the majestic Margaret Beaufort, died just two months later, leaving her grandson with no guidance while he had an entire kingdom to control. Immediately after Henry VII's funeral on 10 May 1509, Henry VIII announced he would marry Katharine of Aragon, fulfilling his father's dying wish. Whether the elder Henry ever said such a thing is unknown, as his son was not with him at the time of his death.

While Henry VII was an older man, and never one to show personal flair, he did know how to be generous and throw a good party, even if he was a quiet man himself. But now the realm had an eighteen-year-old to rule over them, a boy filled with hope, enthusiasm and no experience. Henry was a prince among men in every respect; tall, athletic, handsome, calculating, and exceptionally intelligent. Poems started to spring up about how the sun would shine in England again as the crown passed peacefully from a king to his adult son. No sooner than Henry VII's elaborate funeral was complete, Henry VIII already discussed invading France (despite England's claim on the French crown sitting idle since 1453). Countries looked to form new alliances with a bright new king, and the inexperienced ruler could afford to wait and see how ambassadors behaved at the English court. At his side was his father's royal chaplain, Thomas Wolsey, a man less conservative than the older inherited advisors on the King's Council.[34] By June 1509, Henry and Katharine had married in a private ceremony at the Observant Friars at Greenwich Palace, followed two weeks later by their joint coronation on 24 June at Westminster Abbey.[35]

The need to build the Tudor dynasty and bring peace to England dominated King Henry and Queen Elizabeth's lives, coupled with Elizabeth's overwhelming task of birthing healthy heirs. This challenge had put Elizabeth in an early grave, and the pressure slowly cut down Henry VII into a shell of his former self. He had been the man to defeat Richard III on the battlefield and end England's time in the medieval period as the renaissance flooded Europe. Now Henry VIII and Katharine of Aragon faced similar challenges; to find power and influence in Europe, safety, prosperity, and most importantly for Katharine, male heirs.

Chapter 2

Prince Henry, Duke of Cornwall and the Heirs Lost to Fate

It would have been reasonable for the new King Henry to expect his future heirs to grow up in the manner of the finest English princes and princesses. Whether he considered the influence of their mother is subject to conjecture. Henry may have been the first adult son to peacefully inherit the English throne in two hundred years, but it was his choice of wife that ensured his legitimacy. There could be no better selection than Katharine of Aragon. As the daughter of the most powerful king and queen Spain has ever known, Katharine was inspired by her mother, who grew up listening to the eyewitness accounts of Rodrigo Sanchez de Arevalo, who had lived in France during the rise and fall of Joan of Arc.[1] Isabella of Castile was a fearsome mix of power and religion, traits deep in Katharine's blood. Queen Isabella rose to the top of the nation through circumstance and then ambition, and her daughter was ready to capitalise on that power, as a princess and a Spanish ambassador, destined to be queen.

In a happy, healthy, young marriage of equals, it was little surprise Katharine managed to fall pregnant right away. As Katharine's periods were irregular, she did not announce her pregnancy until her quickening, shared publicly on 1 November 1509, five months into her marriage.[2] Judging by letters going to and from Spain, Katharine had known she was pregnant for some time and would have been observing all the rules of the period. King Ferdinand worried for his daughter, especially since he and his new wife had just lost a newborn son. He wrote to Katharine to 'avoid all exertion, and especially not write with her own hand', as women needed to take care with their first pregnancy.[3] The baby was of much concern in Spain, just as it was in England.

As Katharine acted as Queen of England and ambassador to Spain, influencing alliances with the Pope, the Holy Roman Emperor, and the Scots, she also needed to care for her coming child in the ways of English mothers. Katharine's diet became constricted; while she continued to drink wine and beer, she could only eat tasteless foods; piglets and lambs that had been only milk-fed, pigeons and turtledoves, and nothing with any added spice, and neither salty nor sweet.[4] Rabbit and hare could not be eaten, as it would cause undue urination. Crane and peacock created 'bad blood', fish was off the menu, as was venison, which was rumoured to create melancholy in the mother. While Katharine often dined with her husband in the hall at court, she had her own kitchen staff, who oversaw these changes for her, all working under master cook William Bryce. By late November 1509, Katharine was already considering her lying-in, and Henry had his Great Wardrobe staff send Katharine eight large pillows for her comfort at Greenwich.[5]

Sadly, Margaret Beaufort died before she knew of Katharine's pregnancy, but her strict protocol, *The Royal Book*, followed clear written instructions. Royal surgeon Jehan Veyrier would oversee any emergencies, but Katharine was cared for by women only, her ladies-in-waiting and local midwives with experience. Holy relics were essential, and Katharine sent for the Virgin Mary girdle Queen Elizabeth of York used for spiritual comfort during labour.[6] A groaning or birthing chair was ordered, and even a copper gilt bowl was ordered to receive the placenta. The chosen apartments at Greenwich Palace needed to be emptied and swept, with tapestries of soothing religious scenes covering every pocket of the rooms, including windows (though windows could open if Katharine needed air). It was symbolic rather than practical; Katharine would spend six weeks resting in the womb-like space in the dark, before giving birth to England's heir and then emerge glorious in her success once her child was six weeks old, and freshly baptised in the silver font of Canterbury neatly placed inside the Observant Friars attached to the palace.

As planning went ahead at Greenwich, Katharine expected to enter confinement in mid-to-late February for a late March birth, and the royal couple went to Richmond Palace for Christmas and the Epiphany celebrations, to great fanfare and festivity. By this time, Katharine's dresses remained unlaced for her growing stomach, and the kingdom was one of joy for Henry and Katharine.

Katharine moved back to Greenwich Palace in mid-January to continue her preparations, the final linens and cushions continuing to arrive. But on 30 January, Katharine complained of pain in her knee, and by the following morning, she had gone into premature labour.[7] There could be no doubt of the situation; Katharine was delivering two months early, in such severe pain she swore to donate her finest dress to the Spanish shrine of St Peter the Martyr of the Franciscan Order if she survived. The same day, Katharine gave birth to a stillborn daughter. Her only consolation was that the labour and birth happened in private; only surgeon Veyrier, Katharine's confessor and two of her Spanish ladies knew of the birth other than King Henry.

Katharine's body, swollen from the ordeal she suffered, became the instant subject of conjecture from inexperienced and desperate male physicians. As the new queen's stomach did not quickly return to normal (something women have always known to be the case), it was quickly assumed by doctors like William Adderston and John Chaunte, and Anne Luke, who had nursed Henry as an infant, that Katharine was carrying a second child.[8] Doctors and midwives were wholly unregulated and worked alongside astrologers and fortune-tellers when determining the fate of patients. The realm needed a son and it was easy to lie and tell the naïve royal couple what they needed to hear.

Katharine attempted to brush everything aside and attended a Shove Tuesday event at Westminster with Henry, where he hosted one of his never-ending games of 'hiding' among a show of people, in this instance, performers dressed as Turks among Russian and Prussians fighting the Moors. But little could cheer a queen in such a state. As March dawned, Katharine finally entered her official confinement. The men and women of the court took Mass and proceeded with Katharine to her readied chamber, where they drank spiced wine while the beds received blessings for the coming child.[9] She was shut away with her ladies and midwives to wait out the days, the phantom baby still a month from its time. Katharine could find solace in constant prayer, and blackwork stitching, which was popular with Spaniards, or play cards and dice and watch her ladies practice their dancing. But as time passed, nothing changed for Katharine. Mixtures could be drunk to induce labour, such as a concoction of leek, wine, ale, and rue, but nothing helped. March and April passed, and Katharine's swollen stomach finally began to heal from the January birth. Both Henry and Katharine were deeply humiliated by the situation and did not wish for the story to be public. But by May, rumours circulated that the ladies around Katharine had deceived her, and as they defended themselves, rumours of Katharine's infertility began. By the end of May, Katharine reappeared from confinement and announced her loss. But all was far from lost.

Fray Diego Fernandez, Katharine's confessor, wrote to King Ferdinand and explained the loss of the daughter back in January. He wrote:

> 'all the past time I did not dare to write to your Highness of the condition of the Queen my Lady, in order not to annoy her, and because all the physicians deceived themselves until time was the judge of the truth. The last day of January in the

morning her Highness brought forth prematurely a daughter... the physician said that her Highness remained pregnant of another child, and it was believed and kept secret. Her Highness believed herself to be with child, although she had some doubts.... It has pleased our Lord to be her physician in such a way that (her uterus decreased), and by his infinite mercy he has again permitted her to be with child.'[10]

Diego thought Katharine was around three months pregnant already, while Spanish ambassador Luís Caroz reported Katharine was nine weeks pregnant by 28 May.[11] Henry and Katharine obviously had an understanding that she was not pregnant, as they were sleeping together in mid-March, right when she was due. It would be easier to appear from confinement already carrying another child than to admit defeat. Katharine wrote to her father to tell him of the stillbirth but could also back up the news with a new baby.[12]

Royal women giving birth needed to stay in confinement for around six weeks after birth, carefully stipulated in Margaret Beaufort's birthing instructions. Women needed to stay away from men and be churched before returning to normal life. Katharine and Henry had ignored these customs and returned to their usual marital life within weeks of Katharine's distressing labour. More than anything, Katharine decided to forego these rules to hold onto her husband and her position. She needed an heir to secure God's blessing on the marriage and country, and she needed to persuade Henry away from a rumoured new love interest, Anne Hastings. One of Katharine's favourite ladies-in-waiting, Elizabeth Fitzwalter, admitted that her sister Anne was seen with Henry and his sidekick William Compton. Henry retaliated against Fitzwalter, leading to the first major acrimony between king and queen.[13] But the coming royal baby was the most important person.

This time, Katharine was not prepared to take any risks and would follow suggestions to the letter. Henry drifted off on progress, leaving Katharine at his childhood home of Eltham Palace just outside London. Staying quiet at Eltham with her feet up was exactly what Katharine needed and deserved, and plans for confinement at Richmond Palace did not begin until late September. Henry may have been king, but Katharine was still involved and interested in the potential League of Cambrai, and negotiations for an alliance with the Pope to force the French out of Italy, while her father King Ferdinand looked to create the Holy League with the Pope and Venice. Katharine had no interest in relinquishing her role as an ambassador while she carried England's heir. She and Henry reunited at Greenwich in October 1510, before moving to the Tower of London and then Richmond in early

November, each location hosting marvellous occasions of entertainment for the pregnant queen. At Richmond, a royal nursery was being prepared with purple velvet and green say (silk and wool), with two cradles prepared, one a ceremonial cradle large enough to hold a grown man, and a smaller one where the baby could sleep.[14] The room was ready with all the clothing, blankets and swaddling cloths needed for the expected son. Katharine's rooms were lined with blue say with rich tapestries overlaid, the floors covered in carpets and cushions. Two beds were prepared; an eight-by-eight-foot bed covered in furs, and a smaller pallet bed made of wool and Brussels cloth, probably similar to what was prepared a year earlier at Greenwich.[15] Due to the time of year, keeping Katharine warm was a priority, with rich gowns and robes prepared, along with the finest petticoats. Godparents were chosen, wet nurses sent for, and Henry and his men prayed in the chapel for Katharine's safety. In December, Katharine led a procession to her rooms on the first floor, which overlooked the Thames, with blessings shared over wine, and she was locked away with her ladies.

Given that Katharine was in confinement for less than four weeks, it is likely her baby came a little earlier than planned, but with none of the horror of the previous January. Katharine went into labour with her ladies on 31 December 1510, where she followed all the rituals of the period. Women were encouraged to stay active in the initial stages of labour and made to feel as relaxed as possible; all ties and laces on their clothing were to be loosened and she could not even cross her arms, so she could create sympathy for the natural world. Pregnant stomachs were rubbed with a mixture of dried saffron, date stone, white amber, and cumin seeds. Some midwives administered willow bark as pain relief, but most treatments had no effect, and religious artefacts to hold and focus on gave as much relief as any imagined pain treatment.

For all the pain endured in early 1510, in the early hours of 1 January 1511, Katharine gave birth on the pallet bed to a healthy baby boy, swiftly named Henry. The royal baby was washed in warm water mixed with wine and herbs and swaddled while Katharine could be washed and moved to the larger bed for her comfort. It would be the happiest moment of Henry and Katharine's lives. King Henry set out for Our Lady of Walsingham, known as a shrine for fertility, pregnancy and childbirth, to pray in thanks for the new prince. All of London could celebrate the birth; prayers were said in every parish and every church rang its bells. Free wine flowed while bonfires burned, and the cannons fired from the Tower of London 'for the gladness of the realm'. Ambassadors started sending off letters about the happy news.

Prince Henry's christening four days later, at the Observant Friars beside Richmond, was one of the few things that would not change as Henry's legitimate children were born. A hall from the palace to the friars was created, with rails built along a path measuring twenty-four feet in width, freshly laid gravel to walk upon, decorated with rushes. Golden cloth of arras hung along the south side, and into the church itself.[16] Katharine could not attend the christening, both due to her condition and protocol, and baby Henry was baptised at the silver font by proxies standing in for his royal godparents. The godfathers were King Louis of France and William Warham, Archbishop of Canterbury. Richard Foxe, Bishop of Winchester stood in for King Louis at the christening, while Louis sent a gift of a ninety-nine-ounce fine gold salt holder and cup.[17] Baby Henry, already the Duke of Cornwall, had Duchess Marguerite, Regent of the Netherlands as his godmother (who was also Katharine's sister-in-law as the widow of Katharine's late brother Juan). King Henry appointed his aunt Princess Anne of York as another godmother, to stand at the font. All the ambassadors in London attended; Andrea Badoer from Venice, Luís Caroz from Spain and representatives from France and Rome were all permitted into Katharine's chambers to see her following the ceremony.[18]

The celebrations for the birth of Prince Henry would rival even the double coronation of his parents. King Henry held a magnificent Epiphany banquet on 6 January, the entertainment featuring a mountain covered in gold and jewels, atop it a golden tree bearing gold roses and pomegranates, while children dressed as moors danced around this incredible creation. While Katharine still rested in confinement, Henry designed a magnificent joust to celebrate the baby's birth. On 2 February, Katharine celebrated Candlemas by being churched and purified while wearing purple and crimson velvet and was able to rejoin the court.[19]

Henry and Katharine left the precious prince at Richmond on 11 February and travelled ten miles downstream to Greenwich to enjoy Henry's dramatic event to celebrate the birth. Illustrated plates of the event still survive, showing the elaborate processions and a vast list of attendees. Katharine sat in a special gallery built for her and her ladies while a pageant opened with a golden lion and silver antelope heralding a golden castle twenty-six feet long by sixteen feet wide, surrounded by a decorated golden forest with trumpeters in green velvet, who, in sounding their horns, signalled the castle's opening and showing the four challengers of the joust competition. King Henry was Sir Loyal Heart, his love dedicated to Katharine on his outfit, and won the competition on its second day. The evening on 13 February had another grand pageant dedicated to Katharine, a garden of pleasure decorated in gold as Henry danced an allegory of love before letting everyone present take jewels from his outfit. The crowd went wild with excitement, but Henry and Katharine left in a fit of laughter and passionately kissing at the end of the night.[20]

Just over a week later, England lost its golden era of love. The news came from Richmond Palace that baby Henry was dead, aged just 52 days.[21] The death was unexplained, and Katharine was severely tormented in grief. Henry attempted to stay calm to soothe his wife, but as good Catholics, the sign would have been devastating. They looked to be the new Isabella and Ferdinand of England, and yet Katharine and Henry had suffered the cruellest of blows. Henry arranged a magnificent internment for his baby son at Westminster Abbey on Thursday 27 February 1511. A hearse, banners and gowns were all soon made in black velvet, along with twelve palls and a black canopy to cover the coffin, along with the abbey decorated black for the service, at a cost of 3791 (over £250,000 today). The chief mourner to baby Prince Henry were the most trusted men in the realm; Thomas Grey, Marquess of Dorset, Henry Bouchier, Earl of Essex, Henry Stafford, Earl of Wiltshire, William FitzAlan Lord Maltravers, Lord Edmund Howard, Henry Baron Clifford, Robert Radcliffe Baron Fitzwalter, George Neville Baron Bergavenny, and Thomas Lord Dacre. Hundreds from the households of Henry, Katharine, and the baby prince all attended, from the closest privy chamber members to the kitchen staff. While there would be many more children in King Henry's life, never again would there be the celebration and pageantry dedicated to a queen and her child.

Henry and Katharine had no heir after two years of marriage, only heartache at how close they had come. The loss had not harmed their marriage, as a Spanish delegation wrote, saying they witnessed Henry and Katharine still kissing and embracing in public, Henry professing his love for Katharine to all.[22] They were a happy couple, filled with respect. Katharine was the perfect queen for England, and the finest ambassador the king had when it came to matters of Spain. But 1512 was a difficult year for the couple, with Katharine's father King Ferdinand using Henry and Katharine several times. England sent troops to Spain to assist in the battle against Moors in Africa and the French in Italy, only to be deceived and utilised with disregard. But the royal couple wanted to establish themselves as leaders in Europe. Ignoring the concerns held by King Ferdinand, and all of late Henry VII and Margaret Beaufort's advisors, Henry and Katharine decided to wage war with France in a true Catholic crusade. Not even the new humanist thinkers of the period, such as Erasmus, John Fisher, Hugh Latimer, John Colet or Thomas More's words dissuaded the couple.

Rumours of Katharine being pregnant were about at the time, and given her high fertility, it is possible Katharine got pregnant in 1512, but it was not officially announced or recorded. Other news dominated letters; Henry wanted France, while Katharine would rule England in his place. As King Henry and Thomas Wolsey's war preparations progressed, pregnancy gossip continued, but on 11 June 1513, Queen Katharine was appointed 'Regent and Governess of England, Wales and Ireland during the king's absence in his expedition to France, for the preservation of the Catholic religion and recovery of all his rights'.[23] Within a week, Henry was already in Calais, and a new Pope had been elected, aware of King James of Scotland's plans to attack England. While Katharine had fears for Henry's health in France, King Ferdinand feared for his daughter and a new pregnancy, trying to send Spanish doctors to care for her.[24] Henry met with Holy Roman Emperor Maximilian in France as they shared resources for battle, but the bigger worry was Katharine and her baby. Until she had a healthy child, the heir to England remained the infant sons of Henry's sister Margaret Tudor, Queen of Scotland, but Katharine remained casual in her concerns, happy to wage war on her own.[25] On 3 August, the Scots crossed the border, and Katharine was ready, travelling to Buckinghamshire where she wore armour complete with a golden crown and gave a rousing battle speech just as her mother had done, and was now around six months pregnant. A month of fighting saw Katharine's army kill King James, her sister-in-law's husband, on 9 September, while Katharine was 300 miles away at Woburn Abbey.[26] Katharine rode to Our Lady of Walsingham to pray in thanks for her victory, and more importantly, for the safety of her unborn child.[27] King Henry rode there two years earlier to pray for their son, and the shrine of the Lady was dripping in gold, jewels and silk when Katharine arrived to pray, walking the final mile barefoot to give thanks. While Katharine fought for her country and her baby, Henry was in France, allegedly enjoying an affair with a woman named Etiennette de la Baume, a lady-in-waiting to Queen Katharine's sister-in-law Duchess Marguerite, Regent of the Netherlands.

Rumours of Katharine's stillbirth, around seven months pregnant at the time, entered records around 17 September, though this does not correspond with her arrival at Walsingham on 23 September. James Bannissius wrote to Lord Albert of Carpi, in a letter from Tournai dated 17 September that, 'the Queen of England has given birth to a son', though the letter is now catalogued as 7 October 1513. It was another 115 miles back to London from Walsingham, and it was not until 7 October when the Duke of Ferrara wrote in a letter that, 'a male heir was born to the King of England, and will inherit the crown, the other son having died'. No letters between Henry and

Katharine remain, and if anyone wrote of the pregnancy and stillbirth, it has long disappeared. The reunion between king and queen was loving, but to lose yet another child must have been painful in the extreme.

Henry needed time to recover after taking Tournai and Therouanne in a useless French war. Katharine needed recovery from her ordeals; while she had lost another son, she had won a war and killed a king, which had made Henry's sister a pregnant widow, so Katharine attempted to console Margaret through religious devotion. But the realm still needed an heir, and by spring 1514, Katharine was pregnant yet again. Henry and Katharine's relationship with her father Ferdinand had soured over the years, with the unlikely rumour that Ferdinand tricked Henry into marrying Katharine, an obvious lie. When Henry's sister Princess Mary's marriage to King Charles of Castile stalled due to his ill health, Henry decided to push his sister into marrying the ageing King Louis of France, just months after the end of the war between the nations.[28] Katharine, who announced her pregnancy publicly in June, had no choice but to let Henry give away his sister Mary in a weak match so the old king of France could get the heir he needed, just as Henry and Katharine fought for a child of their own. While visibly pregnant, Katharine was described abroad as 'lively and of gracious disposition' but sad to lose her sister-in-law and friend.[29]

But this time, Katharine stayed quiet during her pregnancy as Henry continued to sour relations with Spain. Katharine attended Princess Mary's proxy marriage to King Louis before the poor eighteen-year-old travelled to France to marry a sick fifty-two-year-old she had never seen.[30] As Henry sought to destabilise relations with King Ferdinand and Emperor Maximilian, Katharine neared her time with her baby and Italian gossip whispered Henry would divorce Katharine, due to Henry's hatred of his former Spanish alliances. Another rumour persisted Henry had some kind of affair with fourteen-year-old Elizabeth Bryan, daughter of one of Katharine's favourite ladies, Lady Margaret Bryan. But Katharine was kind and polite with this rumour, unlike her previous anger at her husband's philandering, and young Elizabeth was married off to Sir Nicholas Carew. With Katharine politically isolated, she needed to concentrate on her position as wife and mother.

Preparations for the royal baby began in October 1514, with Katharine requesting a scarlet and blue cradle,[31] while Thomas Wolsey told the king of France he could be a godfather to a new prince. It appears this pregnancy went almost to full term, with Katharine preparing for her confinement in mid-November at Greenwich.[32] But in an undated December letter by Venetian ambassador Andrea Bodoer wrote that, 'the Queen was delivered of a stillborn child of eight months, a great grief to all the Court'.³³ Just as life was looking up for Katharine and relations between England and Spain were improving, she lost yet another son, an immeasurable loss. Rumours suggested Katharine was no longer a beauty due to her suffering, and that Henry teased Katharine about his affairs, causing a miscarriage. However, there are no sources for such accusations.³⁴ Henry arranged a procession of dancers to enter Katharine's chambers on New Year to cheer his recovering wife, four men and four women dressed in blue velvet with cloth of gold and silver. Henry was one of the performers for his wife, and she enjoyed the surprise, kissing him in thanks. Henry was partnered with fourteen-year-old Elizabeth Blount, who had joined Katharine's household, coming from a family Katharine knew from her time with Prince Arthur at Ludlow.³⁵

Katharine rejoined the court for the Epiphany on 6 January 1515, attending the celebrations depicting valiant knights fighting in the forest, alongside the news that King Louis of France had died, and Mary Tudor, now Queen of France, could return home.³⁶ England and Spain could continue to strengthen alliances, giving Katharine hope for the future. She reluctantly sent word of the stillbirth to her father Ferdinand and got back to work as her husband's diplomatic advisor. Katharine stayed away from the fiasco caused by Henry's sister Mary secretly marrying Charles Brandon on her way home from France, before attending their second wedding at Greenwich in May 1515. The court had another visitor at the time; Sebastian Giustinian from Venice, who recorded much about the king and queen. Giustinian wrote of the May Day celebrations, seeing how much Henry still loved his wife despite all their pain and spoke in Spanish to Katharine about international relations and flattering Henry's many athletic skills.³⁷ Tales that Henry may have engaged in an affair with Jane Popincourt in recent months, a French courtesan who had served both his mother and sister, likely had not reached Katharine's ears. Soothing difficulties at court, Katharine became pregnant again, though Nicholas Sagundino called her 'rather ugly than otherwise' when he relayed the news to Venice.³⁸ Finally, England would gain its much-needed heir.

Chapter 3

An English Princess

Despite all the political difficulties of 1515, the year ended with Henry and Katharine based at Eltham Palace for Christmas and the Epiphany. Henry arranged a massive pageant featuring a castle, a banquet of one hundred dishes, and an evening of dancing for his pregnant queen.[1] Henry's sister Dowager Queen Margaret of Scotland had newly given birth to a daughter named Margaret Douglas, which must have been encouraging for the English royal couple, as Margaret had given birth seven times but only had two surviving children. This birth had been horrific for Margaret and returning home to England was her only option, fleeing her monstrous second husband, leaving her son, the child Scots king, behind.[2]

Meanwhile, Queen Katharine managed to carry almost to full term and left Eltham at the end of January to begin confinement at Greenwich. All the usual ceremonies could be performed this time, with Katharine able to complete the procession and ceremony of her lying-in period and blessing before being closed in with her female attendants. Katharine had been unwell for some time, complaining of pain which was likely sciatica.[3] There was one vital piece of news Katharine missed as she went into seclusion; the death of her father King Ferdinand in Madrigalejo on 23 January.[4] It was a month before the dispatches reached England, but Katharine was spared the news as she awaited England's heir. She had lost her anchor to Spain, with most of her close relatives dead, and many of her Spanish servants returned home or married. Without her father, Katharine was no longer the great ambassador at Henry's side. A child was more important than ever.

The wait was not as long as expected, and at four o'clock on the wintry morning of Monday 18 February 1516, Princess Mary was born, full-term and healthy.[5] Katharine sent off a letter the same day sharing the good news, and Henry swiftly got his men to prepare the christening.[6] Again, it would be the Observant Friars who would host such an event, this time at Greenwich. The freshly laid gravel path was covered in rushes, with rails covered in arras built along the paths to keep the winter at bay while the baby and guests made the procession. Mary's godparents took her to the chapel on Thursday 21 February.[7] The ladies and gentlemen of the court began a great procession, the noblest of the realm preceding Elizabeth Howard, Countess of Surrey, carrying the royal daughter. Amid the beauty and ceremony, a golden canopy hung over the princess, held aloft by Davy ab Owain, King Henry's great-uncle, and three trusted knights, Thomas Parr, Thomas Boleyn, and Nicholas Vaux. They stopped at the door of the chapel, covered in tapestries laden with jewels, the canopy aloft as they sang Psalm XVI, The Prayer of David. Baby Mary was handed to her godmothers at the church door, Agnes Howard, Duchess of Norfolk, and her great-aunt Princess Katherine of York. Thomas Wolsey, made a cardinal in 1515, stood in as godfather to the girl, as the king of France was in a foul mood with Henry and refused to send a proxy in his place.[8] Mary was held over the silver font from Christ Church in Canterbury, which had been used to baptise King Henry and the ill-fated baby Henry, Duke of Cornwall five years earlier. Mary's conformation took place as soon as she was baptised, her godmother for this being Lady Margaret Pole, Countess of Salisbury, a loyal family member who would support Mary until her dying day. The princess was plunged into the font water, anointed, and swaddled in a baptismal robe. Te Deums were sung through the church and trumpets blown, and Mary's title was announced; 'the high, right, noble and excellent Princess Mary, princess of England and daughter of our most excellent dread sovereign lord the King's highness'.[9]

While the ceremony was lavish and followed the strict Catholic wishes of her parents, Mary's arrival celebrations were small. Henry and Katharine had thrown their heart and soul into celebrating the birth of their son Henry, only to lose him, and while Mary was welcome, the royal couple were desperate. There was no precedent suggesting a woman could not rule England, but Henry ruled with a fragile new dynasty, and the potential unrest of a female ruler would not serve the Tudors. Katharine however, while aware of the need for a son, would have felt less disappointed. She was an established queen, and her mother had conquered and ruled over Spain in her own right. While Henry could not see the value in a healthy daughter, Katharine certainly could. Unable to attend the christening, Katharine recovered in her cocoon of confinement, among the heavy and soothing tapestries, lush carpets, soft pillows and a large, canopied bed covered in crimson satin bearing the royal arms.[10] Among the gold and silver, the crucifixes, candles, and relics all specified by Margaret Beaufort's *The Royal Book*, Katharine would have welcomed a living child, born just several weeks too late to be shared with her grandfather, King Ferdinand.

Outside the confinement chambers, King Henry did not stage large banquets and pageants as he so often threw; without a son, there was little need for celebration. The Venetian ambassador Sebastian Giustinian wrote home, saying there was no need to rush to congratulate the news of a daughter. Giustinian was foolish enough to say directly to the king that it would be a disappointment to have a daughter and Henry replied with those well-known words, 'we are both young; if it was a daughter this time, by the grace of God sons will follow'.[11] While Henry was not angered to have a daughter, his disappointment must have been obvious, as Lord Mountjoy, who watched over Katharine's confinement outside her chamber, wrote, 'beseeching our Lord to send you as much rejoicing of my Lady Princess, and made you as glad as ever was king, as after this good beginning to send you many fair sons to your Grace's comfort and all your true subjects'. Mountjoy arranged for bells to ring at Mary's birth and had bonfires lit in celebration, as Henry had only marked the occasion with the mere basics.

Queen Katharine was churched and able to spend time with her baby at court within the month, just in time for her daughter's namesake Mary Tudor, Dowager Queen of France, to give birth to a son she named Henry, with her husband Charles Brandon, the new Duke of Suffolk. At the May Day jousts, Henry sat with his wife Queen Katharine of England, and his sisters, Queen Mary of France, and Queen Margaret of Scotland, the jousts and pageantry dedicated to Margaret's return after thirteen years in Scotland. Yet, as Henry sat surrounded by three queens, he still did not see the value in having his daughter Mary. Henry's father Henry VII had a claim to the throne before he won it in battle, but through his mother only. Henry's mother Elizabeth of York was not the heir to the throne, and yet it was her royal blood that steadied her husband's stability on the English throne. While women had placed Henry VIII on the throne, and women sat alongside him now, he still expected a male heir.

The year carried along in relative peace for the royal couple. King Henry was only twenty-five and Katharine thirty-one by the time Christmas came, with the promise more children could be born. The Christmas celebrations were dedicated to Katharine, though she shared the honour with sister-in-law Queen Margaret. While there was peace at court, Katharine remained at Henry's mercy. The exceptionally intelligent queen had now given the king at least five children and had gained significant weight, her red hair dulling to brown. She was no longer the young Spanish princess, but the queen slowly ageing with time and the stress of her position. Yet more children had to follow.

While the birth of a royal daughter could only serve as a consolation, Henry certainly never looked at Mary with any disdain. The king and queen needed an heir, but Mary received the love and respect of a princess. Her nursery was one of great opulence and comfort, with Elizabeth Denton, who had served as the Lady Mistress during Henry's childhood (and bizarrely rumoured as a lover to then-teenage Henry), running the nursery for two years.[12] Her second-in-charge was Lady Margaret Bryan, who would later become head of the household when Denton retired just before her death in 1519. She may have been an infant, but Princess Mary was a jewel; while she had an everyday cradle, and also a 'cradle of estate' draped in ermine, the royal arms emblazoned on the canopy.[13] The baby needed to look her best when presented to visitors.

Henry Rowle became Mary's chaplain and clerk, and Katharine Pole was Mary's wet nurse, paid 20l for her services. Mary had four women to rock her cradle; Margaret Cousine, Ellen Hutton, Anne Bright, and Margery Parker received a salary of 80s (around £2,000 today). A rotation of seven women also worked for Mary in her household, women who had served Henry and his sister in their youth, including Henry's own nurse Anne Luke, and Eleanor Verney, sister-in-law of Mary's godmother Margaret Pole, Countess of Salisbury.[14] The princess was surrounded by those who had treated Henry well as a child, a show of how important Mary was to her parents.

By the time Mary was seven months old, and living at Ditton Manor in Buckinghamshire, King Henry was already suggesting Mary would be a great ruler of Europe. He suggested a marriage for the baby girl, to her cousin King Charles of Spain, in the hope Spain did not ally with France. Henry still wanted France for himself, and if Mary were to be the only heir of the royal couple, she could rule England and France while Charles remained in Spain. The suggestion came to nothing, but many more suitors would follow.

Mary's household, neatly placed close to Windsor Castle, and accessible by the Datchet Ferry to various manors on the Thames cost King Henry 1,400l (almost £1,000,000 today) in its first year.[15] For Christmas, Henry ordered ten yards of white tinsel and ten yards of silver tinsel to decorate Mary's rooms, twelve yards of white satin and eleven yards of white damask to be made into four white gowns, with three of them lined with ermine, reserved for only the most royal of subjects. The details of Mary's first Christmas are not recorded, but given she was so elegantly dressed, she would have been with her parents at Greenwich where she was born. At Mary's first birthday on 18 February 1517, her nurse Eleanor Verney received her yearly tun of wine, a note of delivery given to Verney at Westminster, where the court was staying, suggesting Mary spent her birthday with her parents in central London.[16]

While Henry and Katharine would have been undoubtedly thrilled to have a daughter who survived her perilous first year, 1517 pushed their difficulties to a new level, with pressures at home and abroad. The first came at Easter when tensions between locals and foreigners living in the city came to a head. London was a richly diverse city, with merchants from all over Europe and beyond. The east of the city had held connections to Italian, French, German, and Flemish traders for hundreds of years who gathered in a tight-knit community. The locals 'not only despised the way the Italians live, but curse them with uncontrollable hatred,' and that the English had a great antipathy of foreigners, and 'imagine that they never come into their island, but to make themselves masters of it, and usurp their goods'.[17] A plan to attack these communities on May Day exploded into an impromptu riot in the eastern quarter of the city. Upwards of 2,000 men began attacking foreign-owned businesses along St Martin's Le Grand and Cheapside, to the distress of Sheriff Thomas More who had been on patrol. The attacks began in the French and Flemish areas, which naturally defended themselves, pouring boiling water on the locals, causing outrage and widespread rioting.[18] The men left the Italian streets alone, knowing them to be wealthy and well-armed (among them, newly married Thomas Cromwell living a quiet Italian life). The king's men quelled the rebellion in the night, and Henry and Katharine staged the situation to their advantage; when four hundred men and eleven women were placed in nooses, Katharine publicly begged her husband to spare them, which he did.[19] The pre-arranged plea made the foreign queen look like the saviour of the locals. However, such a situation must have rattled Henry and Katharine. Spanish antipathy had been high for several years, and Henry had grown up with a father plagued by rebellions and plots. Until now, Henry had suffered precious little resistance within his country or against his laws. An uprising was not a reminder an 'heirless' king needed.

Henry pressed on in his typical luxurious manner, hosting a banquet at Greenwich on 7 July 1517, to celebrate England's new League in Defense of the Church, a three-sided treaty with King Charles of Spain and Holy Roman Emperor Maximilian.[20] This treaty specifically excluded France, but also defended the Catholic faith. The rise of questioning faith gathered pace aboard; Martin Luther was just months away from nailing up his ninety-five Theses in Germany. Andreas Karlstadt had just done similar in Wittenberg over the Easter period. But in England, the festivities of St Thomas' Day celebrated the alliance; dinners, banquets, jousts, dancing, music, and a buffet thirty feet long, with meals brought out on elephants, panthers, and lions.[21]

It would have been a wonderful time for the royal couple to announce another pregnancy. Princess Mary was eighteen months old but the royal couple, for the first time in their relationship, had a large gap between pregnancies. Katharine possibly conceived in this period, but the pregnancy was too short to receive a public mention. Instead, among the glorious celebratory jousts,[22] the worst possible scenario occurred, a huge outbreak of sweating sickness. The international pageant was not over, but ominous news of sudden deaths arrived at the court. While the disease did periodically spring up in England, it is also possible the hundreds of international visitors may have transported the illness. Two of King Henry's younger privy chamber men, Thomas Baron Clinton, and Lord Grey of Wilton, died suddenly at Richmond. Henry and Katharine fled immediately to Windsor and did not see their daughter for months. The last thing they needed was their precious daughter succumbing to the illness, not unlike the illness that killed Prince Arthur fifteen years earlier. The illness spread through England and then Europe, and deaths quickly ran into the thousands. Cardinal Wolsey fell sick with the illness for the fourth time and vowed to take a pilgrimage to Walsingham if he survived. The illness killed noble and common-born subjects with impunity, and with the king away, the locals of London planned more attacks on foreign merchants.

Henry and Katharine passed the months in seclusion, but those around them kept dying, and they fled to Farnham Castle to allow Windsor to be cleaned. Again, Princess Mary does not feature in any of the mentions of pestilence. Mary does gain a mention over the New Year period and stayed in seclusion near her parents at Windsor. The princess accepted a gold cup from Wolsey, a gold spoon from Elizabeth Grey, a gold pomander from her aunt Queen Mary, and pears from Lady Alice Darrell, one of Mary's favourite foods, while Lady Alice Blunt and Lady Mountjoy made gowns.[23] Many of the women around Mary were people beloved by Katharine during her time in England.

Princess Mary stayed with her parents at Windsor, celebrating her second birthday, and met Venetian ambassador Sebastian Guistanian on 28 February 1518. The sweating sickness was still out of control, but the ambassador touched Mary's hand, given more deference and respect than Katharine. It was at this meeting where Henry uttered his well-known boast that Mary never cried, and Mary's first public word, 'priest', was uttered when she saw Henry's Venetian priest turned-musician Dionysius and demanded he play music for her.[24] After the meeting, Henry and Katharine, and likely Mary too, left for Woodstock Palace to continue running from the sweat.

While Henry wrote his first book in seclusion, a collection of refuting claims against Martin Luther's works, Katharine was finally pregnant. The queen took a pilgrimage to St Frideswide's in Oxford, to give an offering to Christ Church cathedral's relics. Having multiple children gave Henry and Katharine options; if Katharine had a son, England would have an heir, and Queen Claude of France had just given birth to a son, and Mary could marry him and be Queen of France. This time, thanks to the illness and the resulting isolation, Katharine kept her pregnancy quiet,[25] and Mary returned to Ditton to remain safe, as even Henry's bedchamber servants were dying. Mary's future marriage to infant Francis, Dauphin of France was agreed upon between King Henry and King Francis on 30 June 1518, despite Mary being a toddler and Francis still under a wet nurse's care. At once, this upset King Charles of Spain and Emperor Maximilian, the same rulers Henry had painstakingly entertained only months earlier with a new treaty.

Around the time of the marriage treaty, the sweating sickness infiltrated Princess Mary's household, when one of her servants fell desperately ill.[26] Henry ordered Mary's household to move to Bisham, eleven miles northwest of her home at Ditton, before travelling to The More in Hertfordshire, where he was staying with Katharine. By this time, Katharine would have been visibly pregnant, and news of her pregnancy had spread. After time with her parents and staying well, Princess Mary's household continued to move through summer homes, stopping at Havering, Hatfield and Tittenhanger, before heading back to Ditton.

Young Mary would have no idea, but she was about to be propelled into a daring plan to create universal peace in Europe. The paperwork discussing the marriage with Dauphin Francis was ready, all the terms agreed upon. But not only this, but the rulers of Europe were courting Henry. By late September, Katharine was nearing full term with her pregnancy, and England simply needed a healthy boy. Henry was planning the future on this very fact. Pope Leo wanted an alliance with England, sending Cardinal Lorenzo Campeggio to England, and making both Campeggio and Wolsey papal legates to negotiate official matters. Campeggio wrote of Henry and Katharine in the highest of terms.[27] But with England and France joining with a marriage contract, King Charles of Spain wanted an English alliance; his Burgundian lands north of France, and Navarre lands south of France, were both at risk of French invasion and needed English troops. The Pope could not offer a deal as peaceful and widespread as the one Cardinal Wolsey managed to negotiate with Spain and France.

On 23 September 1518, a French delegation rode into town to formalise Mary's marriage, a group of more than one hundred people, including wrestlers, tennis players and musicians. Henry met the group at Greenwich after soothing King Charles' feelings over the matter, and on 2 October, the Treaty of London was signed between England and France.[28] Princess Mary and Dauphin Francis would marry after his fourteenth birthday in February 1532. At the same time, signatures were being put to Cardinal Wolsey's Treaty of Universal Peace.[29] There was a catch; Mary had to be formally named as Henry's heir. Katharine was almost ready to give birth and not undertaking any stressful activities. A healthy son was needed to ensure the French did not one day inherit the English crown. The day after signing the contract, Henry and the Bishop of Paris were followed by one thousand knights as they rode in procession from Westminster to St Paul's to swear oaths upon the Treaty of London, followed by a celebration at Wolsey's York Place. Queen Katharine could not attend, and retired early to rest with her baby, so Henry's dancing partner was one of Katharine's ladies, twenty-year-old Bessie Blount, who was newly pregnant (or hours away from becoming pregnant). Henry threw a party to rival the one he devised on the celebration of his son's birth years earlier; from the outside, it looked as if England could not be happier.[30]

It was Princess Mary who was centre stage on 5 October, when the official betrothal took place in Katharine's Great Chamber at Greenwich.[31] Princess Mary wore cloth of gold like her father at the following banquet, accompanied by a little black velvet cap laden with jewels. With Katharine and Henry convinced a healthy son was on the way, they allowed this proxy betrothal to go ahead. It was a risk; naming Mary as heir to the throne and giving her away in marriage at the same time. They surely felt God would deliver this time.

On 25 October 1518, Venetian ambassador Giustinian remarked that Katharine looked to deliver her child, the likely time she entered her confinement at Greenwich.[32] Again, the ceremonial tapestries and carpets had been laid, a luxurious bed to welcome mother and baby after giving birth on the small pallet bed, the room filled with earthly riches to denote status and religious relics to provide comfort. The procession to the chambers and the ceremonial spiced wine would again be taken; Katharine would have known the rituals by heart now. On 9 November, Katharine signed paperwork permitting Mary's marriage.[33] But on the morning of Wednesday 10 November, the news broke that Katharine had given birth prematurely in the night. Again, she delivered a baby girl, either stillborn or had died soon after the birth. Reporting the news, Ambassador Giustinian wrote from Lambeth, 'the Queen was delivered of a daughter, to the vexation of as many as know it; the entire nation looked for a prince. Had the event taken place before the conclusion of the betrothal, that event might not have happened; the sole fear of this kingdom being that it may pass into the power of the French through this marriage'.[34]

While Katharine and Henry dealt with their devastation, Mary's marriage contract received an equally sumptuous ceremony in France; it was too late to change anything. Queen Claude of France was already well-advanced in her pregnancy, despite giving birth ten months earlier, while King Francis agreed to the marriage while draped in cloth of gold, the occasion witnessed by the noblest Frenchmen at court. For King Henry, he had given his daughter in marriage, and it would give his crown to the French. Coupled with the death of their final child, Katharine, who was about to celebrate ten years as a wife and a queen, was about to get an explosive addition to King Henry's indulgent nursery.

Chapter 4

A Son at Last

When John Blount and Katherine Pershall had their first child in 1498, there was little expectation for the girl. Named Elizabeth, possibly after the queen, the girl soon became known as Bessie. The older generations of the family were still in prominence in their area of Kinlet in Shropshire, and in 1501, Bessie's great-grandfather, Sir Richard Croft, was awarded a role fifteen miles west of their home, at Ludlow Castle.[1] Prince Arthur and his wife Katharine of Aragon were setting up their household and Croft was to be the steward and one of Arthur's advisors. Croft found a role in the household for his son-in-law Sir Thomas Blount, and when it came time to find local ladies to serve Princess Katharine, Blount put forward Katherine, his grandson's wife. Three generations were suddenly propelled into a royal household, with everything ruined months later when Prince Arthur died. Both Sir Richard Croft and Sir Thomas Blount stood at Prince Arthur's coffin for the funeral, with Croft breaking his ceremonial stave over the coffin as it was lowered into the ground. While the men arranged the finances of the now-broken royal household, Katherine Blount would have still been caring for Princess Katharine, who was too ill to attend her husband's funeral. When Princess Katharine left Ludlow for London, Katherine Blount stayed behind with her family.[2] But within this period, as Prince Arthur was carried to his burial site in atrocious weather, the procession stopped at Bewley, where four-year-old Bessie Blount lived with her extended family. In a time of grief, this would be Bessie's only brush with royalty.

By the time King Henry VIII ascended the throne in 1509, Bessie still lived in Shropshire, the eldest of a dozen children. The girls were raised in a typical style of their rank at the time, skilled in all the practicalities of being a good wife, though Bessie and her sisters could also read and write and must have received some education. The Blount men had continued their work in the region, and by 1509, both Sir Thomas Blount and his son John were commissioners for the peace in Staffordshire, and Sir Thomas was the sheriff of Herefordshire.[3] John Blount was given a role at Henry VII's funeral as an esquire of the body, as a representative of their home region. Soon after Henry VIII's ascension, he appointed Blount to his new league of the King's Spears, an elite bodyguard group, which mostly served as ceremonial. Blount naturally had to live in London, and his wife Katherine possibly visited, though the family officially lived at Knightley in the Pershall family manor in Staffordshire.

It would have made sense to look for a position at court for young Bessie, aged twelve by 1510, the minimum age for a lady at court. Bessie was exceptionally beautiful, likely blonde with blue eyes, traditionally attractive for English girls in the period. Queen Katharine had many of her own ladies, so waiting for a position would have been paramount. Bessie had to live in London for a period, which would have been dramatic for a girl from Shropshire. Bessie lived either with her father in London or with her grandmother Isabella Stanley. The Blount family had other relatives at court, distant cousins William Blount, Lord Mountjoy, Sirs Henry and Edward Guildford, and Sir Edward Darrell, who was vice-chamberlain to Queen Katharine, and a Spear alongside John Blount.[4] With all these connections it was only a matter of time for Bessie.

Bessie Blount's name as a lady of the royal court shows up in a wage account at Michaelmas (September) 1513, receiving 100s, so she had likely started working for the queen around Michaelmas 1512.[5] Given that John Blount had to ask for a year's wages in advance in May 1513, it was likely to be ensuring his daughter was correctly attired to be a lady in the queen's household.[6] King Henry would also send quality fabric for gowns to Katharine's ladies, a prestigious gift rather than assistance to those who could not afford the finest damask and furs. Bessie's father John went to war in France with the king, while her grandfather worked with their cousin Lord Mountjoy. Bessie made her life in the queen's household, and by October 1514 is mentioned by Charles Brandon, Duke of Suffolk as a friend in a note of remembrance.[7] Queen Katharine had four levels of ladies in her rooms; the highest rank was the most powerful ladies, rarely at court, women such as Margaret Pole, the Stafford sisters, and the countesses of the country. The second level of ladies were those married to barons or notable knights, such as Lady Elizabeth Boleyn and Lady Elizabeth Carew. Bessie Blount was a third-ranked lady, among the unmarried daughters of the gentry, doing the basic tasks for the queen, fetching and holding items, and delivering messages, while the fourth-ranked were the maids and cleaners. Bessie gained a room at court, had her own servant and was given permission to keep pets in the royal household.

The early years of Henry VIII's reign were filled with banquets and pageants, usually in honour of the queen. As a lady, Bessie was to be part of these occasions and is listed at Christmas 1514 as a dancer on one of

Henry's elaborate displays of festivities, when he arranged a group to burst into Queen Katharine's rooms and perform for her after a recent stillbirth.[8] In 'disguise', King Henry, the Duke of Suffolk, Nicholas Carew, and Henry Guildford danced with Margaret Guildford, Elizabeth Carew, Lady Fellinger, and sixteen-year-old Bessie Blount. Accompanied by knights and singers, the whole event was well-received by Queen Katharine. Bessie dressed in a Savoy gown while the men dressed as lavish Portuguese knights. This is the first time Henry and Bessie were recorded together, but as Henry had not long finished an affair with Bessie's friend Elizabeth Carew and was embarking on another with Jane Popincourt, who danced with Henry at the Epiphany celebrations a week later.

Princess Mary was born on 28 February 1516, to the relief of her parents, who now knew they could have healthy children. But the sweating sickness outbreak of 1517 changed everything, meaning the king and queen were constantly on the move to stay safe, and Bessie would have been one of the ladies who accompanied Queen Katharine as they sought to evade the deadly illness. Servants rotated in and out of the royal isolation bubble, and John Blount became an Esquire of the Body to the king in 1517. Bessie's father had been out of the royal picture since the suspension of the Spears' operations, so to gain such a dramatic elevation suggests King Henry's interest in Bessie by this time.[9] Agreeing to be Henry's mistress cannot have been an easy decision, but Henry was considered the most handsome king in Europe, charming, beloved, and well-read like Bessie. They may have had a casual relationship, as Henry was still eager to have a child with Katharine, who got pregnant in February 1518. Having a mistress during this period would have suited Henry, knowing there was a royal baby growing, and so he could have his fun elsewhere.

Just before Queen Katharine entered confinement, the court hosted an intricate banquet to honour Princess Mary's French engagement, with Bessie as Henry's dancing partner while Katharine retired early.[10] It would have been around this time Bessie became pregnant. As a pregnancy could not always be recognised until the quickening, especially in a woman having her first child, it could have been months before Bessie realised what had occurred, and Queen Katharine had already delivered another stillborn daughter.[11] Bessie is not recorded again at court, and by the time she needed to alter her dresses to accommodate a child, Bessie needed to leave. What excuse she gave Katharine is unknown; perhaps Henry told his wife the bitter truth. Queen Katharine had been the perfect wife for Henry and was to suffer a cruel fate; he got a bastard child on his mistress, one of Katharine's own ladies, own friends.

A Son at Last

Cardinal Thomas Wolsey took an interest in Bessie and her pregnancy, and King Henry gave her father the keepership of Cleobury Park in February 1519, likely the date of Bessie's quickening.[12] Soon after, Wolsey moved her northeast of London to Priory of St Lawrence at Blackmore, a few miles outside Chelmsford. In the Essex countryside just twenty-five miles from London, Wolsey organised for Bessie to live in the prior's house on-site rather than in the priory overseen by the prior and its twelve ordained priests. The clergymen of Blackmore had a reputation for not being especially pious, and they were in no position to be judgemental about an unmarried woman. The building where Bessie stayed was nicknamed 'Jericho', known as a place King Henry hid his more inappropriate behaviour. The king had purchased the blandly named manor home of Newhall just eight miles north of Blackmore from Thomas Boleyn years earlier, and set about completely rebuilding it into a palace, which he later renamed Beaulieu or 'beautiful place'. Henry seemingly visited Bessie at Blackmore during and after her pregnancy, and while nothing suggested Henry wished to keep the situation a secret, no visits were officially recorded. Rumours suggested Henry rebuilt Newhall into Beaulieu specifically as a home for Bessie, but she is never recorded as visiting, so was more likely a base for Henry to visit Bessie and her child. Henry had owned Newhall for two years and had already started the rebuild when Bessie moved to Blackmore, but after her arrival, renovations increased, and the palace was described as of the highest royal standards after its completion. By 1522, Henry lived at Newhall more than Richmond Palace and Windsor Castle combined. Newhall was among Henry's hunting grounds, and with only eight miles to Bessie's new home, there is every suggestion Henry and Bessie continued their relationship for some time.

The ornate lying-in and confinements endured by Queen Katharine were a world away from what Bessie could have expected, even when having the king's child. She would have had midwives of good character selected, but even queens had attendants with no regulated qualifications. There would be no luxurious carpets, beds, and tapestries for Bessie, though Cardinal Wolsey was known to visit Bessie, so spiritually she may have been well-provisioned. Her mother, who had only just finished having children after enduring decades of childbirth, may have visited, along with her mother's sister, Katherine Smyth, who lived close to Hampton Court Palace.[13] Bessie likely had a wet nurse to feed her baby, giving her relief after going through a birth.

Bessie's labour and birth went unrecorded; she was simply not important. Bessie gave birth to a healthy son in June 1519, likely full-term. Cardinal Wolsey was seen with Henry at Windsor Castle on 18 June, but rather than travelling to Hampton Court as expected, Wolsey disappeared for ten days, suggesting he was north with Bessie at Blackmore during this time.[14] As both Bessie and her baby were given grants and elevations on 18 June several years in a row, this is the assumed date of Henry Fitzroy's birth. Naming her baby Henry was not unexpected as many babies were named after the king. Wolsey was the godfather to the baby, but all other godparents go unrecorded. The king did not attempt to hide Bessie's son; baby Henry received the surname of Fitzroy, meaning son of the king. While fiction has suggested Henry made a big show of his son and forced Queen Katharine to acknowledge the baby, there is no evidence for this. Henry would have been thrilled he finally had a healthy son, as he believed it showed he was not the reason he and Katharine had so many failed pregnancies. Both Queen Katharine and Bessie Blount were fertile women from fertile families, and it is more likely that Henry Fitzroy's birth was luck rather than King Henry's prowess. Either way, Queen Katharine's devastation would have been heartbreaking when she learned the news. Of all the things she had accomplished, nothing held the high esteem of giving a king a son.

When Henry Fitzroy was born in June 1519, the king was on progress. In addition to his usual palaces of Windsor, Richmond and Greenwich, Henry spent most of the summer travelling through Sussex, only moving north to Essex in August. King Henry and the court stayed at Havering for three nights, less than twenty miles south of Blackmore. Newhall then hosted the banquet of the summer, where the king spent 200l (over £100,000 today) on a masque to be performed, and this is likely when the myth Henry boasted of a son was born (in truth, he toasted King Francis' new son Henri).[15] Henry then moved to Heron Hall, just six miles from Blackmore between 12-14 September, and likely met with Bessie and her son at this time, or indeed several times during these close movements around her home in August and September. Assuming Bessie had a straightforward birth, by mid-September, Bessie would have recovered and been able to resume her relationship with the king. What came next is subject to conjecture. One theory is Henry had no interest in Bessie once she had a child, but there is nothing to suggest Henry lost interest in women once they gave birth. Bessie and Henry possibly thought a return to court life would be possible once the child had his own household. The king was not a man to use and discard women; despite the later image of a gluttonous tyrant, Henry was once a charming, popular, athletic, and intelligent man who loved to love. There is nothing to suggest Bessie was tossed aside. Given that Bessie then gave birth again, likely at Blackmore in mid-1520, her relationship with Henry was still ongoing, and baby Elizabeth could have been conceived during Henry's September visit to the area. Bessie's second child shared the surname of her first husband, whom she married several years later. Baby Elizabeth possibly had no surname for a time, living quietly with her mother at Blackmore. An illegitimate daughter would give Henry no added status, and thus did not need to publicly acknowledge the child. Lord Herbert of Chirbury, who wrote of King Henry with the benefit of now-lost evidence, recorded, '(Henry Fitzroy), roving so equally like to both his parents, that he became the first emblem of their mutual affection'.[16] Whether Herbert meant the literal 'first' emblem or its sixteenth century meaning of 'foremost', both suggest there was more than one result of their relationship. In June 1520, King Henry and the entire court attended the Field of Cloth of Gold in France, including Bessie's father John Blount and all their extended relatives in royal service. Bessie Blount is the notable exception. Given baby Elizabeth was twenty-two in 1542,[17] she was born while the king was away. Bessie's absence in France is suddenly much easier to explain.

Meanwhile, given baby Henry Fitzroy's illegitimacy, his early life is notoriously difficult to track. Soon after Fitzroy's birth, Princess Mary's household was reorganised, with Margaret Pole, Countess of Salisbury taking over the girl, and Lady Margaret Bryan becoming the Lady Mistress for Fitzroy, alongside several cradle rockers which had been previously assigned to Mary.[18] If a household, albeit small and unremarkable, was set up for Fitzroy, Bessie likely still had much say in her son's upbringing, especially while she was able to do little else while carrying her daughter at Blackmore. It was two more years before Henry had Cardinal Wolsey find a husband for Bessie, though some historians suggest Henry wanted Bessie married off as soon as Fitzroy was born, and baby Elizabeth was not Henry's daughter. There are things to suggest that was not true. Given that Bessie did not fall pregnant again after her daughter Elizabeth's birth in mid-1520, her relationship with the king may have cooled. Rumours flared that Henry had an affair, or at least an encounter, with a woman named Arabella Parker, the wife of a London merchant, though how gossipers came to this is a mystery. Rumours of a 'Mistress Parker' appeared, and while there was Margery Parker in Katharine's household, and Alice Parker was wife to Henry's Jewel-Master (and mother to Jane, later Lady Rochford), records show nothing.

Where Fitzroy's little household was set up is unknown but was either with Bessie at Blackmore or nearby Newhall. Bessie and her family had not received much in the way of gifts or grants from the king, but Henry could help her find a good marriage. Cardinal Wolsey, who had been overseeing

Fitzroy's life and housing, arranged for Bessie to marry one of his wards, Gilbert Tailboys. Tailboys was a suitable husband and would gain the barony of Kyme after his father died. The date of the marriage goes unrecorded, but Bessie and her husband received the Tailboys' lands in Somerset, Yorkshire and Lincolnshire on 18 June 1522, Fitzroy's third birthday. This suggests the marriage had recently taken place, with the land worth 200l and with an annuity of 40l (around £20,000 today). Within six years, Bessie and Tailboys had lands and annuities to the value of £342 (around £175,000 today).[19] As a favour, the king also granted permission for Tailboys to receive his inheritance and titles before his mentally incapable father's death, a large financial reward in itself. This deal would have made marrying Bessie even more attractive. While Bessie's many sisters were doomed to the fate of simple marriages and provincial lives, Bessie was safe for life. More sons for Bessie quickly followed, with George born in 1523 and Robert born in 1528, and at least three tragic losses between the two. Meanwhile, Fitzroy's sister Elizabeth, while named Tailboys, was not forgotten by the king, even if she was not acknowledged. King Henry visited Elizabeth once she was grown, helped her gain the title of baroness in her own right, and backed her in legal battles against her terrible first husband. Elizabeth was able to live the life of a titled and wealthy heiress, and married Ambrose Dudley, becoming the Countess of Warwick. Elizabeth was never welcome among the Tailboys family but was certainly welcome in noble circles throughout her life.

While Bessie's relationship with King Henry ended amicably, Fitzroy's birth affected the royal couple. Henry thought God could grant him a healthy legitimate son, for Fitzroy was proof. But 1518 was Queen Katharine's final recorded pregnancy, though Henry and Katharine surely continued to hope, even if Henry also continued to stray. Fitzroy's birth also gave rise to the question of whether Henry could end his marriage to Katharine. The idea of annulment had come up in the past, nasty salacious rumours made whenever Katharine suffered stillbirths. In 1522, the question was asked, could Henry put aside his wife? The answer was a firm no, and everyone dropped the issue. While Bessie Blount proved the king could have healthy sons, she was not suitable to be a queen (though Henry's choices rarely were). No one could beat Katharine of Aragon, the finest of women.

After her marriage, Bessie moved to South Kyme in Lincolnshire with her husband, and baby Henry Fitzroy lived at Durham Place, a manor on the edge of the Thames less than two miles from Westminster. While Bessie and King Henry had parted on good terms and continued to send one another New Year gifts, the young boy was about into come his own thanks to his father's affection. On 18 June 1525, Fitzroy's sixth birthday, he travelled the four miles from Durham Place to Bridewell Palace on the bank of the Thames in central London, to stay in the royal apartments. The royal chambers shone with cloth of gold and silk, culminating in a golden throne under a gold cloth of estate. With King Henry at the head and Wolsey at his side, the Dukes of Norfolk and Suffolk stood ready with the invited marquess', earls, viscounts, barons, and knights. Flanked by nobles of the court, young Henry Fitzroy entered wearing the robes of an earl. Fitzroy knelt before his father and king and rose as Henry handed the patents to the Speaker of the House of Commons, Sir Thomas More. More read the patent, and when he said 'gladii cincturam' (literally girdle of the sword), little Fitzroy knelt again and his father 'the King put the girdle about his neck, the sword hanging bendwise over his breast'.[20] Once the patent was read aloud, Fitzroy was Lord Henry Fitzroy, Earl of Nottingham. No illegitimate royal child had been placed in the peerage for four hundred years. Fitzroy left the chamber to change, now entering in the robes of a duke. They went through the process again and this time, Fitzroy became the 'right high and noble Prince Henry, Duke of Richmond and Somerset.'[21]

A double dukedom was an unmatched honour in Henry's time as king. The selections were careful; Richmond had been Henry VII's earldom, then given to Margaret Beaufort while she was in power with her son. The dukedom of Somerset once belonged to Margaret's father and grandfather, heirs of John of Gaunt and Edward III.

Queen Katharine was now forty years old, and Henry had to look elsewhere for an heir. Sadly, for Katharine, Henry would soon try yet again for a longed-for son.

Chapter 5

Princess Mary: Queen or Empress?

As Princess Mary celebrated New Year 1519 with her parents at Greenwich and prepared for her upcoming third birthday, news from Europe; Emperor Maximilian was dead.[1] This was no simple message, for the Holy Roman Emperor was not an inherited position. Seven electors, all from Imperial states in the German area would vote. Immediately, Maximilian's son King Charles of Spain put his hat in the ring, as did King Francis of France. This meant a lot for Princess Mary, even if she did not know it, for Charles was her cousin, and King Francis' son was her betrothed. Mary was still the heir-presumptive to the kingdom of England; would she want her future husband's country surrounded by Imperial powers? France and Spain already clashed along their border, as well as along the French northern border with the Spanish-ruled Netherlands. Charles wanted an alliance with England, but Mary's betrothal locked in England's treaty with France. If Francis won the title, Mary would be daughter-in-law to the Emperor, and ruler of England herself. It was possible that if King Francis became Emperor, his son the dauphin, Mary's future husband, could become Emperor after his father, making Mary the Empress of the Holy Roman Empire. Charles winning the election did not guarantee her as much prestige. King Henry had no interest in the role, despite suggestions from outsiders looking to gain money from any bribes Henry would have paid to Germany.

The election was lopsided from the beginning. King Charles' sister Mary of Austria was engaged to King Louis of Bohemia, and Charles quickly had his step-grandmother (and rumoured lover) Germaine de Foix marry Louis' legal guardian, George, Margrave of Brandenburg. These two men were both electors. Charles claimed he had these men and two others in his pocket. Thomas Boleyn, French ambassador for King Henry reported the French king believed the same four men were in his pocket. King Henry, already having a treaty with France through Mary, decided to sign the Treaty of Universal Peace with King Charles, the lavish ceremony going ahead in March 1519 at Greenwich, with Cardinal Lorenzo Campeggio standing in for Charles. Strangely, Queen Katharine was not allowed to attend the ceremony, but she did meet with the ambassadors separately to give her goodwill. Soon after, Charles became Holy Roman Emperor, leaving King Francis to sulk and blame his mother for the failure.

King Henry was still too scared to admit Princess Mary would be his heir, but the princess certainly continued to live like the future queen regnant of England. Lady Margaret Bryan was still the Lady Mistress of Mary's household through 1519, and now paid 50l a year (five times the average skilled wage), plus an annual tun (252 gallons / 1150 litres) of Gascon wine. Mary's household had been women acting as nursery staff, and others needed to run the basics of a home, but King Henry then ordered her household be expanded, with twelve grooms for the household, four grooms for the chamber, nine valets, and six gentlemen added at the end of the year. The roles could be quite varied, with a gentleman earning 10l a year, a valet only half of that, and grooms earning around 2l a year.[2] While Mary's household was still based primarily at Ditton, she spent the summer with her parents as they travelled to avoid the plague, and then stayed on at Greenwich with them and her aunt Queen Mary Tudor until December. With Henry expanding Bridewell Palace in London and Newhall in Essex, Mary's household looked tiny in comparison to other royal expenses. In December, Mary's household received all the essentials. Mary had a gold cloth of estate to sit behind her own velvet chair, with two cushions of cloth of gold and red velvet, with a valance of red and gold silk, accompanied by thirty pieces of tapestry. Mary needed six blankets for her room, along with three dozen pairs of sheets and eight long down pillows. She received luxurious carpets and pewter bowls and plates for her room, accompanied by endless pieces of high-quality fabric, and six brushes specially made for her gowns.[3] The nine tuns of wine hopefully were not at her disposal, unlike her favourite strawberries and cherries.

Judging by the King's Accounts, Mary must have spent much of January 1520 with her parents, her household surprisingly frugal. Henry and Katharine were at Greenwich for the first half of the month, Richmond for the second half, close to Mary's home at Ditton. By the time her fourth birthday arrived, Mary was back in her household, which needed 200l (£100,000 today) just to get through the month. Mary received birthday gifts from King Francis and Queen Claude to the value of 40l. Henry and Katharine were eager to settle alliance negotiations with Europe, as Henry and Francis had been planning to meet for months, growing beards for one another (though Katharine had urged Henry to shave, upsetting Francis' mother Louise of Savoy[4]). Henry's ambassador Thomas Boleyn went back and forth to France to plan the meeting, but Queen Katharine had not warmed to the idea of her daughter marrying the dauphin.[5] The French acted as if they already had one hand on the English crown, with Louise of Savoy teasing that France had so many healthy royal children they could afford to send the young dauphin to grow up in England. Louise making cruel jibes at Queen Katharine's pregnancy losses did nothing but undermine the entire meeting. Katharine wanted an alliance with Spain and Burgundy, not France. Her nephew was the King of Spain and Holy Roman Emperor while her sister-in-law Marguerite controlled The Netherlands. Katharine did nothing to hide her opinion from Henry.

May 1520 heralded a big shake-up for Princess Mary. Lady Margaret Bryan moved away to care for Henry Fitzroy, rapidly approaching his first birthday. Into the void stepped Margaret Pole, Countess of Salisbury.[6] There was no higher-ranked woman in England to care for the princess. Margaret was Mary's godmother, had been at Ludlow with Katharine and Arthur, was the niece of King Edward IV and King Richard III, but had been loyal to the Tudors for over thirty years. The Countess had never remarried after her husband's death and was the richest woman in England. Known for her noble piety, her children were high in royal circles and her daughter had married the Duke of Buckingham's son. Princess Mary's new household required 500l a month (£260,000 today) and was too busy to travel when her cousin Emperor Charles landed at Dover to meet with his aunt Queen Katharine and her husband.

All the planning and overly-flattering letters finally heralded the Field of Cloth of Gold meeting in France, and Henry and Katharine, with an entourage of 5,172 people set out from Dover to Calais, and then to the temporary palace made of cloth of gold between Ardres in France and Guînes in the English Pale of Calais. But Princess Mary stayed behind in England; it made no sense to have the young heir make the trip, so Mary stayed home in case anything untoward occurred and the Tudor dynasty suddenly needed a new leader. Henry made a point of taking two important men with him, the 'backup' heirs to the throne: Henry Stafford, Duke of Buckingham, the most senior Lancastrian heir, and Henry Courtenay, Earl of Devon, the most senior Yorkist heir. Mary was only four and did not need a coup on her tiny hands. Henry Lord Montagu also stayed in England, son of Margaret Pole, a senior safeguard in case of disaster.

The Field of Cloth of Gold took place between 7 and 24 June, while Mary stayed at Richmond Palace. Thomas Howard, 2nd Duke of Norfolk stayed behind in England to continue work for the royal council. Howard and the Council regularly went to visit Princess Mary and report back to her parents. Letters throughout the month reported on how well Mary was doing:

'we have sundry times visited and seen your dearest daughter the princess, who God be thanked, is in prosperous health and convalescence, and like as she increases in days and years, so does she in grace, wit and virtue...[7] on Saturday last were at Richmond with the Princess, who, lauded by Almighty God, is right merry, and in prosperous health and state, daily exercising herself in virtuous pastimes and occupations'.[8]

The Field of Cloth of Gold achieved precious little among its splendour, pomp, ceremony, and copious wine flowing from gold fountains. Mary's marriage to the dauphin was again ratified, making Mary the heir to the English throne and future consort of France.[9] As soon as the expensive event ended, Henry, Katharine, and Cardinal Wolsey set out for Calais to meet with Emperor Charles and Charles' aunt Marguerite, Regent of the Netherlands. At once, they suggested that little Mary break off her engagement to the dauphin, and instead marry her cousin the Emperor. They had a sixteen-year age gap, meaning it would be an equally long engagement as the one Mary had with the dauphin. Emperor Charles was engaged to the dauphin's sister Princess Charlotte, herself just an infant.[10] The new plan suggested Charles would attack France and put Henry on the throne, and then head south to conquer Milan. A letter written by King Henry to King Francis recalled the meeting, where Henry bravely stood up to Charles, defended France, and ensured there would be no war or broken alliance.[11] Whether Henry actually said these things to Charles' face is a matter of dispute.

While her parents negotiated in Calais, Princess Mary had her own delegation to consider. The French sent three ambassadors to England and after visiting London, travelled to Richmond Palace where Mary hosted an event. On 2 July, Lords Berners and Darcy brought the French ambassadors, where Mary had Lady Pole at her side along with high-ranked women in the realm. Princess Mary got up before the French delegation and, 'welcomed the French gentlemen with most goodly countenance, proper communication, and pleasant pastime in playing at the virginals, that they greatly marvelled and rejoiced the same, her young and tender age considered'.[12]

Her success complete, Mary travelled to Windsor to await her parents' arrival back in England. However, the plague was rampant at the height of summer, so Mary returned to her household at Richmond Palace to see out the season in safety. The household continued to receive around 200l per month before she rejoined her parents at Greenwich for Christmas and New Year celebrations. For now, Mary remained betrothed to France. Technically there was a peace treaty, even if the French king and the Emperor wooed England for peace if only to prevent each other from gaining England's allegiance.

Four-year-old Princess Mary would have no idea her future marriage was causing agitations with international rulers. But she needed to be prepared for a life of leading multiple countries. When it came to the start of Mary's education, she was especially fortunate. Queen Katharine had an exceptional education herself, as her mother had to rule Spain without even the basics. As a daughter with an older brother, Queen Isabella was uneducated and had to bring in tutors in adulthood so she could effectively rule once she had won by force.[13] Queen Isabella had a book commissioned; *De erudition nobilum puellaru* (On the Education of Noble Girls) by Alessandro and Anthonio Geraldini. Isabella could not even speak Latin when she became queen and had to learn quickly to rule her newly formed kingdom of Spain.[14] Consequently, all of Isabella's children, including the youngest Katharine, received a fine education. Isabella set up a classics school within her palaces, ensuring high-born orphaned girls were educated separately from their male classmates. By the time Katharine was fourteen and nearly ready to leave Spain, there was a new curriculum in place for both genders studying 'grammar, canon and civil law, and poetry', among others.[15] While Katharine may have participated in these classes, she was far above the rest of her mother's students, having her own tutors and being surrounded by ladies who had also received formal education. Consequently, Katharine was the first English queen in almost four hundred years to read, write, and speak Latin.[16]

Naturally, Katharine wished for the same formal education for Mary. When Katharine moved to England, she could already speak Spanish, Latin, French, and Greek, studied history, canon and civil law, scriptures, religious and classical works, genealogy and heraldry, philosophy, religion and theology, and mastered horse riding, hunting and falconry.[17] She had mastered more feminine subjects as well, sewing, embroidery, weaving, spinning, music, dancing, drawing, lacemaking, and even cooking. Katharine famously made King Henry's shirts herself with a complex and intricate black stitch, something her mother also did for her husband. Mary was likely expected to follow this simple family tradition. All these things could begin for Mary by age four.

Henry was not as educated as Katharine, for a king needed language skills like Latin and French, history, basic math, a smattering of law and religion, and little else given that they could call on experts at any time. Henry had always been an intelligent man and had no shortage of scholars to call upon for his daughter's education. Latin was Mary's first subject with her mother, and with Katharine's chaplain Richard Fetherstone.[18] French began younger than four as well, as the Royal Librarian, Giles Duwes, had assisted in King Henry's education. Princess Mary was an important influence on Duwes' works, as he was on hers; he later published a book on learning French called *An Introductorie for to learn and rede, to pronounce, and to speake Frenche trewly*, the book dedicated to Mary, as she commanded Duwes to create the book.[19]

Another of Mary's teachers was Thomas Linacre, a scholar admired by her parents. Linacre learned ancient Greek in Padua while studying medicine. Linacre was Prince Arthur's tutor but became King Henry's physician in 1509 and a founding member of Henry's Royal College of physicians in 1518. Linacre cared for Mary's learning and health, and while teaching Mary, authored a book called *Rudimenta Grammatices*, a collection of his Latin lessons with Mary. Linacre sadly died in 1524, with his book dedicated to Mary published a year after his death.[20]

Among the many scholars Mary could access, the finest Spaniard for the role was Juan Luís Vives. Vives hailed from the University of Valencia (then in the Spanish Aragon region), but after the death of his Jewish family at the hands of Isabella and Ferdinand's purge of Spain, Vives fled first to the universities of Paris and Leuven before meeting Queen Katharine's nephews Emperor Charles and King Ferdinand in Brussels. Vives went to England by invitation after dedicating his new book, *Augustine's De Civitate Dei*, to King Henry. While a Doctor of Law and Philosophy at Corpus Christi College at Oxford, Vives also taught Latin and philosophy to Princess Mary. Vives believed education produced better wives (meaning less likely to sin against their husbands). Vives regularly corresponded with friends Sir Thomas More and Erasmus, and his curriculum with Mary was heavy in religious works, as well as classical and modern authors, and learning to read Spanish and Italian thoughts on said subjects. Vives, like Erasmus, studied the Old and New Testaments, and Mary would have access to both. Vives drafted a book, commanded by Katharine and dedicated to Mary, called *De Institutione Feminae Christiane*[21] (Instruction of Christian Woman), a guide for young women, wives, and widows, heavily leaning on the notion of chastity and women being constantly controlled (and in some cases only ever physically viewed) by her father or husband. Princess Mary would go on to do the very thing Vives believed a woman should never do: rule.

There were plenty of works for Mary to absorb; she was proficient in mathematics and may have used Cuthbert Tunstall's *De arte supputandi libri quattuor* (The Art of Arithmetic), written in 1522. William Cornish, King

Henry's choirmaster, provided musical education for Mary's great enthusiasm, learning the virginals, lute, rebec, and harpsichord. Likewise, Mary developed a love of dancing at an early age, with a household of ladies well-trained to teach and amuse the young student. Meanwhile, Vives published two more books showing Mary's learning, first *De Rationo Studdiis Puerlis* (On a Plan of Study for Children), outlining her education and needs, and showing that translation of Latin to English was an effective way for Mary to learn. Vives included a reading list, and while the book was published when Mary was just eight years old, it showed heavy reading for the princess; Thomas More's *Utopia*, Erasmus' *Education of Christian Princes*, works by Horace, Cato, Lucca, Seneca and Plato's *Dialogues*. Another book soon followed, *Satellitum Sive Synbla*, a collection of mottos and expressions, among them *Veritas tempoeia filia* (truth, the daughter of time), Mary's personal favourite. At least among all this heavy work, Vives suggested Mary have classmates, a handful of students her age, which must have been a great delight for the only royal child. Mary's half-brother Henry Fitzroy remained firmly in his own small household, educated by John Robinson, who would have had similar works to draw upon for the boy, but Mary's household took precedence and lacked for nothing. Mary's work showed her intelligence, as by eleven years old, she had translated an intricate Latin prayer into English, placed inside the royal *Book of Hours of the Virgin*. St Thomas of Aquinas was a complicated prayer even for an adult to manage, about devotion to God in all things, and yet Mary mastered it as a child.[22]

New Year 1521 shows records of Mary's gifts, where she spent the festive season with her parents at Greenwich. Her godfather Thomas Wolsey gave Mary a gold cross, while godmothers, Agnes Howard, and Katherine of York, sent silver candle snuffers and flagons. Queen Claude, Mary's future mother-in-law sent a gold pomander, and Humphrey Dykers, one of the men in Henry's household, made miniature bows so Mary could practice archery now she was almost five. Musicians played, cakes, dresses, flowers, and Mary's favourites of oranges, capons, and grapes all arrived, while her nurse Margaret gave her a satin purse. Mary only returned home to Ditton for a fleeting period before returning to Greenwich for her fifth birthday, and a gift had arrived from the French royal couple in late January, perfume and dresses from Francis and Claude. Five days after her fifth birthday, Mary travelled to Richmond and then Southwark, to visit her cousins Henry, Frances, and Eleanor Brandon. A season in the warmth of her parents' company continued for Mary through until Easter, before she took a trip to Hanworth, first offering 12d at the altar of a Bridgettine convent at Syon, and then returned home to her studies at Ditton.

Princess Mary: Queen or Empress?

While Mary concentrated on her education, her parents had to defend her interests at home and abroad. With only a female heir, there was always the chance there could be another with a claim to the throne who may see himself as a more suitable ruler than a five-year-old girl. The biggest threat to the crown was undoubtedly Edward Stafford, 3rd Duke of Buckingham, whose mother was Catherine Woodville, sister of King Henry's grandmother Queen Elizabeth Woodville, wife of Edward IV. Stafford's father, the 2nd Duke of Buckingham, conspired against King Richard III, planning to stab him to death in a private meeting. King Richard had the duke killed, and young Edward Stafford remained hidden until Henry VII took the throne. Stafford received his father's title of Buckingham and remained close with Henry VII and Henry VIII, though the latter never grew to like or trust him. Buckingham had made the mistake of speaking too freely around people he thought he could trust and then started seeing a Carthusian monk, Nicholas Hopkins, who prophesied Buckingham would take the throne, as Henry VIII would have no male heir. Multiple plans, bribes to solicit support, and prophesies ensued over several years, until Buckingham made a mistake. Sir Charles Knyvett, estate official for Buckingham in Wales was fired from his post for no meaningful reason, prompting Knvyett to lash out, exposing Buckingham's loose lips over the years. A panel of judges pronounced Buckingham guilty of treason and he was beheaded five days after the trial.[23] Henry had ended the biggest internal threat to his crown and inherited lands worth 6,045l a year (well over £3,000,000 today). Knvyett, who heard Buckingham say he planned to stab King Henry to death just as his father planned to murder King Richard, got his job back managing the Welsh estates, assisted by his lawyer Thomas Cromwell, who lived in the Italian Austin Friars neighbourhood where Buckingham was buried as a traitor. Not all was settled, as Buckingham's son, Henry Stafford was married to Ursula Pole, whose mother was Margaret Pole, Princess Mary's godmother and governess. The relationship simply had to end, and Mary lost the woman who had been raising her for around eighteen months. Given the vast retinue around the princess, Mary may not have felt this loss to any great degree, but in time, the association would rekindle, as would the perceived betrayals.

For now, all those within England who felt they would serve as a better heir than Princess Mary felt humbled by Buckingham being a head shorter. A new governess arrived for Mary; her father selected Jane Lady Calthorpe, with her husband Sir Philip Calthorpe as Mary's chamberlain. Jane Calthorpe was Thomas Boleyn's sister, one of Henry's most trusted knights, and Lady Jane received a 40l annual salary to oversee the princess' household, slightly less than previous governesses.[24]

International influences offered no respite. The constant skirmishes on the border with Scotland remained, with Mary's nine-year-old cousin King James, ruled by the Duke of Albany, also a contender for the English throne over a female heir. Rumours of the French aiding the Scots persisted, against the alliance England and France had settled. Mary was still in line to marry the dauphin, but serious plans were afoot. Princess Mary was the prime pawn in a game of European rulers, with her cousin Emperor Charles offering a new proposition as various wars threatened.[25] Emperor Charles suddenly wanted to marry Princess Mary and for England to take up arms against the French while Charles prepped to take Milan.[26] By August 1521, negotiations were serious; but Charles wanted Mary at age seven, in February 1523.[27] Cardinal Wolsey would not take such a risk with Mary, for the threat to her safety, her 'reputation' and potential vilification or disgrace remained foremost in Wolsey's mind before any peace agreement. Wolsey called the Emperor's bluff; he could have Mary at age seven if Charles gave Flanders (and enough paid troops to hold it) to England as security. Naturally, Charles would not hand over a country. Charles wanted Mary and a dower of 250,000l (£130,000,000 today) in instalments, which was the offer made by Isabella of Portugal, but England would not budge. Mary's dower was 100,000l in ready money, and Henry was not prepared to sacrifice his daughter and heir. Charles could not fight the French in Navarre without England's help, nor could he accept the marriage alliance without upsetting his Spanish subjects, who wanted Isabella and her alliance with Portugal.[28]

Princess Mary would have no idea of all the rumblings, treaties and battles fought around Europe as she was paraded as a future French queen or Holy Roman Empress. She had spent most of the year at Ditton, including the festive season and New Year 1522 celebrations run by the Calthorpes. It is not recorded if her parents visited, though she spent time at Richmond with Henry and Katharine. Mary gained all the usual New Year gifts, a silver cup from her father, a gold salt bowl from Wolsey and a gold cross from Katherine of York. A gift came from Sir Richard Weston, who gave the princess twelve pairs of shoes, which must have been far more interesting for the young girl. John Thoroughgood, the Lord of Misrule, attended Mary's festivities and produced a play for the princess, a mock naval battle with real weapons and gunpowder for dramatics.[29]

With the usual festivities out of the way, Ambassador Lachaulx and his men arrived quietly in England to entreat Henry and Wolsey over a new Bruges alliance. Henry and Lachaulx met at Greenwich for a private meeting before Henry left to take part in a jousting event, a combination of celebrating Mary's birthday and the arrival of Imperial ambassadors. The evening entertainment meant Katharine and Mary could meet the envoy. Mary presented herself in the finest of gowns, wearing a golden brooch, with jewels spelling 'the Emperor', as Mary said he was her Valentine and was interested to hear about her potential new husband. Queen Katharine was eager to discuss important business on serious terms.[30] Several days later, Mary again met the group, and on being asked to dance for the group, delighted in showing off her skills, with Lachaulx writing:

> '(Mary) did not need to be asked twice... performing a slow dance and twirled so prettily that no woman in the world could do it better'. Mary then danced the galliard and then turned to her spinet (small harpsichord), and 'showed such unbelievable grace and skill and such self-command as a woman of the twenty might envy. She is pretty and very tall for her age, just turned (six) and a very fine young cousin indeed'.[31]

Among the many banquets and celebrations, Wolsey held one at his York Place home, a banquet with a pageant named Chateau Vert (Green Castle), or The Assault on the Castle of Virtue.[32] Henry again was one of the 'hidden' masked performers, though Katharine's interest in pretending she did not recognise him had probably waned. Among the ladies were Thomas Boleyn's daughters, Anne Boleyn, who had freshly moved home from the French court, and her sister Mary, wife to William Carey. Carey was a man in the king's chamber and was appointed the bailiff and Keeper of the Wardrobe of Newhall Manor, close to Bessie Blount's home at Blackmore. The young Carey couple received the use of the manor and other homes in the area, and more rewards would come again in July 1522.[33] Bessie Blount had just married Gilbert Tailboys and the king had ended his relationship with his long-time mistress. Carey now had several respectable posts from the king, and his father-in-law Thomas Boleyn had recently become Treasurer of the King's Household and received Fobbing Manor in Essex as a gift. Now that Henry had moved on from Bessie, either through lack of interest or out of decency, these promotions for Thomas Boleyn and William Carey hint at Mary Boleyn becoming the king's new mistress. Mary Boleyn possibly played the figure of Kindness in the play, while Anne Boleyn possibly played the figure of Perseverance, though records are far from specific.[34] Mary would come to have something of a reputation for her time living in France, all based on one line written by Rodolfo Pio, Bishop of Faenza, who heard King Francis call Mary Boleyn a whore, an easily discredited lie.[35] Pio boasts a long list of lies in various letters, including that Anne Boleyn faked her 1536 miscarriage (and that Mary Boleyn had been involved), and the lie that Henry had been unconscious for two hours after his jousting fall. The same situation is relevant in 1522; nothing suggests Mary Boleyn became King Henry's mistress at this time, as the benefits gained by Thomas Boleyn could have been for his tireless loyal work. Mary Boleyn may have been the woman of Henry's affections; he jousted several days later with woes of love on his costume rather than vows to Katharine, but simply nothing, ever, puts Henry and Mary Boleyn together.

The party atmosphere continued in England; after years of entreaties and correspondence, it was time for Emperor Charles to finally visit England and meet Mary. After the Field of Cloth of Gold in France, it was Henry's chance to lavishly splurge on an elaborate international event at home. King Francis must have been white-hot with anger over such an event, which marked the best point in relations between England and Katharine's family in Spain. Emperor Charles and his enormous retinue arrived at Gravelines on 25 May 1522, before heading to Calais led by English nobles, with Thomas Grey, Marquess of Dorset at the head.[36] Emperor Charles brought men from all over his realm to impress his potential in-laws, the Duke of Alba from Spain, the Duke of Cleves from the northern German regions, and likewise the Count of Nassau and the Marquess of Brandenberg. Charles had eight trumpeters to announce his every move, councillors from Aragon, Castile and Flanders, his doctors, cooks, tasters and even a sommelier. Charles had considered himself frugal in only bringing 1,000 people with him as they crossed the channel to Dover two days after their arrival. King Henry rode to meet Charles with all his closest men, and together they viewed English warships and sent messages to tell the French that England now supported Charles over France. France had been supporting Scotland, in contradiction with the Treaty of London, which broke Mary's betrothal to the dauphin.

On 2 June, Queen Katharine and Princess Mary met Emperor Charles at Greenwich Palace, the Emperor kneeling before mother and daughter.[37] The constant partying took a toll on the wine and food merchants of the city, with all 809 pipes of wine available in the city emptied (over 460,000 litres / 120,000 gallons). They dined on the finest veal, hare, quail, pigeon, sole, salmon, carp, crab, mullet and oysters. All the favourites were present too with oranges and lemons, olive oil, and capers. Parties and dances filled the nights, while jousts, pageants, hunting, and processions filled the days as they travelled between royal palaces.[38]

Princess Mary attended many events. She would seal the alliance that her father and cousin signed as the Treaty of Windsor. Mary was formally betrothed to Emperor Charles, and would one day be Empress, and Queen Regnant of England, with a dowry of 400,000 crowns (around £50,000,000 today).[39] Charles and England would go to war with France,[40] and Mary would receive a handsome jointure upon marriage. Emperor Charles' brother King Ferdinand of Hungary wrote of Princess Mary on their final day as they bid farewell that, '(Mary) promises to be handsome lady, although it is difficult to form an idea of her beauty, as she is still so small'. Mary was the only subject in which Ferdinand wrote generously, calling the English food, jousts, roads, and weather appalling. He believed his brother would never really marry Mary; neither Henry nor Katharine had responded to Ferdinand's help with the Turks in Hungary, souring his own experience of the event. By the end of June, the enormous fleet left England and regular life could resume for Mary, no longer the future Queen Consort of France, but now the future Holy Roman Empress alongside being Queen of England. Princess Mary returned to her studies at Ditton but spent more time at Windsor where she was learning falconry with her new goshawk received from her parents. Lord Bergavenny, back in the king's good graces after the Buckingham saga, brought Mary a horse to learn to ride. The royal family then continued to Richmond. For a while, Mary's life seemed as normal as she knew it to be.

By the time of her seventh birthday in February 1523, Mary was enjoying her studies and time with her parents who adored her. Henry called her 'his pearl', while Emperor Charles called her 'well-beloved future Empress'. Mary was still a child, but Charles needed a wife and the money that came with her to continue his wars to conquer Italy. England was technically in the battle, organising small invasions in France in 1522, only to back out with no success. But 1523 was supposed to be the dramatic battle invading France.[41] Charles was attacking France on all sides while they battled one another in Italy as well. Wolsey struggled to find the 800,000l (well over £400,000,000 today) needed to fund the invasion of France and even summoned parliament for the first time in eight years. If Henry wanted to keep his betrothal between Mary and Charles, he had to support the war. The nobles supported the war, though they had no interest in paying the extra taxes (only junior minister Thomas Cromwell dared to suggest the war was a bad idea[42]). King Henry invaded France anyway while Charles' troops staged multiple attacks in the east and south, and the Duke of Suffolk took an army into Brittany. The French would not engage, and the Emperor's backup troops never arrived, so Wolsey pulled the financing from the endeavour and Suffolk's army retreated only eighty miles from Paris.[43] The entire plan was a failure. Wolsey also missed becoming pope in the latest round of cardinals' voting, which could have significantly changed the battle lines in Italy. Christmas and New Year would not be celebratory affairs. With a new pope now comfortable on his throne, Pope Clement VII reconfirmed King Henry's title of Defender of the Faith, and Henry countered with a request for a dispensation to marry Princess Mary to Emperor Charles, permission needed due to their close relationship.[44]

France and the Empire were constantly at war over regions in Italy, with England having a negligible effect on European movements. While men fought, Louise of Savoy, in charge of France while her son King Francis (who lost his wife Claude to childbirth in July 1524) was in battle, wrote to Henry and Katharine. Louise suggested Mary abandon her marriage to Emperor Charles and return to marrying the dauphin once again, and Charles could marry one of Francis and Claude's daughters, all younger than Mary.[45] But with King Francis now widowed, he could remarry and make his own alliance, and another player stepped in – King Henry's sister Dowager Queen Margaret in Scotland. Margaret wrote to her brother and suggested Princess Mary marry her son King James V of Scotland (who was only a few years older than Mary), uniting England and Scotland.[46]

Upon all these discussions, Emperor Charles panicked; he wanted his ambassador Louis de Praet to take Princess Mary to Spain immediately, as she was nearing puberty and so old enough to live as a wife, where she could be a symbol of unity between the countries. Henry and Katharine flatly refused to send the 'treasure of the kingdom' away.[47] This time, everyone across Europe could see Henry never intended to give Mary to anyone. The year wore on, and Mary hid away from illness, much like Henry and Katharine, though Mary could continue her studies, unlikely unaware of any of the international movements that risked her future.

But less than a week after Mary's eighth birthday on 24 February 1525, Emperor Charles won the Battle of Pavia, which meant he controlled Italy, and captured King Francis. All discussions with France and Scotland ceased, and Queen Katharine was at pains to make sure her nephew knew England remained on his side.[48] Henry still believed he could go to war in France and take the country for himself now Emperor Charles had so much control. Mary met with the Imperial ambassador alongside Henry and Katharine, showing off her Latin skills, considered to be far beyond her tender age.[49]

But all was not well for young Princess Mary. English ambassadors went to Spain to start negotiations, as France would be split between England and Spain now King Francis had surrendered. Emperor Charles received an emerald ring, claiming to be from Mary, a symbol of their future marriage.[50] Charles was in trouble; Spain wanted Mary there to act as regent and ruler of the country as Charles was so often away. Charles desperately needed money and wanted Mary's dower, despite the fact he already owed England 150,000 crowns. Henry and Katharine would never send away the only heir to the throne, even if she were to rule Spain. For better or worse, they had only a female heir.

The royal marriage had little likelihood of bearing more children; King Henry had been rumoured to have continued his affair with Mary Boleyn on and off for some time. Christopher Coo recorded in his accounts of the king's ships that one was named the Mary Boleyn,[51] though all of Henry's ships had Mary in the name, and this particular ship was leased from Thomas Boleyn, just as the Anne Boleyn was leased a few years later. Mary Boleyn had given birth to a daughter, Catherine in approximately 1524, rumoured to be the king's daughter, but since Mary was married to William Carey, the king was under no obligation to acknowledge the child. As with his daughter with Bessie Blount, the child simply took his mistress' husband's name. The mysterious and entirely undocumented 'affair' between Henry and Mary Boleyn ended at this stage. Henry had enough to think about; he still did not have a male heir and Katharine would never bear one; the queen was now forty and had suffered more heartache than any woman should have to bear. Henry had his illegitimate son Henry Fitzroy named Duke of Richmond and Somerset, but that would never be enough. There were no other daughters to send to Scotland or France as wives to promote peace. Princess Mary could have gone to Spain to rule as she prepared to become the Empress of the Holy Roman Empire. But the pain suffered in the indulgent confinement rooms and nurseries of Henry and Katharine had taken away their children, and their dreams.

Princess Mary's future rapidly started to crumble. Emperor Charles needed a wife, and Mary was at least five years too young to go to Spain. Charles felt remorse for turning away from marrying his cousin but felt he had no choice. The Reformation was spreading wildly in the German regions,[52] and Charles needed to be there to stop it and needed money from a dowry to do it but wanted Henry's blessing on a different marriage.[53] King Henry demanded Charles make peace with France first and repay outstanding debts to England. But in July, Henry did the right thing, and rescinded the Treaty of Windsor, allowing Charles to break his betrothal to Mary, in return for gaining repayments of money owed.[54] Princess Mary was supposed to be the Holy Roman Empress and Queen Regnant of England, which would own a large chunk of France in its own right thanks to the Treaty. Now all was reduced to ashes, and even Henry's sister Margaret would not marry her son King James to Mary, as she had secured a French alliance. Had Mary not been an only child, she could have gone to Spain and embraced her mother's homeland, and instead stayed in her English household, while Charles married Isabella of Portugal and her huge dowry.[55] One can only hope Mary did not feel her parents' crushing disappointment or realise the brightest opportunity of her life slipped away.

King Henry had been fighting for Mary since she could walk, but now he needed to change his plans. Henry Fitzroy was a duke, but Fitzroy could not become legitimate by law, not at least while Katharine sat on the throne. Mary needed to prepare to be the heir and become the Princess of Wales. The Marches of Wales had been a constant problem; English rule was ineffective, the Welsh lords also fought each other, and lawlessness was rife. Edward IV had set up a Welsh council to control the area, headed by his young son Prince Edward, who mysteriously disappeared before his coronation aged twelve. Prince Arthur had this council re-established for him when he and Katharine went to Ludlow after their 1501 marriage. After Arthur died, the council continued in the region, but King Henry, the Prince of Wales since 1504, had never visited. Now, Princess Mary could begin training to be queen by controlling Wales and heading the Princess' Council.[56]

A woman could lead, and a woman could claim a title in her own right, though history had few examples. Mary was not officially Princess of Wales via letters patent, so the title would be informal but appeared in paperwork as early as August 1525 when the Princess' Council began their work. The Prince of Wales had been the heir to the English throne since 1301, and now Mary had the title, if not the official paperwork. Yet the king still had not accepted he would have a female heir.

Chapter 6

Henry Fitzroy, Ruler of the North

While Henry and Katharine prepared the new household and future for their daughter, they were still on good terms as a couple solely due to Katharine's immeasurable patience. Henry had recently spent 4,000l (over £2,000,000 today) on Henry Fitzroy's investiture as Duke of Richmond and Somerset. The day had been an all-male occasion, though Fitzroy's mother Bessie had her husband Gilbert Tailboys give her a first-hand account of the event. Katharine, of course, would not have attended the event, as she stayed at Windsor when Henry travelled to Bridewell to ennoble his son, whom he loved 'like his own soul,' claimed Lorenzo Orio, the Venetian ambassador.[1] From his prime position at the royal court, Orio could see the state of the relationship between Henry and Katharine, writing to the Doge and his council in Venice:

> 'It seems that the Queen resents the earldom and dukedom conferred on the King's natural son and remains dissatisfied at the instigation, it is said, of three of her Spanish ladies, her chief counsellors... so, the King has dismissed them from the Court, a strong measure, but the Queen was obliged to submit and to have patience.'[2]

A lesser woman could not have sustained the rebuke Queen Katharine suffered as Henry built up his son's new household while also working to send Princess Mary to Wales. The new household for 'Lord Henry' was prepared in time for his investiture, complete with the new motto 'Duty Binds Me'. Six-year-old Fitzroy had a household of 245 people to wait upon him, and it must have taken his father months to prepare the large retinue and household items required. Henry began to panic when his plans for Princess Mary and Emperor Charles started to fall apart and began putting together Fitzroy's new life as a backup plan. Just a week after his investiture as a duke, Henry Fitzroy had his official ceremony at Windsor Castle as he joined the Order of the Garter, ranked third on the list, only below Emperor Charles and King Francis. Fitzroy received a great mantle of purple velvet, a cross of St George, accompanied by purple silk tassels and sundial-shaped gold buttons. The tiny duke had arrived wearing a gown of black satin lined with sable, which he gave away at the end of the ceremony in customary fashion.[3] By this time, as a duke and member of the Garter, something Henry would never bestow on any legitimate son, Fitzroy would have looked even more like an heir to the throne. The only other illegitimate royal was King Henry's uncle Arthur Plantagenet, Viscount Lisle. He was the illegitimate son of Edward IV and yet he received nothing until age fifty when he entered his nephew's household and took a noble bride before being raised into the peerage another decade later. By comparison, Fitzroy looked perfectly acceptable as an heir.

All was a highlight of Henry's cruelty, and yet he probably never realised the pain he inflicted on Katharine, who never mentioned Fitzroy to her husband after an argument that saw three of her favourite Spanish attendants banished from court. Princess Mary was being prepared for Ludlow in Wales, and Henry was using his son with Bessie Blount as a little side project to nurse his ego for the losses in Europe. Both Katharine and Mary had been everything King Henry could have hoped for; a loyal and intelligent wife and counsel, followed by an exceptionally intelligent daughter who had all the early makings of a ruler. Yet Henry's vanity simply could not accept the situation. Raising Fitzroy within the nobility was for Henry's pride more than anything dynastically pressing. Fitzroy was six, past the age of most child mortality fears, looked healthy, had 'gravity and good manner', and was Henry's 'worldly jewel'.[4]

Despite claims by the Imperial ambassador, Fitzroy was not legitimate at this time, but Mary was not officially Princess of Wales either. But being Duke of Richmond and Somerset was seen as an implication of inheritance of the crown. Fitzroy also got the titles of Captain of the Town and Castle of Berwick upon Tweed, and Warden General of the Scottish Marshes,[5] also titles that tended to belong to royal heirs. More titles followed, as Lord President of the Council of the North, Governor of Carlisle, and Lord High Admiral of England.[6] Thomas Howard, 3rd Duke of Norfolk held the latter post, a prestigious public role that oversaw the entire country, and had to give it over to a six-year-old.[7]

The only main difference between Princess Mary and Fitzroy was that King Henry was not financially supporting his son, as the lands and titles received would generate income, a whopping 4,845l in the first year alone (over £2,500,000 today).[8] Mary was fully supported by the royal purse, which keep her close to the royal household; the king had carefully prepared everything. While Fitzroy had been living at Durham House on the Strand courtesy of Cardinal Wolsey (and granted the titles High Steward of the Bishopric of Durham and High Steward of the liberties of the Archbishop of York), it was time for Fitzroy to stop living in the care of women and move north to live like a prince.

Fitzroy's destination would be Sheriff Hutton, a northern base used by Richard III and his family before and after his coronation. King Henry needed someone in the north, even if it was his six-year-old son as a figurehead of power. The lords of the north could not be trusted to be loyal, law and order regularly got out of hand in the region, and the Scots were a constant threat. Usually, the region was held by the Archbishop of York or the Bishop of Durham, but Cardinal Wolsey held those posts. The rational thinking of placing Fitzroy as a figurehead in the north was likely Wolsey's idea, rather than Henry's.

The first expense account for Fitzroy's new household arrived at the end of July 1525, showing six weeks' worth of costs while he moved between Durham House and Merton Abbey, costing 523l (over £270,000 today).[9] It also shows costs at Hampton Court and Windsor, incurred while Fitzroy was visiting his godfather and the Garter investiture, respectively. The expense forms show Fitzroy's council; Sir Henry Wyatt, William Bulmer, Geoffrey Foljambe, Thomas Tempest, Brian Higden, William Franklin, Thomas Dalby, William Tait, Fitzroy's tutor John Palsgrave, Richard Page and George Lawson. All were men loyal to the king and especially to Wolsey, and Lawson was in-law to Wolsey's new lawyer Thomas Cromwell.[10] The expenses sit along another bill for fabrics needed for the household, a separate cost of 1,193l 8s 9¾d (£620,000 today).[11] Wolsey had given Fitzroy a litter, which was decorated in black velvet and cloth of silver, with copper buckles, and gold and silver gilt reins bearing silk buttons. Luxurious altar cloths were sent, along with a special vestment of purple velvet, and blue and yellow liveries for Fitzroy's councillors and servants. While this still paled in comparison to Mary's costs in the same period, it was certainly not minimal.

Even Fitzroy's diet was well organised in advance. It varied throughout the year, though generally, the boy could have whatever he liked at breakfast, while his advisors and servants were on a strict diet for every meal.[12] For Fitzroy's afternoon meal, the first course was pottage, boiled beef, mutton, geese, capons, veal and custard. The second course consisted of lamb or kid, rabbits, pigeons, wildfowl, a tart or baked meat, fruits and four gallons of ale and two pitchers of wine, hopefully for those dining with him. The dinner meal was equally heavy, with pottage, chickens, roast mutton, roasted capons, rabbits, and twelve sweet desserts. The second course was again lamb or kid, roast chicken, pigeons, wildfowl, two tarts, fruits and again the same huge volume of ale and wine, all accompanied by a range of salt, sauces and spices. One can only hope the boy had copious others at his table when this food was prepared each day. During Lent and other religious meat-free days, the meals would substitute with ling, cod, salmon, salt eels, boiled pike, sturgeon, sole, shrimps, crayfish, or a mix of other fresh and saltwater fish as available. All levels of the household had strictly measured diets, from Fitzroy's daily buffets down to the lowest-ranked grooms, whose meals would be little more than pottage, sliced cold meat, and some ale. The estimated costs of household food alone came to just over 2,900l a year (£1,500,000 today).

By the end of July 1525, it was time for Fitzroy to leave for Sheriff Hutton. The huge train of 245 people plus copious carts to carry all they needed, left in the blue and yellow livery showing the Richmond crest of a lion demi-rampant bursting from a Tudor rose. While Henry's illegitimate son was known at court, now he was about to be known everywhere. They left Stoke Newington in Middlesex on 26 July and travelled to Northampton before passing through Buntingford, Shengay and Huntington before reaching Collyweston in Lincolnshire on 1 August, a trip of eighty-five miles. Fitzroy took the journey well but enjoyed the break at Collyweston, one of Margaret Beaufort's favourite locations. The litter Wolsey had made went to waste; the boy sat in it for only three or four miles, before wanting to ride his pony for the rest of the trip, which seemed to brighten his spirits.[13] Fitzroy reportedly killed a deer at Cliff Park outside Collyweston.[14] They set off for Grantham in Lincolnshire on 7 August, heading north to Marton Abbey in Stillington, reaching York on 17 August. Eleven days later, the local gentry of the area welcomed the great train as Fitzroy headed to his new home at Sheriff Hutton, a 200-mile trip from London.[15]

Sheriff Hutton Castle, the stronghold of Richard III, a glorious three-story castle overlooking the area, had fallen into serious neglect by the time Fitzroy arrived. The gatehouse lead through into three courtyards, and a staircase took little Fitzroy to his rooms, but other than his area, much of the castle to fallen in disrepair, with damaged roofs and chimneys, collapsed walls and rusted iron gates.[16] The household had 320l (around £150,000 today) to spend on repairs, and the castle had a good water supply, enabling the small village that was the Fitzroy entourage to make themselves at home. Once Sheriff Hutton was set up, the walls heaved in lavish golden tapestries, red or green velvet chairs laced with green silk, and gold thread embroidery showing Fitzroy's arms.[17] Little Fitzroy sat on a gold chair with a gold cloth of estate above him when guests arrived.

The castle was set up as an administrative base for the north, though Wolsey still controlled most things from London. Tutor Palsgrave and Fitzroy's nurse Anne Partridge were the only suggestions the new ruler of the north was a child.[18] It was a mostly male household since Fitzroy would never see the servants in the kitchen and laundry, and after being raised gently and in the presence of his nurses at Durham House, it would have been a huge change. Palsgrave set to work immediately, looking to teach Fitzroy Latin, French and Greek and called on colleagues Sir Thomas More and Archdeacon Stephen Gardiner for advice. Palsgrave had already published his book, *Lesclarcissement de la languine Francoyse*, on how to teach French and had once taught the king's younger sister Queen Mary. William Saunders joined the household, Fitzroy learning to play the virginals at once, and also singing and dancing. Palsgrave was a tutor who gently nurtured his students, allowing the child time to play in his learning, and he punctuated time spent reading and writing with archery, horse riding, hunting and falconry, all expected of a prince. All would have been most entertaining for Fitzroy, who had classmates in William Parr, Fitzroy's chamberlain's son, and George and Henry Blount, Fitzroy's uncles who were his age.

No sooner than the house was set up, cracks began to appear. While the boy had a marvellous Christmas and was lavished with gifts, visitors and praise, John Palsgrave was fired from his post. Many looked to gain favour with the child and would offer Fitzroy the chance to go riding or play games at the expense of his learning. Palsgrave fell into financial trouble and by Christmas, Palsgrave was removed, and Wolsey's friend Sir Richard Croke took his place. Palsgrave accepted help from friend Thomas Cromwell, limped home to London and accepted a post teaching Cromwell's son Gregory.[19]

Fitzroy himself was on the move. He stayed home for Christmas at Sheriff Hutton, and travelled to Collyweston for Candlemas in February 1526, but was back home by April, where he received a letter from his half-cousin, King James of Scotland.[20] Travels like these would allow Fitzroy's homes to be cleaned in his absence. While he then spent more time throughout the year at Sheriff Hutton, winters and the festive seasons were spent thirty miles south at Pontefract Castle, which also needed extensive repairs.[21] The Council of the North would travel between places and do the work needed on Fitzroy's behalf, the boy signing papers he likely had little interest in reading or understanding. Sir Thomas Magnus took care of official business in the council, leaving others to run the Richmond household.

But education remained the biggest issue. Croke's appointment was no better managed than Palsgrave's. King Henry had sent his son to the north to rule, but without supervision, Fitzroy answered to no one. The boys would taunt Croke, calling him a bastard and running off to play rather than learn. Wolsey had made up a strict guideline for teaching, but the boy preferred inappropriate songs in his privy chamber with fools and players rather than learning anything worthwhile. The household's chamberlain Sir William Parr forced the boy to spend his evenings in religious prayer rather than study, and Fitzroy got to a stage where no one could control him.[22] No punishment would work, as Fitzroy could beat his staff in retaliation, despite the fact even royal students got whipped by tutors. Fortunately for Croke, by 1527, King Henry recalled him to London, in need of scholars for a thorny issue, whether a king could annul his marriage. Croke had done a marvellous job given the circumstances, as Fitzroy had perfect handwriting skills and could send eloquent letters when he so felt, even sending Croke home to London with a hearty letter of recommendation.[23] Fighting for the king's divorce in Italy probably felt like quite a relief in comparison.

Fitzroy spent New Year 1527 at Pontefract Castle, sending his father a gift of two small gold pots engraved with branches, and the household spent the occasion quietly with few visitors. Fitzroy received a gift from the king in return, a gilt bowl with a cover, weighing forty-eight ounces. This was not a gift that could delight a seven-year-old, but Fitzroy was forced to write a thank you note in return, writing, 'beseeching your grace to accept and take this, my letter, penned with mine own hand, for a poor token at this time'.[24]

A new visitor arrived in February 1527, a messenger from King James in Scotland. James was about to have his fifteenth birthday and lived as a prisoner under the power of his stepfather Archibald Douglas, Earl of Angus. James had almost escaped several times over the years, but each plan failed. Now, there was an attempt to foster a relationship between James and his cousin Fitzroy, his nearest royal neighbour over the border. Fitzroy was excited to receive the message and wrote back at once that he would send his ten best hounds, along with servants, including dog trainer Nicholas Eton, to King James as a gift.[25] In return, King James also fell over himself with praise, treating Fitzroy's servants with great respect and sent a pair of hounds and a promise to send red hawks.[26] At once the two rulers began an open conversation, requesting each other's help with issues on the border. But by the end of 1527, Fitzroy's education had broken down, the eight-year-old boy doing as he pleased, when he pleased.

By the beginning of 1528, England was suffering many changes. Fitzroy was isolated from the realities of court and his father's movements. Henry had started to reject Queen Katharine, obsessing over his latest mistress

Anne Boleyn, while looking to develop a marriage alliance with France for Princess Mary. Cardinal Wolsey was overwhelmed with negotiations. Fitzroy featured none in the 'Great Matter,' but with marriage negotiations taking place for Princess Mary, Fitzroy could potentially gain an alliance too. A suggestion first came in March 1527 that Fitzroy could marry Catherine de'Medici, Pope Clement's niece.[27] This was no easy alliance; Catherine de'Medici was a force of nature, eagerly wanted by the Empire, Scotland, and France. Catherine had lost her parents as an infant and was raised in the bosom of the powerful Medici circles. But Wolsey had another idea; marry young Fitzroy to Emperor Charles' niece, Infanta Maria of Portugal.[28] This was not easy; the Portuguese dowager queen and her daughter, Eleanor and Maria, strangely were to marry King Francis and his son the dauphin, respectively. Their cousin Isabella was already married to Emperor Charles, and this bizarre plan to marry father and son to a pair of sisters would create a strong alliance between Spain and France. Wolsey looked to break the betrothals of this new Treaty of Madrid (which helped to get King Francis out of Emperor Charles' prison after the Battle of Pavia), and instead get Princess Mary of England again betrothed to the dauphin.

The Emperor and his Chancellor Granvelle were not fooled by rumours King Henry could make Fitzroy the heir to England, or even King of Ireland. They did not believe an illegitimate son of the king was worthy of a Portuguese princess. Emperor Charles was dismayed by the treatment of his aunt Queen Katharine as Henry sought a divorce. Charles had imprisoned Pope Clement and sacked Rome in 1527,[29] so Henry's divorce plans had been on hold, and now threatened Katharine and Mary's inheritance, while treating Fitzroy as an equal in the marriage stakes. As Wolsey fought to create his long-held dream of European peace, he had to make choices between his godchildren. Princess Mary had to take precedence, possibly marrying King Francis' second son Henri, Duke of Orléans. Wolsey wanted peace with France through the new Treaty of Amiens, and when it was close to completion in mid-1527, Emperor Charles panicked and suggested Fitzroy could have Maria of Portugal after all, and the 'gift' of the Duchy of Milan as well as a dowry of 400,000 ducats (almost £35,000,000 today).[30] Charles had no intention of honouring such a plan; he simply did not want France to have Milan, and Wolsey saw through the deceit, despite King Henry's instance at pursuing the false offer. Cardinal Wolsey would have his French alliance and only gain a marriage for Fitzroy if it never dared threaten French peace and Princess Mary's future marriage.[31] As soon as this idea fell apart, Christina of Denmark was floated as an idea for Fitzroy, though she eventually married Emperor Charles' man Francesco Sforza and took Milan as her own, Fitzroy featuring nowhere. All the discussion around Fitzroy was just a rouse to get Mary a French husband.

As 1528 dawned, with Fitzroy staying at Pontefract Castle, England was about to take a turn. King Henry was suddenly trying to get rid of Queen Katharine, after all she had suffered, including Fitzroy's birth and elevation. Seemingly, this meant nothing to Fitzroy's life; he wrote to his father and godfather on 31 January, asking for new armour, as he had been reading about Julius Caesar and wished to emulate the glory.[32] But a letter dated 9 March, from Fitzroy's council to Wolsey showed a prelude to coming disaster when they mentioned they had released a prisoner from York Castle for his safety, 'as the sickness there is so sore and contagious that fourteen prisoners and others are dead'.[33] Fitzroy and his household carried on as normal, spending time in Riddesdale and Newcastle, and corresponding with both the king and James in Scotland. They returned to Pontefract in late April, just as the worst happened; sweating sickness broke out in London, and within weeks had spread through England. With half of all those infected dying, there was no opportunity to be calm. By 31 May, Fitzroy and just five of his household left Pontefract, as Sir William Parr wrote to the king:

> 'six persons have died lately in the lordship of Pontefract, and many young children are sick of the pox. The Council have therefore determined to remove (Fitzroy) to Ledeston, three miles hence. Those that died were first attacked with a great cold, next with a fervent heat and sweating, when they became delirious'.[34]

Parr reminded Wolsey that there were no doctors in the area, and the vacancy for one in the Fitzroy's household had never been filled. Fitzroy and just a few servants went to stay at the Priory of St Johns, part of the Pontefract Priory and hoped the illness would pass them by. Fitzroy was a lucky boy, as he and those around him all stayed well, and on 20 July sent a letter through Thomas Magnus at Sheriff Hutton, to thank the king for the 'goodly apparel' sent north and promised to study as his father requested.[35]

While King Henry and Queen Katharine remained healthy, moving to stay well, many of Henry's closest men had suffered the sweat, including Cardinal Wolsey, who managed to survive his fifth potentially fatal dose of the illness. Thousands did not, such as Thomas Cromwell's wife Elizabeth, but Anne Boleyn, her father Thomas, and brother George all managed to survive a bout of the sweat (though Mary Boleyn's husband William

Carey perished). Fitzroy, having spent his tenth birthday in isolation at the Priory of St John's, returned to Sheriff Hutton in October 1528.[36] Fitzroy had emerged safe from his quarantine and visited Topcliff, the home of the Duke of Northumberland, and was reportedly a well-behaved guest,[37] and also hosted the Earl of Westmorland at Sheriff Hutton, now old enough to conduct 'himself more like a man than a child of his tender age'.[38] The king had sent Fitzroy 'preservatives', medicine he had made for Fitzroy, especially to get them through the period, one of the most practical gifts given by the king, when others were usually golden collars or gold unicorn horns.[39]

While Fitzroy had come through the epidemic unscathed, his household was still in a calamitous state. The household had been running at double the estimated costs, and despite cuts, spending had been out of hand and running at a deficit since 1525. Croke accused multiple men in the household of embezzlement, as accountants sent north failed to understand why the household income was not collected, fees went unpaid, and costs spiralled. Wolsey set up stricter regulations for the household, reducing costs and stopping rumours of theft, as everything from excess meat in the kitchens to used rolls of cloth were inspected, and bills were to be paid. Despite the lack of household management by William Parr, Thomas Magnus and his Council in the North had done their best and made progress by 1529, despite huge obstacles from stubborn northern lords.

Young Fitzroy and his now-rejoined household and council spent the New Year 1529 at Sheriff Hutton, but it was all over for the young duke and his power over the north. The entire household was recalled back to London, Fitzroy arriving back in time for his tenth birthday in June 1529. Given that the divorce of the century was also occurring, Fitzroy returned relatively unnoticed. Fitzroy did still feature a little in the ongoing saga, as Wolsey and Cardinal Campeggio both considered marrying Princess Mary to her half-brother Fitzroy so that the English throne could be safe (religious dispensations could be granted, with missionary sex between brother and sister considered less sinful than other positions with an unrelated partner[40]). But Henry did not feel the need to protect his kingdom by marrying off either of his children, for he would have an heir with Anne Boleyn. Had Henry wanted to put Katharine aside to gain a new marriage for more children, the Pope, and even Katharine's nephew Emperor Charles, may not have objected. But no, Henry wanted Anne Boleyn, a woman considered too inferior to be a queen, and such a marriage brought no diplomatic ties. To top it off, Henry had even allegedly slept with Anne's sister Mary Boleyn. Everything planned for Fitzroy now suddenly crumbled while his father planned for more sons with Anne Boleyn and took the moral high ground in a legatine court, arguing ecclesiastical law against papal legates.

Fitzroy's household and the council broke up, he went back to living at Durham House on The Strand during the royal marriage trial. Perhaps he even got to see his mother Bessie at some stage, and King Henry and Bessie remained on good terms. As the marriage trial collapsed and Wolsey dissolved into despair, Fitzroy's movements and household became hidden under the ongoing drama. But in April 1530, Fitzroy's stepfather Gilbert Tailboys suddenly died, leaving Bessie in possession of a good fortune and a comfortable position. Now was the perfect opportunity; Henry could marry Bessie, legitimise their son Fitzroy and make him the male heir. Henry had loved Bessie for some time. But for all of Henry's complaining about wanting a legitimate marriage and an heir, all he wanted was Anne Boleyn. Fitzroy could easily become legitimate by an act of parliament if Henry married Bessie. The Pope would have agreed to such an annulment from Katharine. Katharine, the rightful queen no matter what Henry believed, would not have liked such a scenario but could have done nothing to argue the case. But Henry's blind devotion to Anne Boleyn, as detested as she was, and unsuitable to be queen compared to Katharine, could not leave Henry's side, no matter how tempting Fitzroy looked as a future king of England.

Chapter 7

The Princess of Wales

Princess Mary's new household in Ludlow was no simple affair. The colours of her household were blue and green, and thousands of yards of damask fabrics were needed for servants' uniforms before they left London. Mary had been disappointed with the palfreys that had been allocated to her, and despite over 100l spent, Sir Andrew Windsor was tasked at short notice to find replacements.[1] Mary's new household had huge facilities to accommodate her, the bakehouse, pantry, buttery cellar, larder, blowing house, spicery, ewry, chandry, saucery and pantry, kitchen, scullery, laundry, almery, stable, scalding house, and counting house all needed a huge fit-out of items, plus fabrics for liveries. Carts came into London from all over southern England to accommodate the volume. The king's armourer William Carter, plus two gunners, joined Mary's household to ensure her protection, and the king's best physician William Butts was to join the Ludlow household.[2] Butts had initially been enlisted to join Fitzroy but was then swapped to Mary, leaving Fitzroy without medical care. Setting up Mary's household with essentials for heating and cooking, plus stable care for her houses cost 972l (just over £500,000 today) for the first year, roughly equal to the costs of her household at Ditton.[3] Besides the officers of her council and their servants, Mary had sixty-two grooms working in the household, at a cost of 40l 4s 8d per quarter.

The most important staff for Princess Mary were her ladies, seventeen of them assigned to go to Ludlow, all given black velvet to wear while working for the princess. While Jane Lady Calthorpe was given dispensation to wear black velvet and spent some time with Mary's household, she was to be replaced as Lady Mistress by her predecessor, Margaret Pole, Countess of Salisbury. The suspicions involving the Pole family during the Buckingham execution had cooled, allowing Mary to have her close ally back, now old enough to form a real attachment to Lady Pole. While Lady Katherine Grey, (daughter of Thomas Grey, Marquess of Dorset who was head of Princess Mary's council) was second in the hierarchy of ladies, alongside Katharine Pole and Elizabeth Pole, daughters of Henry Lord Montagu, and Constance Pole, wife of Geoffrey Pole. They were joined by Anne Knvyett,

Mary Dannett, Cecily Dabridgecourt, Frances Elmer, Anne Rede (wife of Mary's comptroller Giles Greville), plus Marie Wicter, Anne Elmbridge, Anne Darrell, long-time Queen Katherine lady-in-waiting Margery Parker, and three unidentifiable women, Mrs Baker, Mrs Perit and Mrs Geynes.[4] It appears there were no children in Mary's home; she was nine years old by this time and while some of the women in her household were young, all were in their teens by this time.

Princess Mary had been staying at Woburn in August 1525 as her household readied around her. Ludlow Castle was in disrepair and required 45l 17s 9d (£23,000 today) worth of work completed before it became liveable. Mary's parents were not with her when she left and is hard to tell when Katharine had last seen her daughter, despite letters between the pair saying all was well. Mary was taking Master Fetherstone with her to ensure her Latin continued well, but Katharine also wanted to keep a close eye on her daughter's progress. Mary and her enormous train of servants and carts left Woburn on 15 August 1525, heading west toward Kingswood Abbey in Wotton-under-Edge, onto Thornbury Castle in Gloucestershire, arriving on 1 September. Mary sent Wolsey a polite and formal letter of thanks after she arrived, telling Wolsey, 'that you show yourself with continuance unto me a very kind spiritual father'.[5]

Mary and her train of attendants left Thornbury Castle on 12 September, and took a tour through the nearby town, to the breathless excitement of the mayor and one hundred burgesses who lined the streets to greet her. The reverence to Mary took all day, and she stayed the night at St Peter's Abbey, a Benedictine house with the tomb of Edward II, a pilgrimage site where Mary kissed the cross and left an offering of a purse of gold.[6] Princess Mary could not travel anywhere without the crowds looking to catch a glimpse and local officials falling over themselves to shower praise on the royal girl.

By November, Mary was at Tewkesbury, and her council decided upon an appropriate Christmas for Mary, needing particular silver items so she would be served in the manner she deserved, and Bishop Exeter wanted to appoint a lord of misrule to oversee celebrations and entertainment and looked to hire trumpeters and rebecs to provide music. Even Mary's gift list needed preparation; gifts were not for enjoyment but needed to be appropriate for the rank of the recipient. What would a princess give to a king, queen, or cardinal as a suitable gift? Mary stayed at Tewkesbury for Christmas, before moving on to Tickenhall and then Worcester in January, staying until Easter 1526, which fell on 1 April. Mary offered a gold crown at mass where poor Prince Arthur lay at rest.[7]

The Princess of Wales

Records show a royal banquet held at Greenwich on 6 May 1526, stating it was on behalf of Henry, Katharine, Princess Mary, and Mary Tudor. But it is unlikely Mary attended the event, given it was 130 miles from Worcester. More likely, it was in her honour as a member of the royal family.[8] But Mary soon moved on to Hartlebury Castle near Worcester, but the plague began to spread. It was a serious concern, as Mary was constantly visited by people looking to gain favour. Mary remained in the Worcester area, but their options were limited as the household was filled with sickness. Henry, and possibly Katharine, were at Warbington Castle in the south in August but planned to travel to Woodstock to see Mary, but servants began dying of plague there too. Henry was finally able to meet with Mary on 1 September at Langley in Oxfordshire, a fifty-eight-mile trip for Mary. Henry, Katharine, and Mary travelled the remainder of the summer together at Bicester, Buckingham and then Ampthill, before Mary had to return ninety miles to Hartlebury. Cardinal Wolsey had been unable to travel with the royal couple, and indeed, was unlikely to be welcome, as his relationship with Henry had strained over the failure to raise taxes for war in France a few years earlier. Richard Sampson, then an archdeacon and former Imperial ambassador, travelled with the royal couple, and told Wolsey that Princess Mary, 'of her age, as goodly a child as ever I have seen and of as good gesture and countenance.'[9] Mary may not have had the official title of Princess of Wales, but she was treated as such, and consequently as the heir to the throne in every respect, and finally left the royal court to continue her life as heir-presumptive on 1 October.[10]

The Princess' Council changed over the summer season. Thomas Grey, the Marquess of Dorset was in attendance, whereas his rule was usually only ceremonial. John Vesey, Bishop of Exeter remained the president, just as Dr James Denton remained the chancellor. Edward Dudley remained Mary's chamberlain, but soon the role of doctor and apothecary were vacant, with many physicians worried they were not worthy enough to serve the princess. There were plenty of people to care for in Mary's household; her monthly October expenses came to 8951 9s 10½d (£460,000 today).[11] An expense list written up on 31 December shows the cost of Mary's household for the first eighteen months she lived as Princess of Wales, coming to a total of 63881 17s (over £3,200,000 today).

The time had been well-spent. Along with all the needs of a royal household, diets, and strict governance, Mary's education and living standards also had a strict set of guidelines. Henry and Katharine made provisions on how their daughter was to be treated and cared for, though Wolsey wrote the rules of the household's governance. While Mary's education in Latin, French, Greek, mathematics, history, classics, religion and anything else she liked was strictly enforced, all had to be designed to maintain her health and happiness. Mary was to go outdoors every day to exercise in the 'gardens, sweet and wholesome places'. Mary ensured her education was physical as well as intellectual with her dancing, singing and music lessons, but was never allowed to be exhausted by any of her subjects. Mary's life was to be 'pure, sweet, clean and wholesome, and as to so great a princess does appertain'. There could not even be noisy activities, or anything unpleasant to the princess. Even mealtimes were meant to be happy and entertaining, 'in all honour and virtuous manner'. While Mary did complain about missing her parents, she was an otherwise happy child.

By the time Mary turned twelve in February 1527, she was an exceptionally accomplished girl. Her studies had never suffered much disruption, she was intelligent, pious, and talented like her mother. In the time she had been living in the west as Princess of Wales, the international negotiations for potential marriages had not ceased. Mary was approaching the appropriate age that she could be married. Noble girls had to marry much younger than the general population; Katharine married Prince Arthur at fifteen, and her sister Juana of Castile married Archduke Philip at sixteen. Margaret Tudor married the Scots king at age fourteen, Mary Tudor married the French king at eighteen, and Elizabeth of York married Henry VII at the age of twenty. Margaret Beaufort had been married at twelve and gave birth at thirteen, with the harm of that instilled into her son and then grandson; young marriages were unsafe. Prince Arthur had died just months after his marriage at fifteen, and so Princess Mary would not marry young, no matter the requests of international kings and emperors. Princess Mary would not be a child bride.

Still, Europe's leaders continued to fight and look for alliances. King Francis of France had been a prisoner of Emperor Charles for a year and was swapped for hostages in 1526. Francis sacrificed his sons Dauphin Francis and Duke Henri to take his place as hostages. King Francis had promised to marry Eleanor, Dowager Queen of Portugal and sister of Emperor Charles, but looked to renege on this Treaty of Madrid at once and looked for an alliance with England. Emperor Charles held all the power in Europe, but he was not well-liked. The Italian states were looking to ally with one another for protection; France wanted the princes released; Charles owed England vast sums, and in the German States and Low Countries, the Reformation created sweeping changes. Even though Princess Mary had once been engaged to the dauphin, the younger son of France was now more popular. The third option was for Mary to marry King Francis himself, despite the twenty-two-year age gap, and the fact he was the man who swapped his children into a hostage situation. Francis was all for the marriage, except for the fact he would break his alliance with Charles and potentially never see his imprisoned heirs released.[12] Wolsey sent his ambassador John Clerk to entreat on matters in France all through 1526, constantly looking for King Francis to marry Princess Mary and get Emperor Charles to pay England its dues. England was likewise owed money for the last time they gave France a queen; Henry's sister Mary had married a king thirty-three years her senior, and monies owed had never been satisfied. Clerk hounded Francis to create an English alliance, and at one point Francis snapped at the ambassador saying:

> 'I pray you, repeat unto me none of all these matters. I know well enough (Mary's) education, her form and fashion, her beauty and virtue, and what father and mother she cometh of, and how expedient and necessary it shall be for me, and for my realm, that I marry her. And I assure you for the same causes I have as great a mind to her as ever I had to any woman; but I must do my things as near as I can without displeasure of God and reproach of the world'.[13]

As usual, negotiations were weak with King Francis, and his mother Louise of Savoy stepped in to create an alliance. Francis, and France, needed the princes back from Emperor Charles, safe and able to inherit the throne. Thus, King Francis would have to marry Emperor Charles' sister, the rich widow Queen Eleanor of Portugal, despite the fact she was already thirty (and Francis disgustingly liked young children, not grown women), and that no one else would have her. If the dauphin married Eleanor's daughter Maria of Portugal, as was already set in the Treaty of Madrid, Princess Mary could marry the dauphin's brother Henri, who could go to England and be king beside her. King Henry wanted his daughter betrothed but giving his country to France would be a bitter pill to swallow. Katharine for her part never trusted the French or liked a marriage for Mary to any member of the French royal family. But by early 1527, Katharine's opinions were increasingly sidelined while Henry dreamt of getting an heir with someone else. The English ambassadors in Spain did not believe any alliance between England and France would form, considering Francis too weak to commit to anything.[14] But Pope Clement wanted the marriage, to help aid peace in Europe.[15]

Princess Mary spent the winter of 1527 at Tickenhall and Worcester before returning to the court at Windsor on 20 February, and Richmond

Palace in March, to meet French envoys and have her portrait painted for King Francis. Francis even wrote Mary a kind letter on their potential marriage, though Mary, wise enough to have her own opinions on the French, enjoyed the notion of being a French queen as little as her parents. The letter from Francis is now burned and ineligible, but Francis repeatedly called Mary his 'puissante princesse', that everyone involved was 'desiring honour, goodness and prosperity,' and signed off, 'God have you in his treasured and worthy keeping'.[16] Unfortunately for little Mary and her parents, what they liked was not a big consideration in the negotiations.

Stability in Europe was crumbling, well beyond any one person's control. Francesco Sforza wanted a peace alliance between England, the Emperor, Florence and Venice, but it was a tough challenge.[17] The Imperial troops, the French and the Venetians were all looking to the Pope, who was terrified of the French and Imperial troops alike, as the Papal States came under threat. The Imperial army marched on Rome, expecting Pope Clement's support, and 150,000 ducats. Towns would be given as security, and Emperor Charles crowned as Emperor and King of Italy in Rome. King Henry was to be the arbiter of the new treaty and sent Pope Clement 30,000 crowns to help repel the Imperial army. In turn, the Pope backed the marriage of Princess Mary and King Francis.[18] Wolsey, the man desperate to create perpetual peace, met the French ambassador at Westminster in early March, and demanded a new treaty for Mary's marriage; the French could not have Mary without peace. King Henry wanted Boulogne and Ardes for England, along with a 50,000-crown pension, and 15,000 crowns worth of salt a year, in return for Mary. France would not agree and they offered Henri, Duke of Orléans again. Wolsey told the French in no uncertain terms; even if Francis gave up half his realm, they would not give up the Princess at once, but that he should wait till she was fourteen.'[19] Henry, Katharine and Wolsey were at great pains to keep Mary safe and away from marital duties.

All was a mess. No perpetual peace treaty was coming, and Emperor Charles decided to start courting England again, offering to depose King Francis and give France to England. Henry would not have to send Mary to France as she had just turned twelve, and Henry had made it plain several times that she was not yet 'ripe' for a consummated marriage. This angered the French, underestimating how much Henry loved Mary and wanted to keep her safe.

The negotiations had been going in circles, and it was time to bring in the most powerful ambassador of them all; Katharine of Aragon, who would not relent on giving Mary away for anything less than total peace in Europe. Everyone was exhausted after eighteen months of fruitless negotiations, but

Katharine was the queen and would not back down from the demands on her daughter. Universal peace or nothing. The fates of countries and the lives of countless thousands were on the line, but Henry and Katherine would not give up Mary and risk her life, her health or her happiness. Princess Mary was the one true heir of Henry VIII.

Negotiations continued through March 1527 at Hampton Court Palace, but Katharine moved Mary away to Richmond Palace five miles downstream. The French ambassador asked to see her, and Katharine refused, claiming Mary was ill. The French king was getting insistent on having Mary, and his mother Louise of Savoy, suggested they marry in Calais so Francis:

> 'after the marriage solemnised, might abed himself for an hour, or less, with my lady Princess. (Louise) said the King her son was a man of honour and discretion, and would use no violence, especially the father and mother being so nigh, meaning that prudence will be used in attempts have to intercourse with Mary, who is close to puberty'.[20]

After this violation, Mary would return home to England so she could grow older before being submitted to such behaviour again. It would be months before Mary delivered any child created, by which time she could have already turned thirteen (Louise drastically miscalculated Mary's age). John Clerk wrote this proposal to Wolsey but added his own opinion on how bizarre the offer was; even King Francis thought it strange, as the French and English alike found the concept of sleeping with an eleven-year-old disturbing. Henry and Katharine were right to protect Mary, as the Imperial ambassador met up with his French counterpart, and read a letter written by the French king to Emperor Charles, doubting the entire marriage and treaty.[21]

Imperial negotiations were no better. Wolsey wanted to ensure peace and King Henry wanted to be the negotiator between rulers, but multiple bargains went back and forth, marriages for Mary, marriages for Henry Fitzroy, and promises of troops to fight the Turks. Emperor Charles was tired of peace negotiations, especially since the papal alliance troops prepared to take Milan and Naples. All was in vain; Mary was female, and Fitzroy was illegitimate, so England did not have a card to play that would benefit lasting European peace. But Henry pushed on, and at a large banquet for St George's Day, 23 April 1527, where Mary had been staying for a week, the princess appeared before French ambassadors at Greenwich Palace. Mary spoke to the ambassadors in French, Latin and Italian, wrote some French and played her spinet. The French described Mary as 'thin, spare and small,'[22] but this is likely because they wanted to see an older, stronger girl ready for marriage.

A week later, all present ratified the Treaty of Westminster, with King Henry deciding who Mary would marry, either King Francis or his second son Henri.[23] The affair was well-attended with the king on his throne, the knights of the Garter at his side, along with Wolsey and the ambassadors from Venice and the Pope. The following day they held a tournament, and the agreement was signed, followed by a masque performed at a banquet. The entertainment was one of Henry's continuing dramatic events, named the Pageant of the Father of Heaven, with Henry on a platform, Queen Katharine and Henry's sister Queen Mary at his feet. The room was filled with silver plate while Olympian gods acted out an argument of what was better between riches and love. A battle broke out and eight ladies emerged from hiding, led by little Princess Mary. She wore a dress of cloth of tissue and red tinsel covered in jewels and led the ladies to the dancefloor. The ladies performed a figure dance, before another eight masked men joined, among them the king. As Henry danced with his daughter, he pulled off her hat, freeing her long hair to everyone; an ambassador described her hair as silver, though was probably blonde.[24]

All was for nothing; a week later, Wolsey informed the French that King Francis could not marry Mary, as he expected Holy Roman Empress Isabella, who was due to give birth, would likely die during the travail, and Emperor Charles could marry Mary, as was once promised.[25] Mary's fate was traded like she was simply a pawn, only slightly more valued than the French princes still held for ransom. All negotiations were vastly pointless as Emperor Charles, despite signing a fresh alliance with the Pope, allowed the Viceroy of Naples to storm Rome, which had been closed to the barbaric and vicious Imperial troops sent from Germany, and the famous city was sacked. The Sack of Rome saw the heart of Christendom destroyed, the women and children raped, houses and churches set alight, and priests slashed to death.[26] Half the population of Rome, unless they managed to flee, were killed by the slaughterers or the diseases they brought, and approximately 45,000 civilians were gone. Though the Pope managed to survive, he soon became a prisoner to Emperor Charles, who now controlled Italy and much of Europe. Florentines decided to rise and destroy the Medici dynasty in their city, and Milanese and Venetian troops faced off after hearing the news from Rome and Florence.

On 17 May 1527, as news of Rome's betrayal filtered through Europe, another great betrayal took place at York Place. Cardinal Wolsey and

Archbishop of Canterbury William Warham convened on the matter of whether King Henry and Queen Katharine's marriage was truly valid.[27] Theirs was a marriage worthy of a fairytale; a princess from a far-off land came to marry a prince, only for him to die. She was thrown into poverty, only to be rescued by the prince's younger brother, and they fell in love and ruled England together. The Tudor dynasty was legitimate in the eyes of Europe, and the couple was a match of love and power. But the years had been harsh, only one of at least six children surviving. But the couple powered on, without any more children, and survived Henry's various affairs, a testament to Katharine's poise and power. Their daughter was worthy of kings and emperors fighting for her young hand, but now Henry had found a young replacement for his wife and expected the clergymen in his service to toss aside England's great queen. Anne Boleyn had dodged Henry's advances for at least a year and felt safe she would not have to be a mistress. But Henry, who had struggled to accept his female heir for over a decade, decided to end his marriage. Henry was a devout Catholic, the Defender of the Faith, who had read widely and understood doctrine. Yet the passage, Leviticus 20:21, just decided to emerge when it suited Henry: 'If a man shall take his brother's wife, it is an unclean thing...they shall be childless.' Deuteronomy also had a passage stating a man had to marry his brother's wife if they were childless. This second quote was not part of Henry's new favourite bible quote. Time had made the marriage legal, as had the Pope's divine right to give a dispensation to the marriage, just as he had for countless other royal marriages. Queen Katharine swore she never slept with Arthur, but who could trust a woman? Katharine had been prepared to be England's queen since she was a toddler, and no one could be better suited for the role. Her nephew was the Emperor at the head of a butchering army, who would not take kindly to his aunt's humiliation. Pope Clement was a weakling at the best of times but did give out annulments; Henry's sister Margaret in Scotland had managed to boot her atrocious second husband in 1527. But Catholicism was under threat to the reformers of the new evangelical religion, even in England, especially since Wolsey was light on heretics. Undermining Catholic laws and dispensations would only hobble the church's cause. Scholars quietly debated the issue through May, but the Pope was trapped in the Castle St Angelo, and Wolsey wrote that he 'hopes the news of the death of the Great Turk and his elder son is true, though the cruelty of Christian princes is worse than that of the Turks'.[28] Soon Henry would start showing some cruelty of his own.

John Clerk, Thomas Boleyn and Anthony Browne were in France gaining signatures for Mary's new marriage and decided to see King

Francis' thoughts on divorce for Henry and Katharine. Meanwhile, Henry went to Katharine directly, a bold move indeed. It shows two things; either Henry still had respect for Katharine and did not wish to blindside her, or he became entitled and thought he could get an easy annulment and have his way with Anne Boleyn. Sadly, it was likely the latter. Henry once again showed himself to be beneath Katharine, for she had already heard rumours, prepared her answers to the question of her marriage, and while she may have wept, she was also ready to send Henry on his way in shame. Princess Mary was staying at court with her parents, and despite annulment rumours, the family of three appeared to be happy. Mary joined her parents at Beaulieu Palace (formerly Newhall), where it was reported all were well and no illness followed the royal family.[29] In August, Mary returned to her manor in Hartlebury, and Henry and Katharine stayed at Beaulieu. Wolsey told his ambassador in Madrid, Edward Lee, that Katharine had been lied to, told that the marriage validity talk was all to silence the French Bishop of Tarbes, who had brought up the subject during Mary's marriage negotiations.

The annulment situation did not fool Emperor Charles either; he did not want Katharine or Mary dishonoured in such a manner. Charles had the Pope captive and could demand whatever he wished.[30] All the drama of marriage and peace was sealed by Wolsey; Mary would marry Henri, Duke of Orléans, who would be ransomed with his brother the dauphin, and the French king would marry Queen Eleanor.[31] Wolsey thought he had finally achieved peace and ratified all the various treaties made over the years, and Mary gained a husband. Wolsey failed to understand Henry's desire for divorce and said the proceedings would need papal approval when Wolsey could have solved the issue himself with Archbishop Warham. This mistake would impact Mary for years to come. [32]

For Princess Mary, outwardly her life changed little; the Princess of Wales was overseen by her council managing the West Marshes. But she returned to court in November 1527, for a pageant held on 10 November. It was a classic grand affair, the royal table headed by Mary with her parents and godfather Wolsey. Mary danced in a masque in a group of eight ladies, all with gold damask covering their hair.[33] But while the royal family looked the picture of happiness, Wolsey had sent his man Gregory de Casali to see the Pope in captivity,[34] looking to annul Henry from Katharine on the grounds of affinity, and requested a secret dispensation to remarry (this has been taken as a dispensation to marry Anne Boleyn despite also sleeping with her sister Mary, however, this may not be correct, as neither women were mentioned. Henry also referred to his annulment as a dispensation at times, to keep the issue quiet, which Pope Clement was happy to oblige at the time[35]). It was only after New Year that the Pope was safe in France's care, initially willing to entertain annulment and maintain Princess Mary's legitimacy, as the marriage began in good faith. Wolsey stated he was prepared to die to gain this annulment, and likely regretted this choice of words.[36]

Princess Mary spent New Year 1528 with her parents at Greenwich Palace and met with the French ambassador, as always delighting them with her intelligence and manners, as she 'could not have conducted herself with better grace'. Mary was not sent back to the marshes as expected, and on 3 February 1528, just weeks from her twelfth birthday, Mary's household was suddenly dissolved.[37] By late March, everything of value was collected to be sent back to court. As Princess of Wales, Mary's household had been a serious drain on finances, and if Henry were to gain an annulment, Queen Katharine would revert to the title of Princess of Wales.[38] But the ultimate reason Mary's household was broken was that Henry and Katharine simply missed their daughter. Wolsey wrote in a letter to George Throckmorton that 'for her education, and for the consolation of the king and queen, it has been ordered that the princess should reside near the king's person'.[39] Mary was loved, and a valuable asset, but royal life was rapidly changing. Fortunately for the princess and her mother, Pope Clement was still unwilling to immediately sign an annulment.[40]

As soon as Mary returned to the royal court full-time, she caught smallpox, which made its way through several of Queen Katharine's ladies.[41] Naturally, this meant Mary was in her household in isolation from the royal couple but returned to court on 4 August. Mary made a full recovery and showed no signs of the potentially deadly illness and its disfiguring scars. But Mary did not stay long before she and her ladies moved away from court as the annulment case became harder to hide. Princess Mary may have known the king's mistress by now, as Anne Boleyn lived at court. Henry insisted he was only checking on his marriage's validity to ease his conscience, while Katharine's conscience was clear. Regardless, neither wanted their daughter to hear the news. Cardinal Lorenzo Campeggio returned to England, sent on the Pope's behalf, to rule on the marriage alongside Wolsey, who believed they could be successful in freeing Henry to gain a son from Anne Boleyn.[42] While Mary had been ill, the new peace treaty, the Treaty of Amiens, was ready to collapse, as France would not send a prince to marry Mary if she was ruled illegitimate. Henry had completely undermined Wolsey's arduous work for peace and was rapidly diminishing Mary's status in his pursuit to put a baby in Anne Boleyn.

Princess Mary spent New Year 1529 with her parents at Greenwich Palace, and Mary's household was given 40l (£18,000 today) to be shared among them as a gift.[43] Despite everything, the royal family still spent quite a bit of time together; for Mary's thirteenth birthday she was with her parents, and marriage bargains arrived, though this time her cousin King James of Scotland was interested.[44] But marriage for Mary no longer mattered; she had become a young woman, full of virtue, wit, intelligence and talent, and all Henry worried about was lying to a legatine court to gain an annulment. The daughter Henry so often called 'the pearl of my world', was now ushered out of sight as her parents battled one another in a humiliating farce of a court. Henry sat at the Blackfriars court before Cardinals Wolsey and Campeggio, claiming he had always wondered about his marriage's validity, and whether Katharine and Arthur had consummated the marriage, despite the latter detail never coming up before Anne Boleyn caught Henry's eye. Katharine, in a stunning performance, begged the king publicly, while speaking the truth with her clear conscience and scripture evidence, before telling Wolsey and everyone else in court they could take their annulment and stick it up the Thames. Queen Katharine immediately sent an appeal directly to Pope Clement.[45] Many clergymen and courtiers gave depositions suggesting Katharine and Arthur slept together, yet none had any evidence apart from distasteful assumptions about the sleeping arrangements of two naïve teens. Katharine had not needed to worry about her fate, for Campeggio had no intention of ruling the queen an illegitimate wife.[46] But Mary's life was about to come crashing down.

Princess Mary's summer movements are incomplete, but by October, when Henry lost control of his annulment proceedings, and international leaders jostled with opinions and plans for war and peace, Mary was at Windsor, while Katharine stayed at Greenwich, Henry keeping them apart. Henry's new secretary Stephen Gardiner had spoken with colleague Thomas Cranmer from Cambridge University, who had an idea to annul the marriage without papal intervention. Cardinal Wolsey, Mary's godfather, advocate, promoter of peace and the man able to keep King Henry under control, was banished from court, in agony at Esher Place, ousted from all his powerful roles. Pope Clement and Cardinal Campeggio simply shrugged off any notion of letting Henry divorce Katharine.[47] But someone new arrived over the summer, Eustace Chapuys, the ambassador for Emperor Charles, who reported all the movements of the English court with startling regularity. Among the things he learned in his first few months was that Princess Mary was being considered as a bride for Henry Howard, Earl of Surrey. His father, Thomas Howard, Duke of Norfolk, was uncle to Anne Boleyn, with the idea that Mary could be controlled by the Howards.[48] This was news that caused the Emperor to startle; Mary had been a prize dangled throughout Christendom and was now potentially relegated to the wife of a nobody while the king batted his eyelashes at Anne Boleyn. Emperor Charles heard the allegation that Henry slept with Anne's sister Mary Boleyn, and rumours started he had slept with their mother Lady Elizabeth Boleyn too (a dirty rumour, the Boleyn parents were impeccable). Henry cared nothing for his conscience or having a legitimate marriage, he simply wanted a younger wife, and quickly made a fool of his entire family.

New Year celebrations in early 1530 would have been fraught. Henry, Katharine, and Mary spent the season together at Greenwich Palace, but Henry left his wife and daughter after the Epiphany celebrations, Katharine to Windsor and Mary to Eltham Palace. But Henry relented and the pair were back together as soon as May, meeting at Richmond Palace, the whole royal family there to meet Ambassador Chapuys. Mary's movements during this time are hard to track, as records of the court are scant in 1530 and 1531. Henry, Katharine, and Mary spent time at Richmond, before moving to Hampton Court Palace in June 1530, where they met Milanese Ambassador Scarpinello, who marvelled at how well Henry and Katharine continued to get along together. Henry was planning on bedding Anne Boleyn and ditching Katharine as fast as possible, and yet Katharine put on a brave face in public, even if she had to live at the same palace as her husband's mistress. The person missing was Mary's godfather Cardinal Wolsey, who had been up on charges that could cost him his life after the legatine annulment hearing. Wolsey's friend and lawyer Thomas Cromwell had ensured Wolsey's safety and a new life in northern England. It would not be long before Mary found a new friend in Cromwell, who could advocate for her with the king.

In July 1530, Princess Mary left her parents and returned to her usual homes, likely Eltham and Richmond Palaces. Mary was continuing her diligent education, but at fourteen possibly did not fully understand the situation of her parents' impending divorce. It is unlikely Katharine would wish to bring pain to her young daughter, and King Henry was not known for his bravery. One piece of welcome news was that King Francis finally married Emperor Charles' sister Queen Eleanor. French princes Dauphin Francis and Henri of Orléans returned home after four years of scarring imprisonment, as the Treaty of Cambrai ensured their release and peace in Europe. But the treaty had not been a result of Wolsey's decades of service but created by Katharine's sister-in-law Duchess Marguerite, Regent of the Netherlands, and Marguerite's long-time friend, King Francis' mother, Louise of Savoy.

Without Cardinal Wolsey's negotiations, Princess Mary found herself without active plans since she was two years old. Her father had no interest in Mary's life at this stage, desperate to find a way to get a divorce, though on 7 October 1530, Henry, Katharine, and Mary were again together.[49] Henry remained withdrawn but still 'dined and restored to the queen as he was accustomed and much loved and cherished their daughter the Lady Mary'. Henry was right to be wary, as Pope Clement had warned him to go back to his faithful wife and leave Anne Boleyn alone. Yet Henry had a new secret weapon, the notoriously private lawyer Thomas Cromwell busy in his parlour planning to find a legal way around the church.

Mary continued with daily life, with her new chamberlain John Lord Hussey receiving 66l 13s 4d (£30,000 today) for new saddles and harnesses for Mary and six ladies to go riding, a favourite activity for Mary outside of her studies. In November 1530, news came that Cardinal Wolsey was dead at Leicestershire Abbey, aged fifty-seven.[50] Wolsey had done all in his power to ensure Mary was treated as the princess she deserved, but King Henry was angry at Wolsey for conspiring with Katharine, Emperor Charles, and Pope Clement to ensure the royal marriage remained valid.[51] Wolsey died of illness on the way to his probable execution so at least his death was less dramatic than it could have been for Mary. In the meantime, Princess Mary had a new friend, her cousin Lady Margaret Douglas, who moved to London from Scotland with her father Archibald Douglas, Earl of Angus.[52] Dowager Queen Margaret and her son King James had not consented to Margaret travelling south to London, but at least placed in Mary's household, Margaret could be kept safe. Lady Margaret was born just four months before Mary, and the Tudor princesses, one English, one Scottish, could grow together under King Henry's watchful eye. While the two redheads were different in temperament, education, and restraint (as Margaret lacked any), the pair were soon friends. By Christmas, Mary and Margaret were together with Henry and Katharine at Greenwich for the season, and Henry gave his daughter 20l (£9,000 today) to enjoy herself,[53] unaware of just how desolate her life would become. Not only had Henry supplanted his wife with a younger woman, but that same woman would take everything from Mary as well.

Chapter 8

The Destruction of a Royal Family

The court remained at Greenwich after New Year 1531, awaiting parliament opening at Westminster in February. The royal family remained together, though Anne Boleyn also lived at court waiting to become a wife and queen. King Henry was hell-bent on getting a male heir and had his secret privy councillor Thomas Cromwell looking to undermine the church through law rather than ecclesiastical arguments. It was an odd arrangement; Cromwell had no love for Anne and the Boleyn family but harboured no ill will toward Queen Katharine and Princess Mary. But Ambassador Chapuys, who had been in England only eighteen months, was a confidant of both Cromwell and Katharine and made his feelings plain to the king. In a meeting at Greenwich, Chapuys explained how Emperor Charles would never look to unseat a powerful heir like Princess Mary. Mary's cousin, Queen Mary of Hungary, was the new Regent of the Netherlands (after the death of her aunt), ruling the country for her brother Emperor Charles, showing he believed women could rule effectively. Chapuys went to see Henry and Katharine, who dined together at Greenwich on 10 January 1531. Queen Katharine was at the stage where nothing would surprise her, including Henry simply 'marrying' Anne regardless of a divorce.[1]

Mary stayed at Greenwich for her birthday, now fifteen, technically old enough to be married herself, and certainly old enough to know her father was not looking to validate his marriage with his various commissions. Chapuys noted that 'the Lady' Anne Boleyn was openly acknowledged as the king's future wife.[2] Mary joined Katharine at Richmond Palace on 7 March, mother and daughter happy together while Henry was in London for parliament, where the clergy were expected to bow to Thomas Cromwell's new law stating Henry was the ruler of the church in England. Meanwhile, the Pope mentioned he would only resolve Henry and Katharine's marriage, and Mary's legitimacy, if the royal couple went to Rome for the hearing, infuriating Henry, and delighting Katharine, who had witnesses in Castile who could vindicate her.[3] But Katharine needed to write to the Pope and Emperor, but could not, as Henry was watching her. Their cordial cohabitation had ended.

Princess Mary stayed with Katharine at Richmond longer than planned[4] but had to leave her mother by 2 April, when Katharine returned to Greenwich and the king.[5] The following day, Mary fell drastically ill, the start of a lifelong serious condition of headaches, dizziness, stomach pain and heart palpitations. Ambassador Chapuys reported after eight days, Mary still could not hold down food.[6] While the Venetians started the rumours of menstrual problems or hysteria, Mary was more likely suffering a condition of extreme migraines, anaemia, thyroid dysfunction, or a heart condition, all of which could cause such symptoms. By the end of April, Mary was beginning to improve and begged her father to let her travel to Greenwich to be with her parents. Chapuys recorded that Henry refused, as Anne Boleyn did not want Mary nearby, and had become publicly angry at Henry for praising Mary. Chapuys reported the king had complained to the Duke of Norfolk about Anne Boleyn's outspoken behaviour, while Katharine had never spoken 'ill words' to her husband. The Duchess of Norfolk spoke with Queen Katharine, saying the Duke of Norfolk knew Anne Boleyn would be the ruin of the Howard family.[7] King Henry had spent much of Mary's life ensuring she would have a prime place on the European stage as England's heir, and wife of a ruler, and now all efforts and care ceased. Henry put his full attention into Anne Boleyn and breaking the church out of spite. No wonder Mary did not feel well; she wanted to be with her parents as she suffered and instead Henry sent her 10l to give to the poor.

Queen Katharine wanted to be with her daughter but had to stay with her husband and master at court. The May Day celebrations went ahead, and the royal couple attended a banquet on 4 May 1531, where Katharine put on a brave face. The Marquess of Dorset remarked that Katharine's bravery was supernatural, while the Duke of Norfolk remarked that only the devil himself would promote this terrible idea of divorce. But Henry, in front of Ambassador Chapuys, accused Katharine of cruelty, for not always having her physician at Richmond for Mary. Katharine maintained her composure and the next day, begged Henry to let Mary join them at court. Henry again rejected the notion and said he would allow Katharine to visit Mary at Richmond and never return. Katharine would be abandoning her marriage by leaving court. Katharine had to stay away from Mary.[8]

Henry had little in the way of support for the divorce; the Pope was against it, and the Emperor and French king hated each other but agreed annulment was foolish. Henry's sister Mary and her husband the Duke of Suffolk thought it foolish, as did Norfolk and his family. England already had a fine heir and the king did not need a second wife. But now, Henry no longer cared about any detail; he would have Anne no matter what. Chapuys wrote to Emperor Charles, talking of Henry's regret in marrying Katharine, but added, 'since of (the marriage), there had come such a pearl as the Princess, who was one of the most beautiful and virtuous ladies of the world'.[9] Henry suffered some guilt over his behaviour, and over eight days, he left court to visit Mary twice, visits that were reportedly filled with 'great cheer', and that Henry visited 'to present her such service as he owed her'.

The summer visit to Windsor approached, and with Princess Mary recovered, she travelled from Richmond while her father travelled from Guildford to Windsor Castle, where Katharine had settled in, as had Anne Boleyn. All four were living in the same quarters, and Henry and Katharine had been maintaining all usual polite courtesies, King Henry signing letters stating Katharine was his wife and queen consort. But Henry's moods could not be predicted, and no sooner than everyone was settled at Windsor, Henry decided to set off for the 'chase', moving to other manors to hunt. Anne went with Henry, not Katharine, and after six days apart (when messages were meant to travel every three days), Katharine asked Henry for an update. The king shot back with a vicious letter, furious at Katharine for pushing for an annulment hearing in Rome rather than England. Katharine appeared unbothered by Henry's characteristically explosive behaviour, as she was enjoying hunting and riding with Mary at Windsor. But another letter arrived days later, and Henry effectively kicked Queen Katharine out of Windsor Castle.[10] Princess Mary was to be removed from her mother's care, and sent home to Richmond, while Katharine was given a royal but reduced household of her own at The More.[11] The pair did not know it, but mother and daughter would never see each other again, despite The More being only fifteen miles from Richmond.

Henry had finally done it, he had banished his wife of twenty-two years, despite the ongoing annulment case. Guilt must have set in, as, in September, Henry ordered an enormous amount of cloth sent to Mary for exquisite gowns.[12] The first one was a gown of cloth of silver, then a gown of purple velvet, only for the royals at court. A third gown was labelled 'a gown of black tinsel', then another of crimson satin lined with cloth of gold, and finally 'a gown of black velvet, furred with ermine.' Each gown took just over eleven yards of fabric and had added kirtles of cloth of gold or silver, with sleeves to match and satin to line hoods and sleeves. Also included was a black velvet nightgown (a lightweight dress for evenings), black and white velvet and satin, ribands and sixteen pairs of velvet shoes, two dozen Spanish gloves, three French hoods, a night bonnet made of ermine, silk of all colours, and all the equipment necessary to makes these into fine creations for the princess.

Mary remained at Richmond Palace without her parents until November, when she moved forty miles southwest to Farnham Castle, where Prince Arthur lived as a child.[13] Henry had sent many courtiers to see Katharine and beg her to reconsider her position and let Henry remarry, and she crushed them all with her wit and intellect. A four-day banquet and celebration of the Serjeants-in-law went ahead at Ely House in London, and Henry and Katharine both attended, though separately and stayed in different chambers, Henry treating Katharine as a queen once again.[14] But it would not last, as Thomas Cromwell was quietly finding a way to break the Catholic Church through civil law, sending all the canon law experts and theology scholars into a panic.

When New Year 1532 arrived, the king's gift list always had the queen at the top, but this time Katharine received nothing, but the space at the top remained for her, with Henry's sister Queen Mary taking the second spot, and Princess Mary taking the third spot, receiving the largest gift of two gilt bowls weighing 102oz, three gilt bowls weighing 104oz, and a 12oz gilt platter dish.[15] Gifts were never sentimental, but rather a reflection of rank. Princess Mary had the most expensive gifts, and the prettiest dresses in the country, but she was a woman of sixteen in February 1532, and could not simply be placated with frivolous gifts. Thomas Cromwell and Thomas Cranmer continued to drip-feed the reformist religion to King Henry, in the hope he would take the bait and oust the Catholic Church from England. Everything Mary and Katharine held dear was being edged out as Henry desperately searched for a male heir. The king knew he would never get his annulment from Rome, and when Cromwell submitted two laws he had quietly been writing to parliament, the Supplication Against the Ordinaries, and the Restraint of Annates, alarm bells would have rung for Mary and her mother. The king now controlled the clergy, and taxes would no longer go to Rome. Cromwell desired to aid the Reformation but had no desire to help Anne Boleyn, and many Katharine supporters were away from parliament due to illness or travel difficulties. Mary and Katharine remained separated, with Mary at Richmond, where she was again unwell with her unknown affliction of stomach pains and headaches. Lady Margaret Pole still cared for Mary as governess at this time, along with her household which had remained unchanged, though Mary's tutor was now Richard Wolman, Dean of Wells, who was deeply trusted by the king. But conversations at home and abroad suggested Mary and Katharine were not safe in England anymore, especially if Anne Boleyn had a son.[16] Vague rumours of potential marriages for the princess swirled, though impractical suggestions like Wilhelm von der Marck, future Duke of Jülich-Cleves-Burg, and János Zápolya of Transylvania, King of Hungary and Croatia. These were mere suggestions, and without Wolsey, there was simply no one interested in finding suitable positions for Mary. Anne Boleyn mattered more than Mary and Katharine combined.

By the time Easter arrived in late March, King Henry sent fabrics from his Great Wardrobe for both Katharine and Mary to use while commemorating the season,[17] but the royal family spent the occasion apart. The king accepted Cromwell's Supplication Against the Ordinaries, dismantling church powers, and the final draft passed in parliament and submitted to the Archbishop of Canterbury. Henry was about to become head of the new Church of England, when Cromwell's bill enforced the Submission of the Clergy on 15 May, giving Henry unlimited power over religious affairs. No matter how much Pope Clement or Emperor Charles resisted an annulment, they were slowly losing King Henry to reform. Princess Mary had never been in such a low place; she was returning to health, but all the work done by the Princess' Council in Wales had been for nothing, and Thomas Cromwell was forced to enact new rules to get the country into shape again. Without Mary as a figurehead for the council, the region had fallen into disarray, and Mary's place as Princess of Wales and heir to the throne looked long gone. She should have been at the king's side, being prepared to rule, and instead, she lived in a permanent state of uncertainty. All Mary had was the Duke of Norfolk ready to fight in her corner, and he married off his son and heir to ensure it did not look like he planned to wed young Henry Howard to the princess. Those at court believed Mary was still a suitable heir, even if Henry did not. Even Thomas Cromwell believed in Mary over any other.

Suddenly, William Warham, Archbishop of Canterbury died on 22 August. He had been in power for thirty years, spent time as Lord Chancellor, and married Henry and Katharine. Warham had been against the annulment but was a weak old man by the time of his death. Queen Katharine's supporters were loyal, but like Warham, Bishop Fisher was old and powerless, and Sir Thomas More had quit as Lord Chancellor in a tantrum over the Submission of the Clergy. Mary's place as the legitimate heir was slipping away. Some talked of marrying her to her cousin King James of Scotland to escape the mess, but they were too closely related.

King Henry felt inspired; he ennobled Anne Boleyn as Marquess of Pembroke, ranking her only below the Dukes of Norfolk, Suffolk, and Richmond (young Henry Fitzroy), and alongside the Marquesses of Exeter and Dorset. The couple and several thousand courtiers set off for Calais and Boulogne, so Henry and King Francis could meet. Some speculated Henry wanted an alliance for Princess Mary and the dauphin again, other suggested Henry wanted to stop the rumoured marriage of King James of Scotland to Francis' daughter Princess Madeleine.[18] But Henry just wanted to present Anne as the future queen of England; Anne was now noble and fit to meet the king of France in the hopes of Francis showing international support for the marriage. The trip, like all grand meetings between Henry and Francis, was lavish, cost an embarrassing sum, and achieved nothing. France had no intention of supporting Henry's folly, while the Emperor was riding high with victory over the Turks, and the Pope again decreed Henry was still married to Queen Katharine. No one supported Henry's choice of Anne, despite rumours the couple secretly married in France.

Princess Mary did not attend the French event, despite propaganda pamphlets talking of the 'Lady Mary' dancing at events (it was Lady Mary Boleyn). The princess moved from Richmond to Windsor while Henry was in France, and then to Eltham Palace, where she met up with Henry only briefly outdoors, without Anne. Chapuys reported the visit just a brisk but friendly conversation, Henry giving Mary a gift of 10l, as Anne's servants were in earshot.[19] The Venetian ambassador suggested they spent the day hunting together. But the Venetians also mentioned another visit between Henry and Mary after the failed trip to Calais, claiming Mary met Henry at the Tower of London in private, separate from the tour the king took of the construction work with Anne a week earlier.[20] If Henry was reduced to meeting Mary only briefly, without Anne's knowledge, it shows the acrimony of the whole situation. Anne was no longer prepared to wait for the throne, already sacrificing her only card, her virginity, to rid Henry of Katharine and Mary.

January 1533 saw Thomas Cromwell's close friend and ally Thomas Cranmer recalled from Europe to be the new Archbishop of Canterbury, and fellow Cromwellian Sir Thomas Audley appointed Lord Chancellor of England. The reformers held a staggering amount of power in government between the three Thomases. Henry played the Catholic Church off against the new religion, setting everything up to annul his marriage. Cromwell knew how to do it; he enacted a new law in parliament, the Restraint of Appeals, meaning Rome had no more power in England.[21] Queen Katharine lost her final lifeline. Reformer Cranmer was now the one to decide on the royal marriage and he was pro-Boleyn, having worked for Anne's father Thomas Boleyn in Europe. The cards were stacked against Katharine and Mary. Anne Boleyn was already a wife, having secretly married Henry again on 25 January 1533, despite Henry being married to Katharine. Ambassador Chapuys was incandescent with rage over Thomas Cromwell's successes (despite the pair's friendship[22]), suggesting Anne wanted to marry Princess Mary to a commoner so she could not inherit, and that Anne's hatred for Katharine was extreme. Chapuys dared to say to Henry's face that the king did not need a new wife and son because Mary was a suitable heir.[23] Henry wasted no time hinting that Anne was already pregnant and that was all he wanted. Even Count of Cifuentes, the Imperial ambassador to Rome, knew that Anne was pregnant, and they expected to remarry by the end of June, so the secret had leaked across Europe.[24]

While Archbishop Cranmer raced to find Henry and Katharine's marriage invalid and Mary illegitimate, Cromwell hastily prepared a coronation for Anne Boleyn, who was crowned at Westminster on 1 June 1533. Katharine was no longer a queen, Mary no longer a princess, now 'Lady Mary' in correspondence, to her shock. Chapuys hoped the royal women could keep their titles out of courtesy, but Henry had no such manners, and Anne Boleyn joked she could make Mary a servant.[25] Katharine refused to believe the situation, even after Mary was threatened. The Pope threatened King Henry's ex-communication and Emperor Charles threatened war.[26]

Queen Katharine and Princess Mary could write to one another, which had been banned earlier in the year,[27] when Mary fell ill once again at Otford Palace in Canterbury. Mary had been informally corresponding with Thomas Cromwell, as had members of her household, suggesting that while he worked for the king, he was on Mary's side.[28] Fortunately, Katharine's physician helped Mary with her illness, and she moved to Beaulieu Palace outside London in late June after she was feeling better.[29] Henry's sister Mary, Queen of France, died after a long illness the same month, and Mary and Katharine were unable to attend the funeral of their beloved family member. But as Mary travelled between Otford and Beaulieu, locals came out to see her go by and cheered for her, to Anne Boleyn's anger, who had not received a good welcome during her coronation.[30]

Things were becoming petty; with threats from the Pope and Emperor, King Henry retaliated by punishing his daughter. He asked Thomas Cromwell, who was in charge of the king's jewels, to send a note to William Cholmeley, Mary's cofferer, to remove Mary's jewels. Lady Pole was there to stand up for Mary, refusing John Lord Hussey's access and he was forced to admit to Cromwell he failed.[31] Henry retaliated again, sending royal warrants to remove Mary's jewels, plate and 'nursery stuff',[32] as if Henry and Anne, who were spending royal money faster than Cromwell could earn it, needed any more items. But 'happy' news arrived on 7 September that Anne Boleyn had given birth to a daughter, not the prince she promised. After all the pain and fear and waiting and fighting on behalf of so many, Anne gave birth to Princess Elizabeth. Mary thought she had sunk as low as she could go, but as the announcement of this baby went out across England and Europe, Princess Mary was about to find her life forever intertwined with this new girl, and things were about to get so much worse.

Chapter 9

A Worldly Jewel Lost

While Henry Fitzroy and his half-sister Princess Mary shared a common enemy in Anne Boleyn, they were to ride out Anne's stunted reign in quite different circumstances. Fitzroy had all the luxuries of being a king's son, with none of the responsibilities or expectations. Fitzroy neatly faded into the background during the annulment proceedings, as Henry did not want to promote his illegitimate son as an alternative for the throne. But as a safety net, Fitzroy received a new title and became Lord Lieutenant of Ireland a few days after his tenth birthday, on 22 June 1529. The plan was Cardinal Wolsey's, still (just) in favour with King Henry at the time. Ireland had been ruled by a mixture of Lord Lieutenants and Lord Deputies for three hundred years, often Irish earls or archbishops holding the role. King Henry (though more likely Wolsey) redesigned the system, with figurehead Fitzroy at the top, though remaining in England while a 'Secret Council' would rule Ireland on Fitzroy's behalf.[1] But Wolsey's disgrace in October 1529 and death in November 1530, left Fitzroy as adrift as Princess Mary. Within months of Wolsey's death, Henry scrapped the plan and made Sir William Skeffington the Lord Deputy of Ireland, ruling on Fitzroy's behalf.[2] Some speculated Fitzroy could be something of a king of Ireland on his father's behalf, but Anne Boleyn would have liked that as little as Henry. The king would never relinquish power, especially to an illegitimate son when Anne promised a better option.

Fitzroy attended parliament in 1529, in the White Chamber at Westminster, seated high on the left in accordance with his rank.[3] Whether he was living at Durham House on The Strand or other empty properties in London is unknown. Whether he attended Christmas at Greenwich also goes unmentioned, though it was likely, even with Queen Katharine and Anne Boleyn in attendance. Fitzroy received a high-ranked gift from his father, a two-handled gold cup engraved with dragons and flowers, a large standing cup, and two gilt pots.

King Henry kept his son close in the early months of 1530, despite also having his wife and mistress in his household. In April 1530, Fitzroy participated in the 23 April ceremony of the Order of the Garter, and after the ceremony at St George's Chapel at Windsor, Fitzroy stayed on with his father, the pair spending time in various outdoor activities over the next month. Henry also dismissed Fitzroy's nurse Anne Partridge when she retired and was replaced by Joan Brigman.[4] That way, while Fitzroy no longer needed a full-time female carer as children received, there was still a woman overlooking his day-to-day care in the otherwise male household.

Throughout 1530, Fitzroy was on the move, bouncing back and forth between royal manors to see his father, who would also send him gifts, everything from cheap bows for his archery, to a gold collar enamelled with white roses. Anne Boleyn tried to gain the boy's favour at times, sending him a bay horse with saddle, though Fitzroy did not ride the horse, considering it unsafe and in poor condition. Whether Anne sent a poor horse on purpose can never be known. Princess Mary would never fall for Anne's attempts at a relationship, and Fitzroy did not either.

Fitzroy remained popular; he received gifts and visits from nobles and joined his father at Hatfield in April 1531, where the king gave his son a new horse and took him on a hunting trip. Fitzroy's movements are hard to track during this quiet period, as the household had been reduced by at least one hundred staff by this time. George Folbury had been the boy's tutor since 1528, things calmer than in previous years. A few staff remained in the north, in case Fitzroy was sent there again, but Henry's indecision meant this project also slowly unravelled. With Wolsey gone, someone needed to take over the management of Fitzroy's life and homes, and the job fell to the Duke of Norfolk, deputising to his son Henry Howard, Earl of Surrey. Howard was only two years older than Fitzroy and had a household of staff to manage affairs while the boys lived and grew up together. Fitzroy needed a strong role model, and while only fourteen at the time, Henry Howard was well-educated, intelligent, and had superb Latin skills, according to Ambassador Chapuys. The Duke of Norfolk did not take active participation in Fitzroy's household other than paying bills, but for almost six years, Fitzroy and Henry Howard would remain close, a friendship blossoming from the very beginning.

By 1531, Fitzroy was ready to start living as an adult. His tutor George Folbury received a prebend in Yorkshire as a reward for his work, so it is likely Fitzroy's education ended at this time. After Fitzroy's twelfth birthday in June 1531, servants undertook a household inventory, which had not been updated since its inception in 1525. Hugh Johns, Yeoman of the Wardrobe did most of the work, leaving a detailed list.[5] By now, Fitzroy tapestries were laden with holes, beds not fit to sleep in, while his chair of estate had been damaged during travel. Fitzroy's clothes were aged and torn, and of his twenty-five horses, many had been given away or died, some looking so ill they could not take a rider. Fitzroy grew out of clothes, hats, and shoes as fast as they could be made, and had enjoyed a wardrobe of silk, damasks, and velvets, the finest of the period.

The Duke of Norfolk needed to oversee the household spending now Wolsey was not able to care for Fitzroy, having to shoulder the burden of the cost. Much was given away, some to Fitzroy's younger brother George Lord Tailboys, or sold to recover costs. Norfolk had to purchase new fabrics for tapestries, bedframes made, mattresses created, and red and yellow bedcurtains decorated in cloth of gold. With Norfolk's son Henry Howard overseeing the Richmond household, he was stuck with the bill, and rumours persisted Norfolk wanted to marry his youngest daughter to Fitzroy. The household did not have a fixed residence, so Fitzroy was often at court at Greenwich or Hampton Court and spent time at The More before Queen Katharine moved there at the beginning of her exile.[6] But in mid-1531, Fitzroy was set up at Windsor. Construction began on the northwest corner of the castle for the 'prince's lodging', a permanent home for the Richmond household.

Fitzroy seemingly enjoyed a similar childhood to his father for a time, cloistered from the world, but close to the king. In January 1532, Fitzroy came off his horse in the tiltyard during a rare chance to participate. Fortunately, Fitzroy had gained the horse skills of his father and was tall and healthy, so the injury (which required only 40s of care from a physician) went unnoticed. Only Henry Howard's poetry talks of his close friend's incident.[7]

But King Henry's desire for a legitimate male heir was as desperate as ever. While the battles at parliament, convocations and ambassadors' meetings raged, Fitzroy was still in Henry's thoughts. When Henry wanted to meet the French king and display Anne Boleyn as the future queen of England, the ladies of the French court would not welcome her. King Francis planned to bring his mistress Anne de Pisseleu d'Heilly, but not Queen Eleanor. Women such as Henry's sister Mary Tudor refused to accompany Anne Boleyn. But among all the court snobbery, there was a place for Fitzroy. By the time the casts of thousands, all painstakingly arranged and managed by perpetually exhausted Thomas Cromwell, set sail on 11 October, Fitzroy and forty of his closest men were included in the trip. Henry Howard accompanied Fitzroy and was included in the king's private meeting with King Francis at Boulogne, and Fitzroy was not.[8] Fitzroy remained behind when Henry took Anne Boleyn to meet King Francis, leaving him as the highest-ranked person in the large party at Calais.

The event was pointless, as with all meetings between King Henry and King Francis; they spent lavishly and attempted to outdo each with pageantry and expensive parties and gowns. It was a two-week endeavour to let Anne Boleyn feel like a queen, planned so Francis could endorse the new relationship, which never occurred. But Fitzroy got to sit with King Francis at evening festivities, and after two weeks of talks and false promises, a plan formed; Fitzroy would stay in France with the king's household. Unfounded rumours had swirled for months that Fitzroy would go to France while Francis' son Henri would go to England, but like all plans between the countries, this also fell apart. Perhaps Fitzroy only intended to visit France for a few weeks, as a last-minute plan to move Fitzroy and a household of sixty was made in haste in the early weeks of November 1532. King Henry offered Fitzroy as a bribe to ensure King Francis' favour, after hearing swirling rumours of Francis' son Henri marrying Catherine de'Medici; Henry needed an alliance with France. A King Henry lookalike in the form of Fitzroy at the French court may have been just the token to woo Francis into an alliance.[9] The French princes, Francis and Henri, had suffered from their years as hostages in Spain and had a difficult relationship with their father. But Fitzroy seemingly fit in well with the boys by mid-December, along with the youngest French prince, Charles, who had only been a toddler at the time of the Battle of Pavia and spared the physical and psychological torture endured by his older brothers.

Fitzroy soon became a member of King Francis' privy chamber, though spent most of this time in Paris with the three princes, Henri being the same age as Fitzroy. The dauphin threw parties and tournaments in January 1533, allowing Fitzroy to participate and enjoy French court life. The dauphin was a quiet young man, dressed always in black and preferred to be alone after his time as a prisoner, while young Charles was a short-tempered brat. Henri however enjoyed winter activities such as snowball fights and ice skating with the other boys. The royal household hosted many noble boys Fitzroy's age, with the French houses of Lorraine, Bourbon, Guise, and the German Cleves family all lodging sons there to enjoy a royal upbringing. Henri and Charles both loved having Fitzroy at court, discussing their happiness with him in later years. Despite being a king's son, Fitzroy was not a notable presence, not treated like a spectacle at court, but just another noble boy in Francis' household. The French household was enormous, with vast occasions, gifts, and parties held within the king's, queen's and dauphin's households, and Fitzroy never rated a mention in any of them. But King Francis did hold an party to celebrate St George's Day in honour of the Order of the Garter (of which

A Worldly Jewel Lost

he was an international member) and Fitzroy attended, being the only other Garter member in France at the time.[10]

By the summer of 1533, the French court broke up to go on progress, and Fitzroy, along with Henry Howard and their attendants, were placed in King Francis' group travelling south to meet the Pope.[11] Francis had promised to send delegates to meet Pope Clement to discuss King Henry marrying Anne Boleyn, but the alliance fell through, yet another false promise. France's interests were solely on marrying young Duke Henri to Catherine de'Medici and creating an Imperial and papal alliance. Meanwhile, in England, court life changed when Anne Boleyn yielded her virginity to King Henry, getting pregnant immediately and forcing Henry to marry her despite being married to Queen Katharine. Thomas Cromwell and Thomas Cranmer had set up the Church of England and allowed an annulment and coronation to take place, seeing Anne finally on the throne. Fitzroy missed the entire occasion while enjoying his new French life. The Duke of Norfolk travelled to visit Fitzroy and Howard, and begged King Francis not to ally with Emperor Charles and Pope Clement, who had recently ratified King Henry and Queen Katharine still married.[12] Emperor Charles was considering war against England in retaliation for Henry's wrongs against Katharine. Tense meetings went back and forth, with Norfolk losing on every account, and King Henry threw a tantrum, recalling Norfolk, his son Henry Howard, and also Fitzroy back to England. Suddenly Fitzroy left his comfortable French life, leaving King Francis on 25 August 1533, without a goodbye or explanation.

Norfolk rushed back to England, leaving Fitzroy and Howard in Calais under Lord Lisle's care.[13] Lisle had been Fitzroy's vice-admiral for some time before his elevation to Lord Deputy of Calais and well understood the life of being a bastard royal son. Fitzroy had just celebrated his fourteenth birthday with King Francis, and felt safe as the king's beloved illegitimate son, regardless of the poor showing in France. Any worries about his father's marriage to Anne Boleyn evaporated, as news arrived in Calais that Anne had given birth to a daughter on 7 September. The last recording of Fitzroy and Howard in Calais was on 25 September and Fitzroy paid his respects to Henry and Anne soon after.[14] Still without a legitimate prince, which King Henry had assumed was a God-given right, the fates of the now-three royal children fell into the hands of Thomas Cromwell.

Fortunately for the trio, Cromwell was not a man who harboured ill will to most, despite the constant criticism and cruelty thrown in his direction. He was on familiar terms with Princess Mary, and despite considering Anne Boleyn a non-entity, did all he could for infant Princess Elizabeth. Fitzroy's situation was no different; any time Henry wanted something for his son, it was Cromwell giving the instructions, writing polite letters, and making payments. When the unruly Lord Leonard Grey looked to marry Fitzroy's mother Bessie Blount, Lady Tailboys in 1532, it was Cromwell who talked him out of it (much to Bessie's relief, who then married Lord Clinton). But Cromwell also had to see out King Henry's plans and needed to rule Princess Mary as illegitimate, making her lower-ranked than Fitzroy due to her gender. Princess Elizabeth was the official heir to the throne through Cromwell's new Act of Succession. At the same time, people were signing the Act of Royal Supremacy, stating Henry controlled the church, making Elizabeth legitimate through her mother's marriage. But while Elizabeth soon got her own royal household, Fitzroy still wandered around court in 1533. A baby, who Catholics did not consider legitimate, versus a healthy teenage Henry lookalike, gave people an heir to consider.

The decision to have Fitzroy married came to fruition in November 1533. Rumours had swirled for years, as early as 1529, that Fitzroy could marry one of the Duke of Norfolk's daughters. In retaliation, Norfolk had married his eldest daughter Katherine Howard to the Earl of Derby, but she died of illness soon after. Norfolk had his much younger half-sister Dorothy (coincidently related to the Tailboys family) marry Derby to keep her safe also. But Norfolk still had his youngest child, Mary Howard, only ten in 1529 and spared any negotiations. But Norfolk, who had disliked his niece Anne Boleyn in 1529 and now had outright scorn for her, loathed any idea she had of joining the Howards to Fitzroy. But Fitzroy was growing up to be an esteemed young man, and his children would be grandchildren of Henry VIII. Fitzroy was still close to Henry Howard, Mary's elder brother, and Howard had recently married Frances de Vere, though remained exclusively living with Fitzroy. Fitzroy and young Mary Howard could have the same arrangement. It was a gamble for all involved; Fitzroy was marrying a stranger (suggestions of Fitzroy writing poetry for Mary is imagined), and Mary could see the harm of arranged marriages; her father Norfolk had been abusing his wife Duchess Elizabeth for decades (she was forced to marry Norfolk at fourteen, he thirty years older). But Henry Fitzroy and Mary Howard could do worse than each other; she was well born, her father's family the unshakable dukes of Norfolk, her mother the daughter of the Duke of Buckingham and close personal friends with the unwavering Thomas Cromwell. Mary Howard was intelligent, exceptionally beautiful, and as quick-witted as her cousin Anne Boleyn. She would be a fine wife for a boy still rumoured to be a future ruler of Ireland.

Above left: The mourning of Henry VII. In the background as Princesses Margaret and Mary play, young Prince Henry, far left, mourns on his mother's empty bed, c.1503

Above right: King Henry by Meynnart Wewyck, as seen by his people as he took the throne in 1509

Right: Katharine of Aragon, aged about eleven in 1496, painted by Juan de Flandes prior to her proxy marriage to Prince Arthur

Princess Mary, painted in miniature by Lucas Horenbout in 1525 for Emperor Charles, and wearing her 'Emperor' brooch, a Valentine to her betrothed

Princess Mary, as painted by the so-called 'Master John' in 1544

Queen Mary by Hans Eworth in her first portrait after her 1553 coronation

Queen Mary, as painted in 1554 by Antonis Mor at the time of her marriage to Philip II of Spain

Possibly a sketch of Bessie Blount, c.1532. No portrait remains of Bessie, though her second husband, Lord Clinton, was sketched by Hans Holbein in 1532, around the time as this sketch, which still listed as unknown

Henry Fitzroy painted in an informal portrait by Lucas Horenbout in 1534, possibly in preparation for a larger more complete work. Here Fitzroy is still wearing his sleeping cap

This Hans Eworth portrait painted in the 1550s, once considered to be Queen Mary, is now listed as unknown. The Catholic woman could be the daughter of Bessie Blount, Elizabeth Baroness Tailboys of Kyme, whom Henry VIII visited and assisted in the 1540s. The other possibility is the favoured Etheldreda Malte, daughter of Joan Dingley. The woman's religious pendant symbolises Esther saving the Jews from religious persecution. Etheldreda named her only child Esther (anglicised to Hester)

Above left: Emperor Charles V in his years after his betrothal to Princess Mary was broken. The original was painted by Titian c.1540

Above right: King Francis I of France, as painted by Jean Clouet c.1527

Above left: Katharine of Aragon, in a 1560s recreation by Joannes Corvus, as she was seen in the 1520s

Above right: Anne Boleyn by an unknown artist painted long after her death, likely recreated from a portrait created c.1534 when a medal was struck in her honour

Left: Jane Seymour c.1536 by Hans Holbein

Above left: Anna of Cleves' wedding portrait 1539 by Hans Holbein. Her beauty now hangs in the Louvre.

Above right: Portrait possibly of Katheryn Howard c.1540. Other portraits previously attributed to Katheryn are now believed to be Anna of Cleves and Elizabeth Cromwell

Right: Kateryn Parr by an unknown artist c.1600, a recreation of how Kateryn appeared c.1544

Thomas Wolsey, godfather to Princess Mary and Henry Fitzroy, painted by Sampson Strong not long before his downfall in 1529

Thomas Cromwell, as painted by Hans Holbein in 1532. Cromwell would be Mary's defender at court after the loss of Wolsey

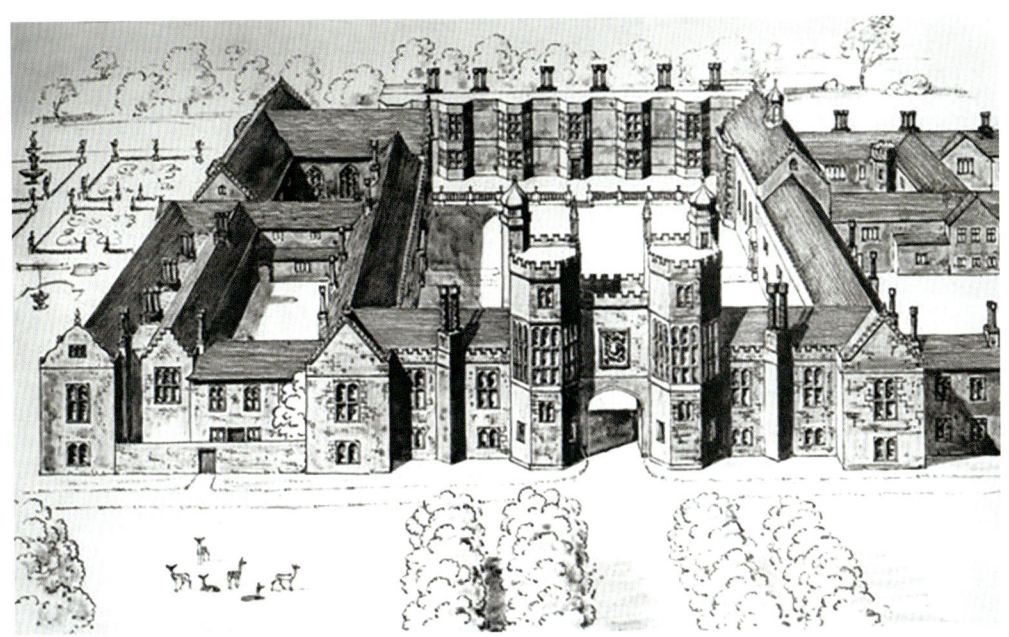

Above: Beaulieu Palace, formerly New Hall, reconstructed to be a permanent Essex palace after Henry Fitzroy's birth, but remained in Princess Mary's hands

Right: Hatfield Old Palace, as it stands today. Hatfield remained a favourite for all the royal siblings

Hunsdon Manor, used by all the royal siblings, remained a favourite of Queen Mary. Queen Elizabeth gave it to her Boleyn cousin Henry Carey, and where they possibly lived together as children. Still stands in a similar state to this sketch, and made of a similar red brick as Hatfield

Princess Elizabeth painted by William Scrots c.1546, the only surviving portrait of Elizabeth prior to her coronation

Queen Elizabeth on her coronation in 1559

Queen Elizabeth in 1572 in the Pelican Portrait, a powerful symbol of Elizabeth as mother of the nation, rather than a traditional wife and mother. Pelicans are known to feed their young with their own blood

Prince Edward's first portrait, painted by Hans Holbein, likely at Hampton Court Palace, in 1538

Prince Edward, again painted by Hans Holbein, likely also at Hampton Court Palace, in 1542 after his life-threatening illness

Right: Prince Edward, painted in the manner of King Henry by William Scrots c.1546

Below left: King Edward, painted in 1550 again by Scrots, another attempt to make the young king as mighty as his father

Below right: The portrait as Henry VIII wished to be remembered, painted by Hans Holbein in 1538

Edward Seymour, Lord Protector and Duke of Somerset, who took over control of King Edward in 1547

Thomas Seymour, who attempted to manipulate Princess Elizabeth and King Edward

John Dudley, later Duke of Northumberland, Head of King Edward's council and father-in-law to Lady Jane Grey

Possibly Lady Jane Grey, who became the queen for nine days between King Edward's death and Queen Mary's ascension

The other illegitimate children of Henry VIII:

Top row: The children of Mary Boleyn: Catherine Carey, Lady Knollys, and Henry Carey, Baron Hunsdon, both painted in 1562 by Steven van Herwijck (often misidentified as van der Meulen).

Middle row: John Perrot, son of Mary Berkeley, in a copy of a 1550s portrait recreated by George Peele in 1776; and *Portrait of a Gentleman 1569* by Antonis Mor, often attributed to Thomas Stuckeley, son of Jane Pollard, though is officially listed as an unknown wealthy man.

Bottom row: Sketch of Richard Edwardes, son of Agnes Blewitt, featuring in *The miscellaneous works of John Dryden* in 1760; and Sir Henry Lee, son of Margaret Wyatt, painted by Antonis Mor in 1568.

At the same time, Ireland was in a state; Norfolk ensured the Earl of Kildare ruled there as the Lord Deputy in Fitzroy's place, which led to murder, lawlessness, and mayhem throughout the country. Norfolk needed to undo his mistakes but also wanted Fitzroy to remain safe as a potential royal heir. Thomas Cromwell stepped in; Fitzroy was an excellent choice to rule Ireland in his father's place, and Cromwell could complete Cardinal Wolsey's plan to reorganise government in Ireland. Much of Ireland's troubles were already tossed on Cromwell's desk, and he was the new blood needed to see through changes. Fitzroy had Cromwell's trust and assurance, but the plan would only fan the flames between Norfolk and Cromwell.

Henry Fitzroy, Duke of Richmond and Somerset, married Lady Mary Howard on 28 November 1533, in a small and simple ceremony. The pair made sense; they were both well-born and educated, even if they did not know one another, and would not live together. Fitzroy and Henry Howard continued their lives at various court palaces, while Mary went home to Kenninghall with her mother. King Henry did not believe in sexual activity in the young, and credited Prince Arthur's early death to possibly sleeping with Katharine of Aragon at fifteen (Katharine mysteriously survived this imaginary deadly consummation without explanation, but this fact was not considered). Either way, the deal spared the fourteen-year-olds the indignity of learning how to have sex while their parents waited outside.

New Year at Greenwich came and went with the usual uninspiring silver and gold utensils exchanged, though Anne Boleyn gave Fitzroy a ring, which he liked and even wore. The first five months of 1534 were spent mostly at Windsor and Westminster, where Fitzroy attended over thirty of the forty-six sessions of parliament, which saw the Acts of Royal Supremacy and Succession voted into law. Princess Elizabeth was to be the only legitimate heir. Princess Mary was not mentioned at all, and neither was Fitzroy.[15] Henry was desperate for everyone to accept that the child currently in his nursery was the lawfully begotten heir, and the punishment for failing to sign the act meant treason, punishable by death.

By St. George's Day on 23 April, Fitzroy was at Windsor, and stood in for the king in the low-key Order of the Garter ceremonies, along with the ceremonial feast on 17 May.[16] It did not go unnoticed that the king had deputised a formal and important ceremony to his almost fifteen-year-old son. It was around this time that Anne Boleyn was noted to have a 'goodly belly' and ready to give birth, though references to this pregnancy are rare.[17] What she thought of having Fitzroy at court with them while she was pregnant can never be known.

At the same time, Ireland was fast deteriorating due to a lack of proper leadership. The Earl of Kildare staged violent uprisings around Dublin to oust English rule. Thomas Cromwell received the news on 27 July that his friend John Aleyn, Archbishop of Dublin was slaughtered by Kildare's men, sending Cromwell into an uncharacteristic rage against the Duke of Norfolk. Norfolk had ensured Fitzroy, the supposed new leader of Ireland, had never established a leadership council, instead kept close to the king and out of harm's way. The violent Irish uprising led to the returning Deputy Skeffington taking extra troops, and Cromwellian loyalists leaving for Ireland immediately to bring peace to the northern areas of Ireland. Cromwell managed to ensure Fitzroy was out of Norfolk's clutches, and sent him on a trip around Dorset, moving between different manors in the area. Enjoying the patronage of the nobles of the region, Fitzroy could finally gain some basic life experience outside the cloister of court and Norfolk's schemes. Norfolk retreated north to his family, disgraced by the whole outburst.

Fitzroy was welcomed as he travelled to his manor at Canford, enjoying the company of those along the way before arriving at his home 100 miles southwest of London.[18] Fitzroy had not been there long before he heard rumours of King Henry travelling to France and asked Thomas Cromwell if he could accompany his father.[19] Henry did not go, nervous about Anne Boleyn's rumoured pregnancy, and he had every right to be nervous, as Anne soon gave birth to a stillborn baby, rumoured a son, at Windsor (though this is entirely subject to conjecture through lack of records. Ambassador Chapuys did record Anne pregnant on 27 July,[20] but then doubted Anne had ever truly been pregnant two months later[21]). No references to the baby appear and as soon as Anne could travel, the king took his wife away on progress for the summer. While the Act of Succession ensured Princess Elizabeth was heir to the throne, in reality, the succession was as fragile as ever. Fitzroy was the only son, Princess Mary was in disgrace as illegitimate, and Elizabeth was only a baby, with a mother no one would support as regent. Henry Brandon, Earl of Lincoln, the king's ten-year-old nephew, had also died earlier in the year, leaving the king no legitimate male relatives other than King James of Scotland. Henry's nearest cousins, Henry Courtenay, Marquess of Exeter and Henry Pole Lord Montagu, who were staunchly Catholic Katharine allies, whispered to the Duke of Norfolk they wanted to spill blood for Katharine and Mary.[22]

Thomas Cromwell grappled with the situation in Ireland, keeping Fitzroy safe and holding court in west England. Henry and Anne's supposed loss of a child remained hidden in a code of silence, hoping for another swift pregnancy, which did not arrive through 1534. The king had taken another mistress, to Anne's rightfully bitter resentment, but as ever, Henry needed to be seen as manly and confident, and having dead male heirs would not help the already insecure king. As part of that, Henry wanted his son close, and Fitzroy moved back to London, joining his father at Richmond Palace, helping with a feast in honour of Philippe de Chabot, the French Admiral visiting to discuss a French betrothal and alliance for Princess Elizabeth.[23] In the wake of still no living son, Anne Boleyn desperately wanted a French alliance for her daughter, and Thomas Cromwell, who loathed the French with a passion, needed someone, anyone to be between him and the French delegation. Fitzroy was perfect for the task.

Fitzroy's life began to follow a routine; after the traditional Greenwich New Year 1535 festivities (where Anne Boleyn gave Fitzroy a silver gilt-covered pot, which Fitzroy sent to Princess Mary[24]), Fitzroy settled either at Windsor or Westminster for newly empowered Vicegerent Cromwell's endless parliamentary sessions. But Cromwell and Ambassador Chapuys, who usually never had anything to do with Fitzroy, produced the plan to besmirch the French delegates still in London for alliance talks. Cromwell planned a large party at his home at Austin Friars, and all the nobles of the court flocked to the event, leaving Chapuys alone at court, where Fitzroy kindly offered to have dinner with the ambassador.[25] All the French saw was the Imperial ambassador dining in private with Fitzroy, the king's favoured son. Cromwell and Chapuys' plan to annoy the French worked perfectly, and Fitzroy looked invaluable and generous. After partaking in the Order of the Garter ceremony at Windsor, helping his father vote King James of Scotland into the order, Fitzroy again acted as a symbol in May. Fitzroy attended the burning of 'heretical' Carthusian monks at Tyburn, the stand-in for the king, something of a royal approval over the grisly event designed to scare clergy into signing the Act of Supremacy.[26]

The 1535 royal progress was to be the largest in some time, King Henry taking Anne on a prolonged tour, the trip all propaganda for the new religious and royal regime. Anne had not been pregnant in a year, and she would have known as well as anyone that she needed a son as fast as possible. Fitzroy did not join the royal progress, instead travelling with his own household to his homes as far north as Sheffield Manor, though was unhappy on his travels. Fitzroy wrote to Vicegerent Cromwell, who was stuck between running the country and following Henry on his endless holiday, complaining there was not enough hunting available in Sheffield.[27]

The twenty-year-old manor was in a deer park and yet was not good enough for newly sixteen-year-old Fitzroy. Why he wrote to Cromwell asking for a better place to stay is a mystery, since the Duke of Norfolk oversaw Fitzroy's household, but Cromwell ordered Norfolk to take Fitzroy to the Welsh Marshes, to oversee his lands there.

Rumours swirled over the summer, at home and abroad, of whether Anne could produce a son. Talk, including at prominent levels, still heavily supported Princess Mary and her exiled mother Queen Katharine. If anything were to befall Anne Boleyn or her daughter, Mary had the support of the people of England, no matter what the Act of Succession claimed. Fitzroy, despite being a healthy sixteen-year-old with the solid backing of the Duke of Norfolk and was 'a goodly young lord... in many qualities and feats,' Fitzroy was simply not considered a serious heir. But Anne Boleyn became pregnant in October 1535, rendering all talk and her naysayers quiet once more.

By New Year 1536, Fitzroy was back at court at Greenwich, this year's silver gifts more impressive than previous years. He received a large silver bowl engraved with his arms, plus a jug with handles shaped like serpents (and with HA engraved, which probably seemed awkward only months later). Fitzroy also received a standing cup engraved with French and an image of a boy carrying a shield, so the king was in a good mood being so generous.[28] While the king kept Princess Mary as disparaged and lonely as possible, Fitzroy did not suffer any consequences for being a rival heir to Princess Elizabeth.

Anne Boleyn, safely pregnant and in the king's affections, had suffered from Henry's affairs through their marriage and had never become popular at court or through the country. The popularity of Katharine and Mary did not drop through these turbulent years, and Anne could never compete. Fitzroy likely felt relieved to remain on the sidelines of such situations. When word came that Queen Katharine died on 7 January 1536, it likely had no bearing on Fitzroy at all. King Henry and Anne Boleyn were openly thrilled to have Katharine dead at last, Anne finally able to feel like an actual queen now Henry's true wife was gone. Disaster almost struck only weeks later, Fitzroy still at court when the king fell off his horse at Greenwich while in the tiltyard, fortunately suffering no injury (despite wild tales told by ambassadors). Tales of a sudden discussion on the succession were also untrue; Henry was back at work the following day. But Anne suffered a miscarriage on 29 January 1536, the day of Queen Katharine's funeral, with rumours of a tiny son reported by Ambassador Chapuys, who almost added a shade of sympathy to his words.

What this meant to Fitzroy was unclear. He had no reason to dislike Anne Boleyn, or care too much about whether his father carried on his flirtation with Jane Seymour (or with Margaret Shelton, a Boleyn cousin, the year prior). Jane's brother Edward Seymour had worked as Fitzroy's Master of the Horse at Sherriff Hutton and had become Fitzroy's Steward of Canford Manor in Dorset, though Fitzroy had wanted to give that role to Sir William Parr. But Fitzroy was married to Mary Howard, his father-in-law the Duke of Norfolk, who supported neither the Seymours nor Boleyns. Fitzroy stayed close to his father, and when the king looked to meet his nephew, King James of Scotland in York, it was suggested Fitzroy attend and be a 'hostage', as surety the meeting would go safely. On 23 April, the Order of the Garter met, and Fitzroy placed two votes for the vacant space, selecting George Boleyn and Sir Nicholas Carew, a Seymour supporter.[29] He had no alliance nor opinion on either side.

By the time the May Day celebrations came to Greenwich, Fitzroy was again near his father. Guards arrested Anne Boleyn on 2 May 1536 and took her to the Tower, while the king remained at Whitehall Palace where he had been during the arrests and subsequent discussions. Fitzroy went to his father that night to ask for his royal blessing, and Ambassador Chapuys wrote that King Henry cried in relief to his son, believing Fitzroy, 'owed a great debt for having escaped from the hands of that cursed and poisoning whore'.[30] Unfounded rumours that Anne planned to poison Princess Mary had appeared from time and time, and occasionally also Fitzroy. Whether these whispers started among Seymour supporters, flamboyant writers, or even the king's volatile imagination is unknown. Even Vicegerent Cromwell, who concocted Anne's murder, did not mention rumours of harm coming to Fitzroy.

King Henry did not put his son on the jury to condemn Anne Boleyn, her brother, and another four men at the court, including William Brereton, one of Fitzroy's former servants. Fitzroy's father-in-law Norfolk sat at the head of the judges' council and oversaw his niece's guilty verdict, and while King Henry did not witness his wife's death, Fitzroy certainly did. Ambassador Chapuys claimed Fitzroy smiled as Anne was beheaded on 19 May 1536, though that may have been wishful thinking. Fitzroy had nothing to gain from Anne's death or Jane Seymour's ascent. But now, with Queen Jane on the throne just days after Anne's death, all three of the king's children were illegitimate, with Fitzroy the only male option.[31] The legitimate line of succession being as it was, the heir-presumptive role fell on Lady Margaret Douglas, daughter of King Henry's sister Margaret,

Dowager Queen of Scotland. Of all the things happening at the royal court, this affected Fitzroy the most.

Lady Margaret Douglas had secretly married Lord Thomas Howard, the Duke of Norfolk's much younger half-brother who shared his name. They had married at Easter 1536, and Fitzroy's wife Mary Howard had been the only witness to the marriage. Lady Margaret was in no position to make a marriage on her own, and now she was the heir-presumptive, it looked as if the Howard family were staging a coup. Norfolk betrayed his brother to the king, and Lady Margaret and Lord Howard were both arrested and housed separately in the Tower. It was a stroke of good luck that King Henry did not turn his anger on Norfolk and Fitzroy's wife too.

With King Henry suddenly married to Jane Seymour, the wait for a new legitimate heir began, but Fitzroy was still an option. The king decided to permanently put his son in Baynard's Castle against the Thames in London, just a short wander along The Strand to Whitehall Palace. This beautiful home, considered fit for princes, and enjoyed by many noble guests, was close to Bridewell Palace where Henry enjoyed regular special occasions. Fitzroy and his wife Mary were finally to live together and given permission to consummate their marriage. They had never lived together and probably spent no time together at all. Mary Howard had stayed at her family home in Norfolk, while Fitzroy and Henry Howard had been together under the king's watch for years. Fitzroy was all but an adult and would finally live in his own castle with his wife.[32]

Vicegerent Cromwell was the one to decide who could be a ruler, making alterations to the Act of Succession so King Henry could choose his successor, rather than an heir-apparent selected by birth. This left Henry to play the factions at court against one another; the Catholics supporting Fitzroy and Princess Mary against the reformers and little Princess Elizabeth. King James of Scotland had a strong claim to the throne, and if Henry did not make serious statements over who would be next, the threat of Scotland banding together with France to take England remained. But if Fitzroy and Mary Howard had a son, then Henry could choose his legitimately born grandson as heir. But the other grandfather to this future king would be the Catholic Duke of Norfolk, the most unlikeable nobleman in the entire royal court, possibly the entire country.

On 8 June 1536, days before his seventeenth birthday, Fitzroy joined his father at the opening of parliament. They completed the solemn procession from Whitehall to Westminster, and Fitzroy carried the official cap of maintenance when they travelled back to Whitehall.[33] All seemed well with Fitzroy; he had just been given the title of Chamberlain of Chester and North Wales, Warden of the Cinque Ports, and Constable of Dover Castle. Ambassador Chapuys discussed how Fitzroy looked solid as an heir, and international rumours suggested Fitzroy could gain the duchy of Milan as part of peace talks.[34] While the Act of Succession was updated in parliament, focusing on the legitimacy of any of Jane Seymour's future heirs, Fitzroy looked consistent and welcomed by everyone. He was liked by all at court, even by those who believed Princess Mary was the rightful heir to the throne.

It was only on 8 July that anyone noticed something was wrong, when Chapuys wrote, '...the Duke of Richmond cannot, according to the prognostication of his physicians, live many months, having been pronounced to be in a state of rapid consumption'.[35] Fitzroy's sudden illness was kept quiet, only referenced almost two decades later when Edward VI became ill and was likened to Fitzroy's state. Consumption or tuberculosis remains the likely source of infection but bears a resemblance to suppurating pulmonary infection. This kind of bacterial infection is easily contracted in patients with bronchiectasis, abscesses in the lungs, or even necrotising pneumonia. A patient would often have little more than a cough, followed by difficulty breathing, dizziness and night sweats as the lung inflammation began. The airways and lungs would slowly collapse under the weight of fluid and swelling, resulting in limb bloating, skin sores and the smell of infected and dying skin on a patient. A lung infection of this nature needed strong antibiotics and lung drainage, but for Fitzroy, there could be no hope of dislodging the infection.

At the time of his illness, Fitzroy's household was spread out over his usual residences, as Baynard's Castle was not yet ready. He had been staying in Tonge in Kent, as well as travelling between his home in Lewes, Sheffield and Godstone. St James' Palace was a temporary place for Fitzroy to stay while he was in London, a suitably adequate home for a potential royal heir. The king was travelling in Kent at the time, preparing fortifications in Dover in case of attack. Fitzroy had not been fit to travel with his father, and within ten days of the first whispers of illness, Fitzroy's health was widely known as being in a steep decline, when John Husee wrote to tell Lord Lisle he feared the worst for the boy.[36]

The final days of Fitzroy's life have been lost to time, but Chapuys wrote on 23 July 1536, 'I just this moment have heard the Duke of Richmond died this morning, which is not a bad thing for the interests of the princess'.[37] King Henry was still in Kent, one hundred miles from his son when the worst happened. How Henry immediately reacted is unknown, but it must have been an occasion of severe horror and lamentation. Henry had taken the deaths of his children, born or miscarried, with great pain, and the loss of his vibrant and loved seventeen-year-old boy would have been horrific. The later reaction showed the depth of Henry's pain, as a week passed without much said, and Vicegerent Cromwell needed to see out Henry's wishes; the king wanted his son's death hushed up and quietly resolved. By 25 July, the inventory of Fitzroy's household began, and Henry had the Duke of Norfolk deal with the body, requesting Fitzroy be, 'conveyed secretly in a closed cart'. Fitzroy received only a modest coffin and placed in an open cart covered with hay, and taken to Thetford Priory in Norfolk, to the tombs of the Howard family. Only two men could travel with the cart, Fitzroy's governor George Cotton, a long-time servant, and his brother Richard Cotton. The men followed the cart dressed in plain green attire eighty miles north to Thetford. Black fabric went to the houschold to wear, but in the end, no souls but the Cotton brothers were present when Fitzroy was buried.[38]

King Henry soon heard of his son's undisclosed burial and flew into a rage even Cromwell could not contain. Norfolk heard of the king's wrath and assumed Henry was mad at the news of the death being shared, or the type of cart or the coffin not being adequately secret. In fact, Henry had changed his mind about Fitzroy and wanted his son properly buried, and Norfolk had 'denied' his king this right. Norfolk wrote to Vicegerent Cromwell on 5 August, fearing he would be thrown in the Tower, and needed someone to come to his aid and even hold his will for him.[39] Cromwell had his son Gregory staying with Norfolk, and the duke, scared and filled with regret, Norfolk pleaded with Cromwell to be spared the king's wrath, promising he would do all he could to appease Henry. Three years later, Norfolk was still in final preparations for having Fitzroy's impressive tomb finished, where Fitzroy and Norfolk would be buried together at a cost of 400l (over £175,000 today) for a pair of tombs lovingly designed and built.[40] Thetford Priory closed in 1539 during the Dissolution of the Monasteries, and Fitzroy's body was moved to Framlingham Church in Suffolk, where it still rests today.

The twenty-nine-page inventory taken at St James' Palace showed the depth of Henry's love for his son, combined with the significant income Fitzroy made each year from his lands.[41] His wardrobe had five gowns of damask, velvet, and satin tinsel, a purple velvet mantle of the Garter, complete with the Garter wrought with Venice gold. He owned nine coats of satin, taffeta, and damask, one of which, in green velvet and taffeta, went to his half-brother George Lord Tailboys. Fitzroy's clothing included doublets of velvet, satin, and taffeta, a whole fur of sable, velvet hats, scarlet cloaks, silver and gold buttons and many pairs of velvet shoes. His plate included copious quantities of gold, including a gold salt with a black dragon and pearls and stones from Cardinal Wolsey. Many New Year gifts from his father, in gold and silver in elaborately garnished and decorated patterns, a unicorn's horn covered in pearls and turquoise stones, a collar of twenty-one garters and twenty-one knots of crown gold, a George set with diamonds, along with a long list of fine jewellery and precious stones. Many of the fine silver gilt work such as pots, ewes, dishes, and the like were sent to Princess Mary for her use, plus Fitzroy's fabrics and plate in his chapel, including 'seven pieces of hangings of the Passion'. Among the bedroom furniture was quite an array of wall hangings featuring Moses and Balaam, 'Lady Plesaunce' surrounded by Virtues and Vices, King Lewes, the Coronation of Honour, Tullus Hostilius, King of Rome, and many more alongside fine pillows, curtains, quilts, and cushions covered in cloth of gold. A fully stocked kitchen and stable were also accounted for, and an extensive list of servants needed to be provided for, and new jobs found, many absorbed into other noble houses, or into Vicegerent Cromwell's service, including Henry Blount. Many had been in Fitzroy's household since its inception in 1525.[42] The sudden loss would have hurt many, and their potential chances of advancement.

Only one portrait remains of Fitzroy's likeness, a miniature by Lucas Horenbout, created around 1533 or 1534. It shows Fitzroy in a state of undress, wearing a beautiful skullcap to hide his red hair, his simple shirt undone at the collar as if he just got out of bed. A portrait dated 1534 shows Fitzroy leading the Knights of the Garter, a line-up which never actually occurred, so perhaps this plain miniature was made to help create the likeness of the king's son for a larger portrait. Fitzroy looked very much like his father, even with the red hair hidden under the cap, though his eyes were a lighter colour. Bessie Blount does not feature anywhere in the story of Fitzroy's death, though she would have been as devastated as any mother over the news, even though he had been separated from her by the age of three. Her other sons had been in their elder brother's household, so contact was regular, but without the funeral worthy of a prince, which Fitzroy should have received, the king's son was suddenly consigned to history.

The country soon fell into chaos with the Pilgrimage of Grace in the north, the constant fighting in Ireland, followed by the birth of a legitimate son in 1537 meant the possibilities and the pain of Henry Fitzroy, Duke of Richmond and Somerset soon faded from memory. For Lady Mary

Howard, her unconsummated marriage meant that she inherited nothing from Fitzroy's vast estates, no matter how many times Cromwell tried to petition the king for her rightful income. Lady Mary lived the rest of her life alone and bitter towards the Howard family for their treatment of her, going as far as testifying against her brother Henry Howard in a trial that saw him executed.

For a brief time, King Henry had the perfect male heir, a symbol showing a nursery of sons could be possible for himself and his dynasty, and without Fitzroy's brief life, Henry may have become even more cruel, even quicker than already experienced by those fated to step in his way.

Chapter 10

A Reformist Princess

During her lifetime, and in the five hundred years since, Anne Boleyn has received many labels. From the woman who stole the king; a seductress, a concubine, 'that woman', to a young woman forced to be a queen; a victim, an innocent, a sacrifice, through to the more bizarre and unfounded; a whore, a feminist, a witch. Anne Boleyn was none of these things, simply a woman who found herself given unusual opportunities which thrust her into the history books.

Born in either 1501 or 1507, depending on differing surviving manuscripts, Anne was the youngest daughter of the three surviving Boleyn children. Her father Thomas Boleyn was the eldest son of a wealthy merchant born of minor gentry, and his wife, a noble Irish heiress. Boleyn married Elizabeth Howard, daughter of the 2nd Duke of Norfolk, a spectacular coup for a man with money but only minor social connections. Thomas Boleyn worked for Henry VII, notably escorting Princess Margaret to Scotland when she became their queen in 1503 and was well in favour at the royal court when Henry VIII came to power, who made Boleyn a Knight of the Bath. Lady Elizabeth Boleyn worked in Queen Katharine's household, quietly aiding her queen while Sir Thomas became a diplomat, visiting Duchess Marguerite, Regent of the Netherlands. They struck up quite a relationship, as Boleyn requested a space in Marguerite's household for his youngest daughter Anne. Why he chose Anne and not his elder daughter Mary is a mystery, though with Mary being twelve at the time, perhaps they hoped she would enter the English court. Anne Boleyn moved to the Court of Savoy in Mechelen with Marguerite, quickly astounding the duchess with her impeccable manners and behaviour. Anne may have been as young as six or seven at the time, and spent eighteen months away from home, educated in reading, writing, mathematics, genealogy, history, dancing, embroidery, music, needlework and singing. The pastimes of a noble court also came easily to Anne, enjoying cards, chess, and dice, along with horse riding, hunting, archery, and falconry. When King Henry's sister Mary became the French queen in October 1514, Anne moved to join this new household, and her sister Mary joined her, travelling with their father for the occasion. Queen Mary was on the throne for only three months and then safely returned to England while the Boleyn girls stayed behind to live in the new Queen Claude's household.

Mary Boleyn returned to England in approximately 1519 before marrying in February 1520, but Anne may not have returned to England until as late as early 1522. Both sisters were soon in Queen Katharine's household, with Anne standing out from the crowd. Her French education and etiquette combined with a confident and witty nature soon endeared her to many, but it was not until around 1526 that King Henry took a shine to the younger Boleyn sister. Within a year, as Anne tried to keep her distance from the king, Henry looked to secure an annulment from Queen Katharine at a time of immense social upheaval in Europe. Another two years passed before the English courts attempted to end the marriage without success, by which time, Anne Boleyn had risen in power beside the king, and yet another two years passed before Katharine was exiled and Anne lived as the queen at court. Anne was not, and would never become popular at court, as her relationship with the king tore at England's social fabric. Only after Anne finally slept with Henry in late 1532 and immediately became pregnant did Henry panic and marry her, despite being married to Katharine. Anne must have felt secure at last by mid-1533; she was lawfully and spiritually married in England, the true wife under England's new laws. Unfortunately, Katharine was also lawfully and spiritually married to Henry, under papal law. The new reformist laws now had precedence in England, but they did not cancel out any rulings made before 1533. Both women had a case for being Henry's official queen.

Anne had no choice but to live as queen and be as comfortable as possible. She was at Henry's side, while Katharine remained in exile. The marriage had its supporters, notably the Archbishop of Canterbury Thomas Cranmer, while Thomas Cromwell (who Anne considered too beneath her to garner respect) had masterminded her legal marriage through strict new laws banning interference from Rome. But all was not well, as while Anne lived as a queen, she was not accepted as one. The general mood was still for Queen Katharine, and the French king continued to talk of an alliance with the Emperor in retaliation for Henry keeping Anne as queen.[1] Katharine had been downgraded to Princess Dowager and her household reduced, and she swore to die before accepting the judgement.[2] Elizabeth Barton had been prophesying that Henry would go to hell for marrying Anne, while international gossip said Henry was governed by Anne, who would give birth to a monster.[3]

When it came time to give birth to the son Anne Boleyn promised King Henry, the birth needed to follow Margaret Beaufort's *The Royal Book*, ensuring the birth prepared for a future king. Everything needed to be at least as elaborate and sumptuous as it had been for Queen Katharine. While avoiding the summer illnesses, Henry and Anne had been travelling from various locations, moving through Windsor and Westminster in August, arriving at Greenwich where Anne planned to go into her six-week confinement through September. The preferred apartments in the palace were emptied and swept, with tapestries and arras of soothing religious scenes covering every pocket of the rooms, including windows. Even the ceilings needed soothing images so the baby would not be affected by any distressing scenes Anne may see. Anne selected the tapestries to help her through this time; the story of St Ursula and the eleven thousand virgins. According to *The Royal Book*, Anne needed to spend six weeks resting in the womb-like space, but given the date of the birth, Anne stayed out of confinement as long as possible, to muddy opinions on whether she became pregnant well before her 25 January wedding, which seems to be the case. Henry had a special French bed placed in Anne's room, an enormous and beautiful item for his precious queen. The bed was a semi-throne for Anne, with a crimson cover lined with ermine and gold, with a gold canopy emblazoned with the crown and arms of the king and queen, much like Henry's mother Elizabeth of York chose in her day. It is unlikely Anne used relics with her strong reformist faith, but there would have been an altar and closet in her chambers, along with a cradle for the baby, matching the stately bed, and a simpler wooden one for regular use. It is likely the baby was born on the pallet bed on the floor, the traditional location for any birth. The Jewel House sent the best gold and silver plate to adorn the room, along with religious icons, so the baby would be born into a space of both religious devotion and rich magnificence.

On 26 August, the official procession into confinement took place, with Anne hearing mass in the royal chapel before proceeding to her rooms, where they shared spiced wine and said prayers for a safe delivery. The men of court departed, and the women were locked into the special rooms for the magic of royal birth. The court would have expected Anne to rest in the confinement rooms for at least four weeks, but it was less than two weeks before word of impending labour came from the rooms. The birth went smoothly, especially for a first child, with Princess Elizabeth born between three and four o'clock on Sunday afternoon, 7 September 1533. Physicians and astrologers alike had been promising a boy, but Henry had to cancel the planned fanfare. Anne had given birth to a full-term healthy daughter, and both were safe and well, a relief for Henry as Te Deums were sung in their honour. The couple both wanted a boy, but their daughter was not unwelcomed.

Baby Elizabeth's birth would have to follow Princess Mary's in pageantry and royalty. Elizabeth's christening was set for 10 September at the Observant Friars, just like Princess Mary and Prince Henry, Duke of Cornwall before her, and even King Henry himself. Thomas Cromwell ensured a perfect christening that mirrored royal protocol. A hall from the palace to the friars was created, with rails built along a path of newly laid gravel embellished with rushes. Golden cloth of arras hung along the south side, and into the church itself. Anne could not attend the christening, both due to her condition and protocol, as Elizabeth was baptised at the silver font by her godparents. Again, the silver font from Canterbury travelled to Greenwich, placed on an octagon-shaped stage three steps high. Red cloth adorned the stage, with a crimson stain canopy fringed with gold hung overhead, while the interior of the church and its doors shone with cloth of gold.[4]

London mayor Sir Stephen Peacock and forty of the chief citizens joined the royal procession, entering two by two, followed by gentlemen, squires, chaplains, aldermen, the king's council, barons, and bishops. Henry Bouchier, Earl of Essex carried the covered gilt basin, Henry Courtenay, Marquess of Exeter carried a taper of virgin wax, and Henry Grey, Marquess of Dorset carried the salt. Lady Mary Howard bore the chism ahead of her grandmother Agnes Howard, Dowager Duchess of Norfolk, carrying the new princess on a mantle of purple velvet, the long train carried by Thomas Boleyn, Earl of Wiltshire, Anne Grey, Countess of Kent and Edward Stanley, Earl of Derby. The Dukes of Norfolk and Suffolk walked alongside the baby in the duchess' arms, with a canopy held aloft by George Boleyn, Lord Rochford, John Lord Hussey, Lord William Howard and Lord Thomas Howard the younger. The Boleyn and Howard families were well represented among the nobility around them.

The staunchly Catholic Bishop of London John Stokesley, surrounded by the abbots of Westminster, St Alban's, Bermondsey and Stratford, christened Princess Elizabeth at the door to the chapel before Elizabeth was taken to the font with her godparents Thomas Cranmer, Archbishop of Canterbury, Agnes Howard, the Dowager Duchess of Norfolk (also Princess Mary's godmother), and Margaret Grey, Dowager Duchess of Dorset. Elizabeth was triple dipped in the warmed water of the font and confirmed by Cranmer, all the torches were lit while the heralds trumpeted for Princess Elizabeth, the now-only legitimate child of Henry VIII. Gifts were given out, along with wafers, comfits, and hypocras, before she passed servants and guards holding five hundred torches.

The king needed a son. Henry broke with Rome for a son. Created a divorce for a son. Exiled his daughter for a son. Henry inflicted intense pain and got a daughter. Ambassador Chapuys wrote of the disappointment of a daughter, while enemies of Anne and the Reformation were thrilled. There is no conclusive evidence of serious disappointment from Henry or Anne. They had a child, they had their marriage, and they could create healthy children. Now the baby needed to be set aside so Anne could get pregnant again as soon as possible. At least the baby was called Elizabeth, not Mary like Ambassador Chapuys feared, who also said 'the christening has been like her mother's coronation, very cold and disagreeable'.[5] Among Cromwell's notes for September, catching up on business, he noted he had a ballad written by Princess Mary, to give to Princess Elizabeth. Regardless of who their mothers were, the girls were still sisters, even if Mary would not call Elizabeth a princess.[6] After Elizabeth's christening, Cromwell retired to his home in Stepney to go hawking, where Ambassador Chapuys joined him, and reported Cromwell was an ally to Katharine and Mary, and they could still be saved from treachery with Cromwell's help.[7]

Princess Elizabeth began her early life staying close to her mother at Greenwich, under the care of Lady Margaret Bryan, who had already raised Princess Mary and Henry Fitzroy in their early years. There have been suggestions Anne breastfed Elizabeth, but there is no firm evidence of this and was inappropriate for a noblewoman. Anne needed to do everything properly to signify her daughter's royal position. Elizabeth was a royal child and needed her own household even as a baby, and Henry soon chose Hatfield. Only twenty miles north of London, Hatfield had been built in 1497 by Archbishop John Morton, a red-brick manor comprised of four wings and a central courtyard, and wide countryside all around, perfect for any royal family member. Elizabeth was to spend her first winter at Hatfield, accompanied by a full household, and her sister, Princess Mary. Baby Elizabeth arrived at Hatfield with Lady Bryan on 13 December 1533, three days before the arrival of her sister.

The birth and christening of Princess Elizabeth must have been a deep shock for Princess Mary, despite knowing well in advance all that would occur. Being reduced from a princess to simply a king's daughter, without her rank and title, would have hurt beyond compare. Mary wrote to her mother at Buckden Palace, seeking solace when they could not be together, and while the letter has not survived, Ambassador Chapuys reported it to be 'wonderfully good'. Queen Katharine wrote back to her daughter on

15 September, telling Mary she heard of Elizabeth's birth and how God would handle Mary well through the situation. Katharine implored her daughter to offer herself to God to find peace and warned Mary to follow any commandment sent from Henry. Katharine wrote:

> 'answer you with few words, obeying the King your father in everything, save only that you will not offend God and lose your own soul, and go no further with learning and disputation in the matter. And wheresoever and in whatsoever company you shall come, obey the King's commandments. Speak you few words and meddle nothing... for I dare make you sure that you shall see a very good end, and better than you can desire. I would God, good daughter, that you did know with how good a heart I do write this letter unto you'.[8]

Princess Mary received two Latin books from her mother, *De Vita Christi*, with the declaration of the Gospels, and the other the *Epistles of Hierome*, the letters of St Jerome, who created the Vulgate Latin bible. She told her daughter to play the virginals or the lute to relax, not to make any risky decisions about her life, and to stay far away from even thinking about a husband. Katharine warned against false friends and seemed pleased Mary was still safe in Lady Margaret Pole's care. She promised to write to Mary and do all she could for her daughter, signing off, 'by your loving mother, Katharine The Queen'.

There had been rumours the baby Elizabeth would be known as the only princess of England, to eliminate all memory of Princess Mary. It was the least of Mary's problems, for John Lord Hussey arrived at her household at Beaulieu and informed them of her diminished state, that she was no longer a princess. Mary had always been quiet about her opinion on Anne Boleyn and the annulment, but now aged seventeen, she was a young woman and told Hussey her thoughts in person, as notes could be used as evidence. Princess Mary told Hussey she was a princess, and she would believe no man bringing such news until she heard it from the king himself. Hussey scurried away and wrote to the Privy Council on 20 September explaining the situation, and naturally, Henry was displeased.[9] The king was a coward; he never discussed his annulment or new marriage with Mary, and never had the guts to personally deliver unwelcome news after Katharine gave him a royal dressing down in 1527 when he mentioned annulment. Mary's refusal to listen to instructions showed Henry to be weak in the face of a seventeen-year-old woman.

Henry sent Richard Sampson, then Dean of Lichfield, along with John de Vere, Earl of Oxford, Robert Radcliffe, Earl of Sussex, and Henry Bouchier, Earl of Essex, to Beaulieu to tell Mary the truth; that she was no longer a legitimate princess and deprived of all the benefits of such high estate.[10] Mary had a meeting with these men, leaving them all simultaneously in tears. Henry loved his daughter, but he had not contacted Mary in a year and now sent others to do his dirty work. Had Princess Elizabeth been born a boy, the situation never would have happened, but with two daughters, one had to be seen as the legitimate heir, and the other diminished and humiliated. The Pope and the Emperor both expected Henry to take back Katharine and Mary, and marriage for Mary was an option to get her the power she needed.[11] No wonder Katharine warned her not to get sad, isolated, drunk, or worse, forced into a marriage. Mary wrote to her father personally on 2 October, shocked to hear she was Lady Mary, as she was born in lawful matrimony.[12]

Princess Mary's household accounts were settled for the year on 30 September 1533, showing a cost of 2,685l 3s 9¾d (almost £1,200,000 today)[13] and 'Lady' Mary's household was established on 1 October. A roll of her servants at Beaulieu counted 162 people. Margaret Pole remained Mary's governess, and twenty-two women remained Mary's ladies, including Lady Margaret Douglas, Katharine Grey Lady Maltravers, Margaret Blount Lady Hussey, plus Mrs Rider, Mrs Aylmer, Mrs Butts, Mrs de Bruxia, Mrs Duwes, Mrs Browne, Mrs Parker, and Mrs Knight, all wives of men in Mary's household. John Lord Hussey was still chamberlain, and Richard Fetherstone was still Mary's tutor.[14] But Princess Mary suddenly received word she would have to leave Beaulieu Palace, as it now belonged to George Boleyn, Lord Rochford; her household would be moved twenty-three miles north to Hertford Castle. Thomas Cromwell was forced to note that any valuable items not suitable for Princess Elizabeth's new household go back to the Jewel House, showing how diminished Mary's status was becoming. Cromwell also received reports that those in Mary's household kept calling her princess, and those with Katharine still called her queen, though Cromwell never punished anyone for doing so, despite King Henry's demands.[15]

The move was pointless; as Mary continued to rebel against her father, he became cruel and petty and took up one of Anne Boleyn's earlier ideas of making Mary a servant in Princess Elizabeth's new household at Hatfield.[16] Until now, Elizabeth had been in a nursery at Greenwich, behind a special wainscot screen where she could be viewed by only the noblest of the court and her besotted mother.

Princess Mary at once became ever more indignant to such a request and discussed the situation with Ambassador Chapuys, who advised her to make sure she made her lack of consent plain. Cromwell promised Chapuys he would do what he could for Mary, but no one could persuade Henry, and on 16 December, the Duke of Norfolk, the Earl of Oxford, and the king's almoner Edward Foxe arrived to give Mary the official news. She was not a princess; she was a servant to a princess. Given only half an hour to prepare, Mary heard she would also lose all but two of her household, not even allowed to take Margaret Pole with her to Hatfield, despite Lady Pole offering to pay for an entire household on Mary's behalf. Mary bravely told Norfolk that she knew of no princess but herself, both at Hertford Castle and again when she arrived at Hatfield, despite saying she would acknowledge Elizabeth as the king's child the same way she considered Fitzroy her brother. Mary also told Norfolk to report to the king that she, a princess, wanted her father's blessing, which Norfolk refused to repeat.[17] Mary was exiled from both parents for varied reasons, and now also from Lady Pole, and in a household filled with enemies. The situation could not get any worse. For extra pain, Lady Margaret Douglas could not stay with her cousin Mary. All while this was happening, the Duke of Suffolk was attempting to evict Queen Katharine from Buckden Palace, where she barricaded herself in her room and refused to get out of bed or dress, making the task impossible.[18]

Christmas meant different things for the two princesses. For Mary, she did not receive any gift from her father at New Year, her remaining attendants were removed, and a Scottish ambassador asking if Mary could marry King James was rebuffed.[19] But King Henry decided to travel without Anne to Hatfield on 17 January, to speak with Mary and get her to accept her position as the illegitimate sibling to the new princess. Ambassador Chapuys claimed that Anne Boleyn commanded Thomas Cromwell, William Fitzwilliam, and William Kingston to go after the king and ensure he did not speak to Mary, lest he be beguiled by her virtues and treat her well. It is more likely the three went with the king in case he became too scared to speak to his daughter. That was exactly what happened; Henry went to visit Princess Elizabeth in her rooms, while Cromwell spoke with Princess Mary. He could do no more than explain the situation as it stood, and that the new Act of Succession he had put to parliament three days earlier would make Elizabeth the sole heir to the throne. Cromwell asked Princess Mary to renounce her title, and she refused, even if her father threatened death. Mary wanted to see the king, and Henry refused, so Mary ran to the roof balcony to see her father leaving Hatfield. Henry saw his daughter, on her knees, her hands pleading, and he returned an acknowledgement, bowing and touching his hat, and all the men in the retinue bowed to Mary.

Anne was furious King Henry had acknowledged Mary, instead of only seeing Elizabeth. Anne wanted Mary controlled more strictly and was concerned she was being led by others in her stubbornness. Rumours from the Earl of Northumberland's men suggested Anne planned to poison Mary, while Queen Katharine wrote to Emperor Charles asking why he was not pressing harder against Henry. Ambassador Chapuys wanted to speak in parliament about Katharine and Mary, but Cromwell could not allow it under the rule of no foreigners allowed. The idea that mother and daughter could be reunited if they renounced their titles was quickly dropped. By this time, Princess Mary was living under the care of Lady Anne Shelton, one of Anne Boleyn's aunts, who received instructions to strike Mary if she used the title of princess. At least poisoning fears dropped when Mary ate at a communal table rather than served privately as a princess would expect.[20] But Anne's other aunt, Lady Alice Clere (sister of Thomas Boleyn and Anne Shelton) was also in charge of Mary and did not use such cruelty. George Boleyn wrote to his aunt Alice, warning her from using 'too much honesty and humility' with Mary. Mary was surrounded by Boleyns, and Lady Alice was her only ally.

Henry and Anne continued their pettiness with Mary; Lady Shelton was instructed to punish Mary more harshly for her behaviour, and yet Lady Shelton refused, saying Mary deserved polite treatment considering her goodness and virtues. Mary found herself running out of clothes as she grew but servants were supposed to only take letters from princesses, and she was no longer one, and thus could not request new items. Mary was not allowed to attend mass in a local parish church; as it was, Mary was cheered as a princess for simply walking along a gallery at Hatfield when spotted by locals.[21] In February, Anne travelled to Hatfield to see Princess Elizabeth and asked to see Mary too, but Mary refused, as she could only see the queen, and her mother lived at Buckden. Mary was not above playing games with her father's wife. The pettiness spilt into international politics when the French ambassador offered an alliance with France if King Henry married Mary to Alessandro de'Medici, Duke of Florence, an ally of Emperor Charles, who believed Mary needed his consent to marry.[22] According to the French, the English king hated his daughter and offered his nieces Margaret Douglas or Frances Brandon to be the Duchess of Florence.[23] A week later, the Act of Succession passed in parliament, making Princess Elizabeth the only lawful heir in England. Cromwell had omitted Princess Mary from the paperwork entirely, but leaving her name out kept her closer to succession than she may have thought. The paperwork did not state Mary was an heir to the throne, but it did not consider her ineligible either, giving her options. Thomas Cromwell and Thomas Cranmer also ensured a proclamation Henry and Anne's marriage was valid, and it was treason to call Katharine a queen, or Mary a princess, though that would do nothing to change people's private opinions. There were still two queens and two princesses in England.

In preparation for Easter 1534, Princess Elizabeth needed to join her parents, but Mary refused to travel, going as far as being forced into a litter by Anne Shelton. Ambassador Chapuys was surprised by Mary's defiance, scared his suggestions she should fight her father had gone too far and she would suffer as a result.[24] Servants then searched Mary's room, a velvet bag of letters taken away, though they contained nothing incriminating. There is no record of her reaction to having her rooms searched when she returned to Hatfield.

Weeks later, on 18 April 1534, Princess Elizabeth went to Eltham to be presented naked to French ambassadors[25] (as deformity was a sign of parental sin and needed to be ruled out). The child was then sent to live in the rebuilt 'prince's' side of the palace, while Mary stayed behind at Hatfield. Princess Mary's daily tasks waiting on her sister were vague, so what Mary could do when Elizabeth was away is even more incomplete. She received letters from Chapuys, who also sent her books to enjoy. But when Thomas Boleyn and William Kingston arrived at Hatfield to force Mary into signing the Act of Succession and swearing her father was Head of the Church, she steadfastly refused. Boleyn's sister Anne Shelton told Princess Mary that her father no longer cared if she renounced her title or not and she faced homelessness for such disobedience, or perhaps King Henry would execute his daughter. Mary asked to speak to Elizabeth's doctor, and speaking publicly in Latin, Mary told the physician of the threats against her. In English, Mary said she could no longer speak Latin properly, as it was not spoken in the household, and the doctor 'agreed' in English, to throw everyone off Mary's desperate plea for help.[26] Soon, Mary's maid and her confessor were both fired, as they were the ones smuggling in letters to Mary from Queen Katharine. The Boleyn faction had made a significant mistake threatening Mary's life, even if they were simply following the king's lead.

Throughout the first half of 1534, England was undergoing massive changes, not that baby Elizabeth would know in her well-appointed nursery at Eltham, and newly eighteen-year-old Mary, still spending her days being a maid to Elizabeth, felt isolated from affairs. The Pope still considered Katharine and Mary legitimate, men such as Sir Thomas More and Bishop

John Fisher were in the Tower for not signing the Act of Supremacy and Act of Succession, and Ambassador Chapuys had been to a huge summit at Westminster to plead Mary's case. Thomas Cromwell quietly promised to Chapuys to keep Katharine, Mary and all Spaniards in England safe from the Acts of Supremacy and Succession, but Cromwell was worried about Anne Boleyn's wrath.[27]

Princesses Elizabeth and Mary remained at Eltham as the world battled around them. Mary signed a written statement she would not bow to pressure and was a legitimate princess.[28] But Mary was starting to feel unwell, as she had first done in 1532 with stomach aches, heart pains, and headaches. Mary was not the only one with issues; Henry and Anne were at Windsor, where Anne had a 'goodly belly' as early as April 1534, but no baby was ever born. Henry was entertaining an unnamed mistress, one sympathetic to Mary, claimed Chapuys, throughout the summer of discontent in 1534. Rumours of Anne threatening to do away with Mary abounded, with Anne's brother George warning against such words. Anne being that outwardly cruel seems more like slander than fact, no matter how nervous Anne felt about not producing a son.

Princess Elizabeth's household was on the move again in August, heading from Eltham to Greenwich, where Princess Mary was allowed to ride, to avoid any dramatic stand-offs. Mary rode hard ahead of Elizabeth's train, and arrived at Greenwich an hour early, taking the prime spot on the royal barge there to fetch Elizabeth and her household. No one would dare touch Mary in public, so she led the barge ride down the Thames as the guest of honour.

So little of Princess Elizabeth's first year exists. Her first Christmas, her first birthday, the women in her household, a lot of information is surprisingly lacking. But Elizabeth did not receive her own independent households like Mary or Fitzroy, she was connected to the royal household, and thus, costs and information are mixed with Henry's own running costs. The overall expenditure was upwards of 2,000l a year (£880,000 today) to keep the princesses together. Costs for Anne Boleyn gives details of Elizabeth's life, as her mother regularly ordered luxurious items for her, like a rich purple satin cap with damask gold detail and edging, a white satin cap with gold edging, a crimson satin cap, a taffeta cap edging with cloth of gold to match the crimson woven linen on Elizabeth's cradle.[29] Elizabeth wore black fur mittens with white ribbon and had a bedcover made of russet damask, and it was details such as these that remained so important. Elizabeth and Mary lived together, but Elizabeth's household needed to appear materially well-endowed to display who was the heir-apparent and the highest-ranked daughter. Mary was not as poverty-stricken as Chapuys liked to point out. Mary had her own privy chamber and staff to assist her with things day to day, even if it paled to the size and grandeur of Elizabeth's lifestyle. The king paid for Mary's household, just as he did for Elizabeth, to ensure the Emperor did not suspect Mary suffered mistreatment. While Mary was ill in the summer of 1534, the household had to ensure they made changes to her dietary requirements to ease her stomach pains, as Mary's physicians and apothecaries ordered.[30] No matter how important Elizabeth needed to appear, Mary gained love from her father, albeit from afar.

Scholars, from the contemporary to the modern day, have made many assumptions about the situation of Elizabeth and Mary's combined household. Chapuys wrote of how Mary became a servant, while today Mary is still often written in misogynistic terms, once described as a teenager pouting and sulking about her treatment. The reality is far less simple. In September 1534, Mary wrote a letter to Sir Nicholas Carew, one of the most esteemed men in Henry's privy chamber.[31] Carew was married to Lady Elizabeth Carew, one of Henry's former mistresses and daughter of Lady Margaret Bryan, Elizabeth's governess. The theory that Mary was being held like a victim or prisoner is not as probable as Chapuys liked to believe, but since Mary had been primed since birth to be above all others, it was natural the new situation made little sense to her. Princess Mary knew no other world, and now that world was being handed to the unsuspecting Elizabeth.

Rumours abounded that King Henry had a new mistress, likely Margaret Shelton, his wife's cousin, and daughter of John and Anne Shelton (the same running Elizabeth's household and watching over Princess Mary). Pope Clement died, ending the futile annulment battle, and George Boleyn had been working as ambassador to France so baby Elizabeth could solidify an alliance through marriage. All these things left the royal daughters in a state of confusion; Henry still loved Mary, despite being firmly on Anne and Elizabeth's side. Even Anne no longer criticised Mary, as many courtiers close to Henry had been hounded by the king for speaking negatively about his daughter. Thomas Cromwell had made clear guidelines in parliament about the treatment of Katharine and Mary, and neither were to be harmed. Cromwell believed Henry loved Mary 'one hundred times more than Elizabeth' and told Chapuys so in secret.[32]

In October, the princesses were staying at The More in Herefordshire, where Queen Katharine had been exiled. Henry went to see Elizabeth but allowed Mary to meet the courtiers who travelled with their king. While it was a simple gesture, to Mary and the court, it was a strong showing that Henry was not angry at Mary. She had not been fighting her father's marriage over several months whilst ill, and Henry had again turned back to his daughter, possibly while being distracted by a new mistress.[33] Either way, Mary was buoyed by the gesture, and the following day, 23 October, Elizabeth and Mary set off for Richmond Palace, and Mary was given a velvet litter to travel in, the same as Elizabeth. She also spent part of the trip on a barge instead of with the royal train, where she was able to see Ambassador Chapuys who was waiting near the bank at a pre-organised spot, showing Mary had access to letters. Chapuys mentioned Mary looked healthy and cared for, propaganda Henry would have been pleased to read.[34]

Recent French negotiations had not been fruitful, and France sent Phillipe de Chabot, Seigneur de Brion, the Admiral of France to discuss alliances. Chabot arrived to discuss the 1518 treaty of Princess Mary marrying the dauphin; the French still considered Mary legitimate. Mary no longer had Queen Katharine advocating against a French marriage, but she did have Thomas Cromwell, who gritted his teeth in meetings and then sought to undermine negotiations behind closed doors. Henry wanted Princess Elizabeth to marry into France, the country Anne loved, but Anne was furious Mary was considered the legitimate heir abroad. Chabot was not even keen to meet with Anne unless Henry enforced the meeting. The king went as far as saying he would give up his dubious claim to the French crown and offer Princess Elizabeth to marry Francis' third son Charles, Duke of Angoulême if King Francis admitted Henry and Katharine's marriage was void. Meanwhile, the Emperor's men were looking to get Mary into Scotland to be queen, safe from Anne Boleyn.[35]

The royal family and the nobles were all at odds over the princess. Anne was angry and ensured her aunt Anne Shelton continued to hound and harass Mary in their household and had one of Mary's servants fired, suspected of sharing secret messages with Chapuys. The Duke of Norfolk was suspicious of Mary sailing past Chapuys' house at the perfect moment for a meeting and knew not who to trust. But when Mary fell desperately ill, Henry again sent Dr Butts, his number one physician, who diagnosed Mary sick due to the conditions in the household, suggesting she should live with Queen Katharine. Thomas Cromwell too lobbied this to the king, but Henry denied the request yet again. Princess Elizabeth's household accounts show Mary needing her special diet again, giving her a good breakfast before being served meat by nine o'clock; Princess Elizabeth's household had refused to accommodate this need until now. Mary ate in private in her rooms, at an additional cost of 26l 13s 4d a year (£12,000 today), hardly a huge imposition in a household with a cost running well over 1,000l a year.[36]

Princess Mary remained ill and even got worse after New Year 1535, especially when she and her mother were threatened with the Tower for not accepting the succession. Cromwell again tried to have Mary moved to Queen Katharine at Kimbolton Castle, the queen's sixth and final home in exile. The situation had become a farce; the king's physicians would not treat Princess Mary without Katharine's physicians present; no one wanted to be accused of any mistreatment or poisoning.[37] Emperor Charles wanted Mary smuggled out of England. Meanwhile, the French were ready to marry Princess Elizabeth to the dauphin or his brother Charles if Henry could prove Mary was not heir to the throne. Mary would not provide such proof by signing the Act of Succession. Anne Boleyn then insulted the French ambassador by laughing in his face at her own joke about how King Henry had excused himself from their dinner to meet his mistress. Meanwhile, Thomas Cromwell hated French Ambassador Chabot so much that Chapuys revelled in watching the king's chief minister try to restrain himself from lashing out in public. Princess Mary was not a child anymore, she could understand the games played by the adults, even when home in bed with her illness. At this point, even Cromwell suspected poison inside the princess' household.[38]

Poor Princess Elizabeth was only nearing eighteen months old and already a bargaining chip. The French agreed to marry Elizabeth to Charles, Duke of Angoulême if Mary could not inherit the crown. New French Ambassador Gontier spoke with Anne Boleyn, who admitted she was scared for her position if the French did not see her as queen and Elizabeth as heir.[39] But Princess Mary was still considered the prize, not Elizabeth. Cromwell and Chapuys planned various marriages and alliances, all for nothing, but in late January 1535, Princess Mary was still desperately ill; King Henry claimed she might not survive and no one wanted to take responsibility for choosing her doctors.

Ambassador Chapuys did not buy this claim and wrote that Mary was well after being able to eat and drink. Queen Katharine was worried for Mary and wanted to nurse her personally, but before anything could change, Mary, still with Elizabeth at Greenwich Palace, fell sick again, unable to eat, and plagued with pains, headaches, and heart issues. Henry travelled there personally in mid-March, and Mary had made some recovery, Chapuys writing Mary, 'is well, better than some would have her. She may be called the paragon of beauty, goodness, and virtue'.[40] He also claimed Anne believed she would not give the king a son while Katharine and

Mary remained alive. Henry and Anne spent Easter at Richmond Palace, presumably with Princess Elizabeth alongside them, while Mary was sent to Hunsdon. Mary remained extremely ill for the first month of her time there, fearing poison and asking Chapuys for help, so Cromwell secured her the king's physicians. Rumours swirled that the king travelled to Hunsdon personally, but without Chapuys' verification, it seems unlikely.

Negotiations paused when Thomas Cromwell fell ill with malaria and almost died in April 1535. Katharine and Mary were at risk of execution for not accepting the Succession, with Anne Shelton still threatening Mary at Hunsdon. King Henry himself visited Cromwell on his deathbed to ensure Charterhouse monks were burned at the stake for not signing the Succession.[41] It was proof those who did not accept the Reformation in England would perish and the burnings were designed to scare people such as Katharine and Mary.

But the Reformation then took another turn when Henry decided that Bishop John Fisher and Sir Thomas More would die at Tower Hill for refusing the royal marriage and new religion. Cromwell, newly appointed England's only ever Vicegerent of England, tried to get the men to accept a pardon and sign the supremacy, but it was too late, and the murders shocked European leaders and the new Pope Paul III. If Henry wanted his daughters married to European rulers, he had made a terrible decision. Cromwell bemoaned to Chapuys that things would not improve until Katharine and Mary died, as both women were smuggling letters abroad to Queen Mary, Regent of the Netherlands and Queen Eleanor of France.

Henry and Anne left London on a glorious summer progress of Reformation propaganda, leaving Princess Mary sick at Hunsdon, and her parents' doctors both attended her, as she was still sick in September. Mary was recovering but what she needed was fresh air, exercise, and her mother. The plague was rife in London, and no one could visit Mary until October when the royal daughters reunited, in time for the new French ambassador Antoine de Castelnau, Bishop of Tarbes to visit and see Princess Elizabeth, newly two years old. Mary tried to present herself, only to be physically restrained by Anne Shelton. Queen Katharine wrote to the Pope, expecting she and Mary would suffer execution, and wanted Emperor Charles to invade England and the Pope to excommunicate Henry.

By late 1535, England needed to pivot priorities yet again. King Henry produced a new plan to dissolve English monasteries, despite Vicegerent Cromwell's protestations to reform them as part of his church valuation plan, and Anne was finally pregnant. Marriage negotiations with France no longer mattered if there was a legitimate son. Ambassador Chapuys could not get a visit with Mary, not even a servant to do a weekly checkup. Anne considered Princess Mary her number one enemy and Henry promised to never marry Mary to anyone. But on 13 December, Cromwell sent for Chapuys, to tell him Queen Katharine was desperately ill, followed by word on 29 December that she would die. Chapuys and Cromwell had been secretly planning an Anglo-Imperial alliance,[42] ignoring Henry's plans for his daughters, but while Chapuys gained permission to visit Katharine, Mary did not.[43] Chapuys sat with Katharine for four days, calming her and explaining all would be well, explaining she and Mary would be safe from Henry and Anne. Chapuys left on 5 January 1536 to report to Mary, but Katharine died only two days later, separated from her daughter.[44]

Henry and Anne openly celebrated Queen Katharine's death, parading Princess Elizabeth at Greenwich where the court had gathered for New Year. Thomas and George Boleyn were 'overheard' saying they hoped Princess Mary would be next. Mary had lost her mother, and with her, international safety and support.[45] The devastation would have been acute; separated and ostracised for five years, Mary got only a quick message of condolence from Chapuys, coupled with Anne Shelton's big mouth blurting the news. Mary wanted to see Katharine's doctors to hear about her final days, but she could not write to her father nor attend any funeral. Vicegerent Cromwell planned an enormous funeral fit for a queen, only to be angrily knocked back by Henry, allowing only a simple burial at St Peterborough Cathedral. Only Mary's cousin Lady Eleanor Brandon and eight ladies-in-waiting could attend. Mary did get her meeting with Katharine's staff and was seen in tears over the Act of Succession.[46]

Days later, Chapuys wrote again saying, 'the King, being mounted on a great horse to run at the lists, both fell so heavily that everyone thought it a miracle he was not killed, but he sustained no injury. I might ask of fortune for what greater misfortune he is reserved, like the other tyrant who escaped from the fall of the horse, in which all the rest were smothered, and soon after died'.[47] Rumours of serious injury and succession fears later popped up without any evidence; Henry was fine, his son Fitzroy was with him at court, and the law clearly stated Princess Elizabeth was heir. But no matter how many letters Anne wrote to her aunt telling her to force Mary to accept her as queen, everyone still preferred adult Mary over baby Elizabeth.

The same day Ambassador Chapuys wrote of Queen Katharine's funeral, he mentioned Anne had collapsed and suffered a miscarriage, possibly a boy a few months old.[48] Mary at been at Eltham Palace at the time and Lady Shelton tried keeping the news from Mary as long as possible, along with news Henry and Anne were having serious marriage problems. Anne had been crying over Katharine's death, as she realised her vulnerability without a son. Chapuys and Cromwell were trying to secure an alliance for their masters and now with the loss of a child, Anne was in danger of losing Henry, and in an impossible situation. She had fought for her position for years while being berated at every turn, and had done her best for Princess Elizabeth while waiting for a son, all for nothing.[49]

Soon after Anne's miscarriage, Princess Mary's treatment started to improve, she moved to a new home about forty miles from Gravesend and received money to distribute to the poor. Vicegerent Cromwell had orders to increase the numbers in her household, and Ambassador Chapuys worried there was a catch, writing, 'I hope no scorpion lurks beneath the honey'.[50] But Mary soon got the news that her old tutor Richard Fetherstone (along with her mother's chaplain Thomas Abel) was condemned to death for refusing the supremacy. It scared Mary, and she wrote to Chapuys with plans to escape from Gravesend and head abroad. Chapuys advised against the plan, for it seemed too easy to escape, fearing a trap, and suggested Mary wait until Easter when staying again at Eltham.

Vicegerent Cromwell and Chapuys again looked to secure an alliance, while Emperor Charles and the Duke of Savoy went to war over Milan. Cromwell desperately wanted to create an Imperial alliance and peace, going behind Henry's back. The Emperor would even accept Anne as queen in the new deal, but Henry had not spoken to his wife in months and was courting Jane Seymour, with limited success. Princess Mary would gain a husband from Cromwell's plan, the heir-presumptive to the Portuguese throne, keeping her safe from her father. Dinner gossip among high-ranking nobles heralded other dangers; Anne wanted to rid herself of Cromwell, and Chapuys was nervous about his friend's survival.[51] Cromwell was Princess Mary's ally at court and the only one looking to ally with the Emperor, though Cromwell told Chapuys he was not scared of Anne but promised to be careful.[52] Ambassador Chapuys had his own problems; he was forced to finally meet Anne in the flesh when attending mass at court. The Easter season had been hard; Anne had her almoner openly criticise King Henry and Vicegerent Cromwell at the Sunday sermon, in front of the entire royal court.

With Princess Mary still at Eltham, Chapuys went to an Easter Tuesday banquet at Greenwich where he and Cromwell were forced to explain their private negotiations of an alliance, caught out when Henry heard rumours. Chapuys ran and hid with Edward Seymour, but Cromwell openly quarrelled with the king in public, refusing to back down. Chapuys reported Cromwell was still stunned into silence by his own behaviour when they licked their wounds the following morning, and Chapuys suggested they smuggle Mary out of England and forget the whole plan.[53] The Privy Council begged Henry to accept Cromwell's plan with Chapuys, but Cromwell disappeared; Chapuys thought he was in bed with melancholy, but he was instead at his Stepney home, meeting with religious leaders on how to annul a royal marriage.

Anne Boleyn was no fool; without anything being explicitly said, she knew the tide was turning against her and Princess Elizabeth. Her husband was in busy council meetings about an Imperial alliance, but Vicegerent Cromwell was missing in action; she feared the worst. On 26 April, Anne met with her chaplain Matthew Parker, and asked him, if anything were to happen to her, to look after Elizabeth.[54] It was a vow Parker took seriously for the rest of his life. A later recollection by Scottish scholar Alexander Alesius recalled waiting at Greenwich for the king late at night and looking up to see Henry and Anne arguing in a gallery, as Anne held Elizabeth in her arms. The royal couple argued for some time in plain view of the court waiting to return to London, the conversation silent to all but the pair.[55] Alesius was a wise man who worked at Cambridge University and as an occasional spy for Cromwell, and his records from his time in England and Europe are generally reliable sources, but there is no record of Elizabeth visiting her parents in April. Princess Elizabeth was at Hunsdon as the May Day celebrations were prepared at Greenwich. Perhaps Elizabeth went to Greenwich without any record, but it is also possible that Alesius mixed up his days when writing to Elizabeth decades later.

To everyone except Vicegerent Cromwell, shock hit the court at the May Day events at Greenwich, when he and the king abruptly left for Whitehall Palace. Anne's ladies were taken away, just as court lute player Mark Smeaton had been a day earlier. The following morning, 2 May, Anne Boleyn was arrested, along with a handful of other men, and then also George Boleyn. Henry cried at Whitehall, telling his son Fitzroy he was glad neither he nor Mary had been poisoned by Anne, who was condemned as a whore. Princess Mary's reaction to the news went unrecorded. Chapuys had informants in Mary's household, so the news would have reached Eltham quickly. Anne had allegedly bedded her brother, plus Henry Norris, Mark Smeaton, Francis Weston, and William Brereton. Thanks to panic, lies, and finger-pointing, comments quickly twisted into 'evidence' of Anne's adultery along with plans to kill the king, and remarks about his all-important virility. There was still no son for England. The royal marriage was declared void on 17 May 1536 by Thomas Cranmer, but his reasoning for the ruling goes unrecorded. All papers on the issue were destroyed and only conjecture remains, and there is no evidence of King Henry's affair with Mary Boleyn was used as justification, nor anything on Anne Boleyn's adultery. Before the trial for Anne's life even began, courtiers were looking to pay favour to Princess Mary. Strangely, Anne Shelton let them in to see the princess, her allegiance to her great-niece Elizabeth suddenly forgotten. Cromwell arranged the trials and executions, with poor Anne Boleyn killed on 19 May 1536, her daughter not yet three and now motherless like her sister.

Ambassador Chapuys and Vicegerent Cromwell thought little of Jane Seymour, but she was prepared to be the new queen and support Princess Mary. Jane dared to open her mouth once in Mary's defence, but Henry was still not ready to accept his mistake with Anne Boleyn and reminded Jane to do as she was told.

Vicegerent Cromwell sent Lady Mary Kingston to see Princess Mary, first to tell her Anne had expressed remorse for the treatment of Mary, and then to give Mary a letter from Cromwell. So many men had gone to Mary over the years, forcing her to bow to her father's demands. Cromwell needed to get it right and wrote a long letter to Mary, less polite than their previous letters, but also more realistic, begging her to copy a second letter he sent, bowing to her father's will.

Mary wrote to Vicegerent Cromwell asking to write to her father, which Henry granted the day he married Jane Seymour on 4 June 1536. A week later Cromwell broached the subject with Mary again, begging her to submit to her father's supremacy. He signed off, 'I take Christ, whose mercy I refuse if I wrote anything unto you that I have not professed in my heart and know to be true'.[56] Mary wrote back the same day, thanking Cromwell for his help, and a few days later, copied out his letter and sent it to the king. Princess Mary considered Vicegerent Cromwell her closest friend after her father and his new wife Jane, whom Mary had never met. Mary had done all she could without offending her conscience.[57]

But Mary and Cromwell's letter was not enough for King Henry, and Cromwell could not physically intervene. The king sent several of his men to bully Mary into submitting to his supremacy and she was locked in her room until she complied. The Duke of Norfolk mentioned he wanted to smash Mary's head until it was soft as baked apples. Chapuys thought she should only relent at the last moment, and eventually, Mary signed the oath that believed in her father's position as Head of the Church, that Rome had no power over England, and that her parents were never legitimately married.[58] Norfolk and the others begged forgiveness and took Mary's begging letters of humble repentance to her father. Chapuys immediately sent off Mary's request for absolution to the Pope.

Princess Mary and Vicegerent Cromwell corresponded as he set up her new household, selecting all those she wanted to be reinstated from years past, a total of forty-two people, while Princess Elizabeth gained thirty-two in her new retinue.[59] Elizabeth retained Lady Margaret Bryan running her household, and while most of Elizabeth's staff were from her usual retinue and members of her Boleyn family, she now also had Katherine Champernowne as a chamber woman and tutor. Now both princesses, technically being equally illegitimate, were back in their father's affections. Cromwell sent Mary a horse and saddle so she might go outdoors and recover her health, and negotiations for peace, alliances and marriages soon resumed.[60] Elizabeth was safe with Katharine Champernowne on hand. How Kat was selected is unknown, but she was from a well-educated reformist family and had contact with Cromwell,[61] so it is likely he carefully placed a strong reformist mind in the household.

Vicegerent Cromwell had recently finished rebuilding one of the finest private country homes in England, just a few miles from London in Hackney. In secret, King Henry and Queen Jane went to meet Mary there on 7 July, a day after Mary arrived from Hunsdon. They ate together, Henry gave her a gift of 1,000 crowns, and Jane gave her new stepdaughter a diamond. Not all was calm; they had spent four years apart due to Henry's rage, but Mary left the night of the meeting with Henry promising she would move to court with him and Queen Jane as soon as he returned from a trip to Dover. Cromwell reported he would die happy now the royal family was reunited, while Ambassador Chapuys remained sceptical.[62]

But who would be the heir? Princess Elizabeth was nothing but illegitimate like her siblings. Mary remained in limbo, as did Henry Fitzroy, but he was male. Mary was now twenty years old and had domestic and international support, but Fitzroy was well-liked and one of the king's advisors. Parliament had freshly ratified all three children illegitimate, but a shock came when Fitzroy suddenly died, aged only seventeen. Mary and Elizabeth had never met their brother and now the realm was back to having no male heir at all. Princess Mary was now an adult, and Henry could gain a worthy son-in-law if he handled the relationship well. But Henry had missed many of his daughter's formative years and their relationship had a long way to go before being repaired.

As for Princess Elizabeth, her life at Hunsdon was as confusing as her sister's. Margaret Bryan wrote to Cromwell, apologising for her boldness, and explained Elizabeth's household and staff were confused about how to raise a girl who was no longer a princess. Lady Bryan wrote:

'when my lady Mary was born, the King appointed me lady Mistress and made me a baroness, and so I have been a mother to the children his Grace have had since. Now, as my lady Elizabeth is put from that degree she was in, and what degree she is at now, I know not but by hearsay, I know not how to order her or myself.'

Lady Bryan explained that Elizabeth grew out of her clothes and begged for gowns, petticoats, kirtles, linen, sleeves, and various other items needed for the girl. Elizabeth's great uncle Sir John Shelton still ran the house and allowed Elizabeth to dine as head of the household, of which Lady Bryan disproved, writing:

'It is not mete for a child of her age to keep such rule. If she do, I dare not take it upon me to keep her Grace in health; for she will see diverse meats, fruits, and wine, that it will be hard for me to refrain her from. You know, my lord, there is no place of correction there; and she is too young to correct greatly'.

Princess Elizabeth was also suffering from a terrible toothache and yet was, 'as toward a child and as gentle of conditions as ever I knew any in my life'.[63]

The people of northern England had different ideas on peace and harmony as Henry reunited with his daughters. The Dissolution of the Monasteries had angered many around the country, and with a new tax law, the Statute of Uses coming into force, groups started to form against monastery inspectors and tax collectors in time for Michaelmas at the end of September 1536. What started as a few individuals rising up in Louth on 4 October exploded into thousands marching towards London to stop the king's councillors from enacting changes to religion. Mary and Elizabeth were still at Hunsdon, but by mid-October Henry planned to bring them to the fortress of Windsor.[64]

With Anne Boleyn gone, the people needed a new person to blame for the Reformation, and Vicegerent Cromwell was now public enemy number one, with upwards of 40,000 wanting his head. By 24 October, Henry sent armies north to stop the rebels and their 'Pilgrimage of Grace', and Mary and Elizabeth were safe with the royal family. Henry had no intention of dumping Cromwell, nor Archbishop Cranmer to appease the rebels and sent the Dukes of Norfolk and Suffolk to end the uprising. An unknown writer sent a message to Cardinal du Bellay in Paris, who had once been the

French ambassador at the English court, talking about Mary and Elizabeth with their father at the time of rebellion. The author noted that Mary sat at the head table at court for mealtimes, across from Jane, and Mary was the one to offer the hand towel to the royal couple before they ate, considered an honour. Mary was served meals second after the king and queen and was shown great deference. Princess Elizabeth did not sit at the head table, but was at court and loved by her father, who was openly affectionate towards her. Queen Jane had begged Henry on her knees to stop dissolving monasteries, and Henry, 'told her, prudently enough, to get up, and he had often told her not to meddle with his affairs, referring to the late Queen, which was enough to frighten a woman who is not very secure'.[65]

Negotiations and demands for peace settled the uprising through November 1536 and Mary and Elizabeth returned to Hunsdon. But on 8 December, Mary wrote to Cromwell to ask for money, as her 40l quarterly allowance (£18,000 today) was not covering costs for her household. A week later, Cromwell had Mary's and Elizabeth's households moved to Richmond Palace instead, and they joined everyone at Greenwich for Christmas. Both Mary and Elizabeth were going to spend far more time at the royal court with their father and stepmother. Mary wrote to Cromwell, addressing him as 'my lord', as he had become the Lord Privy Seal and Lord Cromwell of Wimbledon for his work ensuring the king had a new wife and happier children. Mary told him, 'as I cannot conveniently thank you with my mouth for your daily goodness, I write to advertise you of my goodwill, considering that it is all I have to repay your perfect friendship, of which I desire the continuance', and spoke of the great comfort he gave her.[66] Young Elizabeth would never be likely to say the same, as Cromwell had killed her mother, but both Mary and Elizabeth were back in their father's esteem, a confusing time whether a princess of twenty or only three.

On 22 December 1536, King Henry and Queen Jane rode into London, able to ride their horses over the frozen Thames, to the Great Hall at Westminster to oversee the investiture of a new mayor for London. Princess Mary rode behind them, treated every bit as royal as she deserved. The streets had been freshly gravelled and arras hung from buildings, with priests, friars, and abbots lining the street holding tapers, while the men of the guilds stood in their liveries to salute the royal family.[67] But with the country still at war with itself, for one day, Mary could feel as if she was one step closer to her throne.

Chapter 11

Finally, A Male Heir

All was not well at New Year 1537. Queen Jane, not that she knew it, was newly pregnant, which would change Mary and Elizabeth's lives. A very fragile peace remained in the north, but nobles and commoners alike were beginning to doubt King Henry's pardons against the rebels, especially since he had ignored their requests to have the Cromwellian faction ousted from court. But if Henry was nervous, he did not show it, with parties and celebrations right through to Candlemas in February. The court stayed at Greenwich, where Mary's physician Michael de Lasao and apothecary John Soda gained rewards for their work with the princess. Emperor Charles had bigger plans for Princess Mary; he believed she deserved to be the sole heiress to the English crown and wanted her married to the Infante Luís of Portugal, making entreaties as such.[1] The French had similar plans, with King Francis wanting Mary to marry his son Charles, provided she was declared legitimate.[2] The rebels in the north also wanted Mary as their heir. Some believed it was already time for her to take her place on the throne, marry her cousin Cardinal Reginald Pole (son of Mary's governess Lady Margaret Pole) and the pair could rule England in Henry's place. Several others in the realm were also touted as heirs; Henry Courtenay, Marquess of Exeter and Henry Pole, Lord Montagu were at the front of the line when it came to Catholic substitutes.

Whether Princess Mary had much knowledge of the ongoing domestic and international arguments around the royal succession is hard to know, but Chapuys certainly knew all the gossip. But his letters from 1537 are missing, leaving a gap in Mary's conversations, thoughts and movements. Princess Elizabeth was only three and would have had no idea what was happening. She still had Lady Margaret Bryan, Kat Champernowne and her household of loyal attendants, so it is hard to know if Elizabeth understood the loss of her mother, or at what age she became aware of the world around her, given her private and cloistered environment.

The second wave of rebellions during the Pilgrimage of Grace in early 1537 did not pose the same level of danger as the previous year. The Duke of Norfolk quickly put down the rebels whenever they dared to flare up, and by Easter, all the leaders awaited execution.[3] During this time, Princesses Mary and Elizabeth were constantly on the move. They had been at Hatfield but travelled to Beaulieu and then Greenwich until Candlemas before heading to Whitehall. Vicegerent Cromwell even tried to cheer Mary by sending her a Valentine of 15l (about £6,500 today).[4] Mary also stood as godmother to the first son of Edward Seymour and his wife Anne. In April, the Privy Council gathered under its new formalised system, to discuss Mary and Elizabeth, suggesting Mary be ruled legitimate for the sake of the realm.[5] The princesses were travelling again, through Hatfield, Cholmeley and home to Hunsdon, Mary giving donations to churches along their travels. But the need to put down rebels in the north or gain international alliances suddenly went on hold when Queen Jane's pregnancy rumours began to spread through the court in late April, which the royal family spent together at Greenwich. By May, Mary and Elizabeth were back in London, where Mary corresponded with Cromwell, thanking him for his help on behalf of her faithful servant Randall Dodd. The sisters were still in the same household, with John Shelton still in charge, complaining he had only received 300l of the 600l he needed for the quarter.[6] But they stayed at Westminster through June, as Mary had again fallen ill and her physicians were brought in, along with a surgeon to bleed her.[7] A plan was formed to get the princesses out of the city in the hope it would help Mary's health, the household travelling to Hampton Court, Guildford, Easthampstead and then onto Windsor, where again apothecaries tried to lift Mary's spirits. Queen Jane also sought to soothe Mary with a gift of 50l, quite a boost for her household, especially since Mary regularly gave to churches and clergymen, and sought to give gifts to those she cared for and were kind to her.

Mary and Elizabeth tried to return to Richmond and then Hunsdon, but soon they needed to be at court again, as Queen Jane neared her time. Jane's pregnancy, for being so momentous, seemed to trickle by without complication or even causing mention in news. Finally, the king had no issues with whether this child was legitimate; there were no impediments to the marriage whatsoever, and Jane was the perfect model of a royal wife, even if she had mentioned Princess Mary's welfare too many times early in the marriage. Since her quickening in early June,[8] Jane's pregnancy had been welcome news at court and the king would finally have the chance to have another son. As Vicegerent Cromwell wrote to Thomas Wyatt, who was with Emperor Charles, 'the King is in good health and disposition, the more because the Queen is quick with child. God send her good deliverance of a prince, to the joy of all faithful subjects'.[9] All potential marriage treaties for Mary were on hold as Henry waited to see if Queen Jane could have a healthy son. Jane was worried during her pregnancy; the plague and various summer illnesses were especially bad, and the court had to use complex isolation and distancing measures to elevate Jane's worries as she neared her time. While Jane stayed at Windsor, news came that the new French Queen of Scotland was dead, so soon after marrying King James.[10] Suddenly James was a husband option for Mary, but Henry ignored the offer, the same as with any Portuguese alliance. Within the vast collection of international correspondence discussing alliances and marriages for Mary, it was apparent Henry had no intention of ever allowing his daughter to go anywhere. He may have loved his daughter, but he still feared she would gain a following and take his throne.

On 16 September 1537, *The Royal Book* protocols were used as Queen Jane proceeded to her confinement chambers at Hampton Court Palace, a departure from the royal births at Greenwich. Jane had a little knowledge of the protocol, being in Queen Katharine and Anne Boleyn's households over the years. Jane Seymour was a quiet woman, aged twenty-nine years old, with no previous marriage or even betrothal in her past. The nearest Jane had ever come to having a marriage was when Cromwell noted a request from Jane's father to ask about a marriage for his daughter and Sir Ralph Elderton in 1532.[11] There was no doubt of Jane's virginity, and her traditional country upbringing and education appealed to a king who had already had a genius politician of a wife in Katharine and then a well-educated courtier in Anne. Jane was the eldest surviving daughter of ten children born to a family who could trace their family's nobility back hundreds of years. Jane and Henry shared King Edward III as a relative and a dispensation eliminated this flimsy affinity five generations earlier. Queen Jane had seen her former mistress beheaded, taking her place in the royal bed within eleven days, and struggled with early royal life. Rumours of her being pregnant at the time of the marriage are simply that, with nothing in Jane's behaviour reflecting such a predicament. Henry had stereotypically rebounded from Anne towards Jane, lamenting his haste, and felt nervous when it took Jane six months to conceive, as neither bride nor groom were considered fit for creating children by the time of their marriage.[12]

But through the upheavals of the Pilgrimage of Grace and the new amity with Mary and Elizabeth, Queen Jane became pregnant. This was another barrier to her coronation, already hindered by rebellion and plague. But when it came time for Jane to take to her chamber, domestic and international opinion seemed pleased for the royal couple, and the anger of the past was quickly left behind. Jane had been with the king when he received the news of Henry Fitzroy's death in July, but now physicians and astrologers promised Jane carried a replacement son. By mid-September 1537 all were well, Jane attending mass and having a procession of the court walk her to her tapestry and jewel-laden confinement space for spiced wine and prayers, before being shut away.

As early as 28 September, rumours of a royal mistress appeared, when it was claimed Henry came upon a 'wench' near Eltham, taking her from her male companion and seducing her.[13] Given all the rumours of illegitimate children over the years, Henry simply selecting a low-ranked woman and doing as he pleased would not be considered unusual behaviour.

Queen Jane went into labour on the night of 10 October, labouring another two days and nights through an arduous and painful birth. Rumours of a caesarean or broken limbs were only imaginings, but there can be no doubt Jane suffered. While most of the royal protocol was followed, Jane had something new; men in the birthing chamber, with Doctors John Chambre, George Owen and Henry's best physician William Butts. Men had little to no knowledge of childbirth, and midwives easily could have attended to the queen, but Henry insisted on physicians' intervention and presence. Whether that contributed to Jane's difficulty and poor recovery can never be known.

Baby Edward was born around two o'clock on the morning of Friday 12 October 1537, a strong and healthy child, unlike his mother who lay exhausted, with only enough energy to write to Vicegerent Cromwell, promising England had a son born in lawful matrimony.[14] King Henry rushed to Hampton Court from Esher Place three miles away to witness the sight he had awaited since the death of Prince Henry in 1511. Dr Butts watched over Jane while Dr Owen watched over the baby, Jane's ladies all in attendance. At once all rooms and hallways connected to the royal nursery were swept out and then soaped down for cleanliness to prevent any risk of the plague epidemic getting into the palace walls. Margaret Grey, Dowager Marchioness of Dorset was to be godmother, as she was to Princess Elizabeth, but could not attend due to the outbreak, and was replaced by the grovelling Gertrude Courtenay, Marchioness of Exeter, who managed to dodge plague, to great concern from Henry and grateful acceptance from Courtenay.[15]

The first royal christening at Hampton Court took place three days later with strict social distancing rules. Those invited could only bring a few attendants, ranging from a duke allowed six, ranked down to chaplains only allowed two.[16] The procession from the nursery where Edward awaited with wet nurses to the chapel took an enormous six hours, the christening not beginning until midnight. The silver font at Canterbury was ready to christen Edward in Hampton Court's chapel, this time on an octagon platform with octagonal screens to shield the precious confirmation. The chapel had been newly redecorated with an oak ceiling covered in gold leaf, and new arms of Henry and Jane are still emblazoned on the door today.[17] The walls heaved with rich golden tapestries, with pans of perfumed warmed water awaiting in case the baby was in need. Courtiers walked in two by two in a solemn procession; after the chaplains, household and privy chamber staff came Vicegerent Cromwell and Lord Chancellor Audley, followed by the Duke of Norfolk and Archbishop Cranmer, the boy's godfathers. Robert Radcliffe, Earl of Sussex and Henry Pole Lord Montagu carried covered silver basins, and Thomas Boleyn, Earl of Wiltshire carried a taper of virgin wax beside Henry Bouchier, Earl of Essex, who carried a golden bowl of salt (a gift from Mary to Edward). Sir Edward Seymour carried Princess Elizabeth, who carried the chism of the rich purple velvet. Gertrude Courtenay, Marchioness of Exeter carried Prince Edward, just as she had carried Princess Elizabeth four years earlier. Her husband Henry Courtenay, Marquess of Exeter walked alongside the baby, as did the Duke of Suffolk, and Lord William Howard and Henry FitzAlan, Earl of Arundel carried baby Edward's robes. At the font, the child was proclaimed Prince Edward, Duke of Cornwall and Earl of Chester with his second godmother Princess Mary. Bonfires were lit, church bells rang while Te Deums were sung for days, and two thousand guns had fired at the Tower on the day of the birth. After the ceremony, spices, wines and wafers were served, and Mary and Elizabeth were treated every bit the royal siblings as twenty-four trumpeters heralded the baby's new title. Jane managed to sit up in bed, wrapped in furs and jewels so the court could come in and congratulate her on the momentous occasion, and many men of the court were given new titles, including Edward Seymour made the Earl of Hertford.

England finally had an undisputed heir. All the meetings and negotiations for Princess Mary to rule, marry, or create alliances were suddenly irrelevant, as the baby assumed all rights and responsibilities. All the worries and conspiracies halted, as England had a king to follow Henry. Mary and Elizabeth remained at Hampton Court, only for Queen Jane to die on 24 October, succumbing to a blood infection.[18] Rumours of Jane dying to save the prince, either during or after the labour are all stories born of fear, though even Prince Edward believed he killed his mother by being born, so rumours clearly persisted. The Great Hall at Windsor was draped in black, and a funeral was hastily prepared in Cromwell's offices for 12 November. Princess Mary was the chief mourner, followed by twenty-eight other ladies, including Queen Jane's sister Elizabeth Cromwell (daughter-in-law to the vicegerent), who herself was pregnant and had witnessed Jane's sad demise.[19] As chief mourner, Mary had to lead the funeral procession on a horse draped in black velvet, followed by the ladies of the realm. Mary proceeded to the altar in St George's Chapel at Windsor beside the Dukes of Suffolk and Norfolk, to mourn her stepmother, a queen, the way she could never mourn her mother.

Mary needed to have a tooth pulled at Windsor, before she, Elizabeth and Edward travelled by barge to Richmond Palace for the festive season, while King Henry went to Greenwich draped in mourning and refused all but his closest men. Vicegerent Cromwell needed to draw up a list of brides for the king just three days after Jane's death;[20] with a king and now a prince to betroth, what happened with Princesses Mary and Elizabeth took on a new meaning. It was Mary who held court as the high-ranked woman in England, buying lavish gifts and treating herself to finery, such as one hundred pearls costing 267l (£110,000 today). Prince Edward was now cared for by Lady Margaret Bryan, while Elizabeth was transferred to Blanche Milbourne, Lady Troy of Herbert and her niece Blanche Parry, with Kat Champernowne still at Elizabeth's side. The three royal siblings living together while their father dangled them and himself as prizes in the marriage market would be the near-constant narrative of their coming years.

Chapter 12

Changing Queens, Changing Fortunes

In early February 1538, the household of the royal trio had moved between Richmond and Hanworth to be close to Hampton Court and the king. Princess Mary had seen to it that staff in every household was well-dressed and appointed. Ambassador Chapuys went to visit the royal children, where Mary performed with her lute and spinet.[1] It is Mary's account records that show much of the royal children's household activities during this time, as Mary was in her rightful place, respected as a princess of England, even if she and Elizabeth were still considered illegitimate. Mary was bombarded with requests to be godmother for children, many times being paired with Vicegerent Cromwell as godfather, where he would pay for the midwife and nurses for the child, and Mary would provide a gold cup for the christening.[2] King Henry remained at Hampton Court through the early part of 1538, where Mary stayed with her father and enjoyed parties thrown by Cromwell.[3] By Easter, the royal children visited their father, their mourning black attire long gone, as Henry was actively courting marriages from France and the Emperor as they all looked to secure alliances.

For all the turmoil created so King Henry could have a son, he saw Prince Edward and his daughters infrequently. Mary was now twenty-two, and well aware of the constant whispers and intrigues of the court. Prince Edward lived in royal splendour in his nursery under Lady Bryan, and Elizabeth was only four and yet already showing her poise and intelligence. Lady Bryan wrote to Cromwell in March 1538, complaining the princess was not living with enough luxury. Cromwell sent an extra 5000l (just over £2,000,000 today) to the Lady Mistress for supplies. The sisters spent much of their time in Hunsdon, Cholmeley and Hatfield, while Edward's nursery remained at Hanworth or Hampton Court, though when Mary met with the king, they stayed at Richmond. Henry had been trying to secure Mary of Guise as his wife, though she was to be the new queen of Scotland.[4] Henry was also pushing the idea he could marry Duchess Christina of Milan, while Mary would marry into Portugal and Elizabeth and Edward to children of the Emperor.[5] Henry was watching Princess Mary; Cromwell needed to write to her and report he had heard rumours of strangers (foreigners) visiting her without permission, and Mary easily rebuffed such notions. Cromwell was the one tasked with securing an alliance and Ambassador Chapuys was Mary's most common visitor, and fortunately, both were always on Mary's side.

As King Henry's marriage plans continued to swing blindly around Europe, the notion of Mary marrying King Francis' youngest son Charles emerged yet again, along with possibly marrying the son of the Duke of Lorraine, whose marriage plans to Duchess Anna of Cleves had collapsed. The Emperor then tried pushing Luís of Portugal on his cousin yet again. Mary was not well, and neither was much of England, with outbreaks of sweating sickness and plague, coupled with the monasteries still closing and monks being burned as heretics at Henry's demand. The Cromwell Bible, the first English bible was almost complete and Catholics were feeling increasingly marginalised by Vicegerent Cromwell and Archbishop Cranmer's reformist advances.[6] What King Henry never seemed to notice were the quiet reformers living around Princess Elizabeth and Prince Edward, including Edward Seymour. Shrines burned, religious houses broke up, and while Cromwell tried securing many houses as new colleges,[7] Henry wanted the money and land and favoured foreclosure instead.

Doctors and apothecaries frequented Princess Mary without success as her bouts of headaches and stomach pains ailed her on and off for months. Mary was well enough to visit her father at Whitehall in June, where an idea appeared for her to marry Wilhelm of Jülich-Cleves-Burg, with limited success. Mary could not marry a Lutheran, and Henry never intended to take any meetings seriously. Discussions remained fruitless, and Mary was frustrated. She and Vicegerent Cromwell produced a plan to discuss alliances in August 1538, meeting Imperial ambassadors over a marriage, where Mary showed her intelligence during negotiations but the plan quickly fell through. Ambassadors praised baby Edward at Hampton Court and spent time with Mary and her ladies, but Mary was increasingly aware of the futility of her position. If she were legitimate again, or better, England's heir, Mary could negotiate her position in Europe on better terms. Discussing such things with ambassadors would be treason and yet Mary had little qualms, despite men burning and hanging in the streets for defying Henry. Mary could be heir, or even flee abroad and marry, and return to claim the country with an army, saving Catholicism.

Meanwhile, Prince Edward was thriving as the heir to the realm. By his first birthday, he had grown all his teeth and his (probably relieved) wet nurse was replaced by his dry nurse Sibyl Penne, to work alongside Edward's four cradle rockers. Sibyl Penne stayed with Edward throughout his young years, earning the nickname 'Mother Jak' from Edward himself, and gained a spot in a royal family portrait. Edward lived among the women, while Vicegerent Cromwell kept spies on the lookout for who was creating effigy dolls filled with pins and making rumours about how Edward would grow up to be a murderer like his father.[8] No one with a title lower than knight could enter the baby's presence, and every guest and gift was catalogued and checked by the king himself. No one could touch the prince unless it was a kiss on the hand which Henry personally approved in writing, and even then, the women would hover and monitor everything.[9] The prince's clothes were washed and aired dry beside a fire and scented with perfume, all his food washed and cooked thoroughly, and tested as soon as he began to eat solids. Henry seldom visited the prince, going only for a visit in May 1538, where he held Edward at a window for well-wishers to see him. By contrast, Mary spent much time with Edward, constantly visiting with gifts for her brother and his servants. Even Princess Elizabeth was in Mary's care and affection, Mary's lavish spending habits showed she spared no expense on items for her little sister, who would ride with Mary on Queen Jane's horse. Hans Holbein arrived to paint Prince Edward, who, at fourteen months old, was dressed in full noble attire, his beauty (as considered in the period) showing intensely pale skin, blonde hair and blue eyes, totally unlike his redheaded sisters. As one of Cromwell's servants wrote, 'Heaven and earth could scarcely produce a son whose glory would surpass that of a father,' on the back of the painting.

By the end of 1538, others had been plotting far more than Mary. Henry Courtenay, Marquess of Exeter and Henry Pole, Lord Montagu, who had been rumoured to succeed their cousin King Henry for years, had been conspiring with convicted traitor Cardinal Reginald Pole abroad. Plans to put Mary, Exeter or Pole on the throne had travelled back and forth for months. Exeter, Pole, and Pole's uncle-in-law Sir Edward Neville were arrested and convicted in speedy trials, all executed in time for the festive season in January 1539. If Mary thought she had Catholic support, she was right, but Henry was always one step ahead, and Cromwell, no matter how much he helped Mary, could not defy the king and so organised the executions.[10] Mary's biggest problem now was that Henry Pole and Reginald Pole's mother was Lady Margaret Pole, Countess of Salisbury. Lady Pole was possibly Mary's closest friend and ally, and her governess during the formative years of Mary's life. Lady Pole was also rounded up when Henry went in search of killing off the last Yorkist heirs to the English throne. Gertrude Courtenay, Marchioness of Exeter, godmother to Elizabeth and

Edward, also went to the Tower with her young son when her husband became a head shorter through Henry's vindictive behaviour.

Elizabeth and Edward were able to spend the festive season with their father at Greenwich, but Mary remained at Blackfriars, with her 'old sickness' of stomach pains. They did appear to be stress related, always flaring up in times of trouble with her father. Mary spent New Year in bed and sent gifts to her siblings, Edward receiving an embroidered crimson satin coat covered in gold and pearls. Princess Elizabeth, aged only five, made Edward a shirt herself, far better at needlework than her much older sister.[11] All three siblings received the standard gifts of gold and silver plate from their father, though the Earl of Essex sent Prince Edward a golden bell with a whistle attached, which likely delighted the child and infuriated the nurses.[12] Edward's life was centred at Hampton Court and Hanworth, while Mary and Elizabeth stayed primarily at Richmond, Hatfield and Hunsdon, a routine that would stay in place throughout 1539. The only time Prince Edward needed to be presented was to a German ambassador in February, where he hid his face against Sybil Penne's shoulder, refusing to look at the strangers before him. The Earl of Essex managed to elicit a laugh from the boy, but Edward still would not allow the German men to kiss his young hand. Essex delighted in the whole affair, telling the young prince after the ambassadors left, 'now, full well knows thou that I am thy father's true man and thine, and these others be false knaves'.[13] The king may have been looking for Protestant allies, but this never amused the Catholics of the court.

Edward and Elizabeth were still young, living quiet lives in nurseries run by women, but Mary had no such luxury. Drastically overworked Vicegerent Cromwell, busy executing Henry's imagined enemies domestically and trying to create alliances abroad, looked to the German States for a new queen, as no other nation was prepared to sacrifice a woman to Henry. The Emperor and King Francis went as far as signing a treaty together, leaving England exposed and threatened with a war over its position as a reformed country. Henry was officially excommunicated only a few months earlier, and Cromwell spent the first few months of 1539 sending ambassadors to Germany and preparing to be invaded as Henry commanded the country in panic. A plan Cromwell suggested stated Henry could join England with the Schmalkaldic League, headed by the Duke of Saxony, the King of Denmark, the Duke of Julich-Cleves-Burg and multiple small German States, a group which had a combined army strong enough to repel Emperor Charles. Negotiations over Princess Mary were pointless, though Henry imagined marrying her to Luís of Portugal and them ruling Milan together.

For himself, he looked to marry Christina of Milan, but Christina had made it clear she would not go to England. The Emperor and French king had no other noble women to offer ever-more reformist England. Queen Mary, Regent of the Netherlands, ordered Ambassador Chapuys to be sent to her in Brussels, a sign of diplomatic isolation.[14] King Henry was furious, and Mary would lose one of her great allies, but Cromwell got Chapuys a passport and safely out of the country in private, and in return, Chapuys promised to get England's Low Countries ambassadors-turned-hostages Thomas Wriothesley, Edward Kerne, and Stephen Vaughan freed.[15] Princess Mary would not see Chapuys for another year.

Henry spent Easter 1539 with his children and bought purple velvet for himself and crimson for all three children to use in their Easter processions. But Vicegerent Cromwell had fallen ill again with malaria (and likely stress), leaving King Henry in a confused state. Henry wrote up the Six Articles, six points on religion in England, leaning heavily back towards the Catholic faith,[16] and pushed it through parliament while Cromwell lay on his sickbed. The king simultaneously changed the entire order of presence in England with a new act, making Cromwell the most powerful man in England, and reducing power based on birthright.[17] While no one could outrank Prince Edward, these papers had repercussions for England and Princess Mary. The Articles appeased the Emperor, who looked to invade and put Mary and Reginald Pole on the throne, but the articles clashed with the Lutheran Schmalkaldic League, which had opened negotiations with England for alliances and marriages in good faith. At the same time, Holy Roman Empress Isabella died in Spain, and Emperor Charles truly mourned, which averted the threat of war.[18] But Henry's interest in marrying one of the Cleves sisters also waned.

The summer passed in relative peace for the royal children, while the king went on progress through the south of England. The princesses spent time together, moving between Richmond, Whitehall, and Beaulieu, but Mary then fell ill once again through September. Once she recovered, they moved to Hunsdon, close to Prince Edward at Tittenhanger, where they remained as the weather grew colder through autumn. But as soon as King Henry returned to London, he made a snap decision to marry and wanted Anna of Cleves. The portrait of a beautiful but reclusive duchess arrived; Henry agreed at once, sending Vicegerent Cromwell and the court into a flurry to ensure the match could go ahead.[19] An iron-clad contract was signed in October, and the court prepared to create a queen and have a royal court ready for her arrival. Princess Mary was to be the head of the ladies to welcome the new queen to England, alongside her cousin Lady

Margaret Douglas, Henry Fitzroy's widow Mary Howard, who also brought her young cousin Lady Katheryn Howard. Mary Boleyn also joined the circle of ladies, along with her daughter Catherine, rumoured daughter of the king.[20]

Marriage negotiations for Mary had not ceased, with Cromwell forced to house and entertain Philip, Count Palatine and Duke of Bavaria for Mary.[21] Cromwell had remained suspicious of husbands for Mary, knowing she would not want a Lutheran husband, but Henry always refused Catholic offers. Prince Edward was at Hampton Court Palace, but Mary and Elizabeth remained away at Hertford Castle. Thomas Wriothesley visited the princesses, and Mary gave him a polite reply that she would conform to her father's will despite not wanting a husband. Mary sent off a frank letter to Cromwell about the situation, knowing he understood she would not marry any Lutheran.[22]

But Wriothesley was most impressed by Princess Elizabeth, now six years old, and remarked to Cromwell that Elizabeth, 'replied to the King's message with as great gravity as she had been forty years old. If she be no worse educated than she appears, she will be an honour to womanhood'.[23] Elizabeth had been living a quiet life within her household and was educated by Kat Champernowne. Kat was an exceptionally well-educated woman from a family who believed in steady education and the new religion. Elizabeth was already able to learn Kat's beliefs in an 'elaborate code of politeness and respect to her elders', along with Kat's skills in French, Italian, Flemish, and Spanish, mathematics, geography, astronomy, and history. Kat could also teach the more traditional subjects of needlework, embroidery, dancing, and riding. In addition to these languages, Elizabeth was also able to learn Welsh from Blanche Parry working in her household.

Vicegerent Cromwell took Duke Philip to Enfield on 22 December, where Mary met them. No official record of the meeting took place, though news that Philip kissed Mary gave some impression Mary was interested.[24] As Henry impatiently waited at Greenwich for Lady Anna to make the crossing from Calais in bad weather, he ordered Cromwell to draft a marriage contract for Mary, for her to marry Duke Philip and offered a dowry of 40,000 florins, about 10,000l (£4,000,000 today), a petty sum for such a princess.[25] Mary was to move to Bavaria with Philip and receive an allowance of 10,000l a year during her marriage. Cromwell wrote several drafts, some mentioning her illegitimacy, some not, hedging his bets either way.

Mary and Elizabeth spent Christmas at Baynard's Castle in London, and Mary met Duke Philip again at Westminster, where Philip kissed her again, and gave her a gift of a diamond cross set with pearls.[26] King Henry immediately made his daughter hand it over. Assumptions stated Mary would be married in weeks. Instead, the royal children joined the court for New Year festivities, where Mary gave her little brother, now just over two years old, a coat made of crimson satin with a ruby brooch, while Elizabeth received a yellow satin kirtle.[27] Naturally, the king lavished Prince Edward with gifts of gold and silver no toddler would care for.[28] But the usual celebrations were not relevant this year, as 6 January 1540 was also Henry's marriage to Anna of Cleves. After a private meeting at Rochester on 1 January with Anna (which history would record as a failure thanks to false affidavits later published), and a glorious official welcome to London on 3 January, Henry and Anna married at Greenwich just after 9 o'clock on the morning of the Epiphany.[29] Given the awkward start to the marriage and the busy mood at court, Mary and Elizabeth's movements went largely unrecorded. Within weeks, Queen Anna changed into French fashions to assume a role at court and received compliments from all except King Henry. History would consign Anna to the role of being too ugly to bed, but the reality was her brother Duke Wilhelm prepared to head to war over the duchy of Guelders. King Henry had to ally with the Germans, against Emperor Charles, who also wanted the small German state. Bedding Anna would secure the marriage and alliance, and Henry had found his manhood failing in the face of actual consequences.

Princess Mary's potential marriage to Philip of Bavaria was halted amid war threats, the duke fleeing the country while he still had safe passage home. War again threatened England and Europe, and Henry sent the Duke of Norfolk to France to attempt some reconciliation between the countries.[30] Cleves and Emperor Charles would later go on to settle their anger without war, but by the time they had, King Henry had truly grown to hate Queen Anna over nothing. At the same time, the idea of marrying Princess Mary into a German duchy quickly fell apart. Whether Mary received any official confirmation all talks were off, or felt disappointed, went unrecorded.

But as long as there was a queen at court, Mary could live there despite being unmarried. Mary was given a double lodging, a room in the inner circle of Hampton Court Palace, where Prince Edward, Vicegerent Cromwell and Lady Margaret Douglas all stayed.[31] Life at court seemed calm, with the royal children all spending time around Hampton Court, as Queen Anna tried to adjust to English life. Mary also attended to her siblings, and at Easter at Hampton Court, Prince Edward was described by Lady Bryan as 'in good health and merry, his grace danced and played so wantonly that he could not stand still and was as full of pretty toys as ever I saw a child in my life'.[32] Mary and likely Elizabeth and Edward attended the May Day celebrations at Greenwich, but Mary soon fell sick again at Tittenhanger while ordering many new summer gowns for herself and Elizabeth, while Edward was back at Hampton Court.

But merry times at court were to soon be a thing of the past, as Henry struggled with his new bride. Despite Queen Anna being well-liked and accommodating, Henry could not consummate his marriage, admitting so to Cromwell and William Fitzwilliam of the privy chamber. Cromwell, now the Earl of Essex for all his work for the royal family, needed to undo yet another marriage, which risked war or trade embargoes from abroad, and in his disappointment, mistakenly trusted one of the oldest servants, Thomas Wriothesley, with the secret that the marriage was unconsummated. Wriothesley ran like a child to the king and said Lord Cromwell was speaking of Henry's impotence. The rage of Henry, his fragile manliness, and his panic over his fickle ability to provide heirs, all came down on Lord Cromwell, who was arrested on 10 June, for saying he would fight Henry on the issue of the Reformation if it came to it (a metaphorical battle, not a physical battle as Bishop Stephen Gardiner interpreted).[33] Coupled with King Henry believing Cromwell spoke of impotency (and rumours from enemies that Cromwell wanted to marry Mary), Cromwell was attainted without trial. While imprisoned in the Queen's apartments at the Tower, Lord Cromwell prepared Henry's annulment from Queen Anna and denied accusations of wanting to marry Mary. Lord Cromwell and Princess Mary had been allies for years despite their blindingly different opinions on many subjects, especially religion. Mary had been writing with Cromwell as recently as April 1540, calling him her 'sheet anchor' close to the crown.[34] But nothing ever occurred to suspect romance between the pair, with their thirty-year age gap, political and religious differences and vast discrepancy in social rank, despite Cromwell's recent elevation to Earl of Essex. In a fit of anger, Henry had Cromwell beheaded, thus ending the life of the man who ran the entire royal court, and held all major political, religious and financial offices, leaving the crown to bankrupt itself and make poor choices for the rest of Henry's reign. This also left the princesses without a sympathetic ear beside the king.

King Henry proved his inability to manage alone immediately by marrying teenager Lady Katheryn Howard at Oatlands on the day of Lord Cromwell's death, 28 July 1540.[35] The new queen, one of Lady Anna's ladies, was seven years younger than Mary, someone who had fallen prey to men with designs on pretty, young, orphans in the past. The marriage was a joke; Europe laughed at Henry for his choices, along with his marital bed problems and blatant disregard for Anna. Now Henry had married a child rumoured to be pregnant, so the French Ambassador Charles Marilliac incorrectly claimed. Elizabeth and Edward were still young and kept away from such matters, but the changes appalled Princess Mary, with the added shock her old tutor Richard Fetherstone was hanged, drawn and quartered just days after Cromwell, for the crime of refusing Henry's supremacy under Anne Boleyn years ago. Queen Katherine's old confessor Thomas Abel suffered the same fate that day as Henry went on a religious killing spree to celebrate his new marriage.

Ambassador Chapuys soon arrived back in England, so English Ambassador Richard Pate with the Emperor suggested Princess Mary and Emperor Charles finally marry. But ambassadors all over Europe knew as well as Mary; Henry would never let her go. To compound issues, Mary was disappointed in her father's behaviour with the new Queen Katheryn, while Katheryn believed Mary needed to show extra respect to her young stepmother.[36] Mary was banished from court, and the royal children spent time away from their father. Rumours of Mary having attendants removed on Katheryn's orders did see Mary attempt politeness with her father's child bride. Through the New Year, Henry and Katheryn dominated the court while the royal children were kept far from sight.

Rumours of Princess Mary leaving England to marry Emperor Charles continued into 1541, but Mary needed to be legitimate to marry, and with Lord Cromwell gone, no one in parliament seemed willing to push through legislation in the Commons, Lords, or with the king himself. Philip of Bavaria renewed interest in Mary, sending ambassadors at Easter 1541, but again, King Henry was too infatuated with his new queen to care.

At this time, Prince Edward was still living in his miniature court at Hampton Court Palace or nearby residences. Princesses Mary and Elizabeth had not seen their brother in some time, so Mary wrote to her father in May 1541 in the hopes of them coming back together and the sisters being allowed to see their brother. Henry allowed the visit, and Mary was permitted to live at court again,[37] but not so for Elizabeth, still consigned to households such as Hatfield, which by all accounts, gave Elizabeth a happy environment in which to be raised and educated. But at the same time, Lady Margaret Pole, Countess of Salisbury, Mary's long-time governess and mother figure was butchered at the Tower, dying by the hand of an amateur headsman while she prayed for Princess Mary.[38] Any notion of Mary defying her father or marrying abroad was equally cut short, though Elizabeth was hopefully spared gossip of what was happening in London while she lived in the safety of the Hertfordshire countryside. The summer of 1541 would remain much the same for Elizabeth and Edward, moving around the various homes of Hatfield, Hunsdon, and Ashridge. They shared a friend in the royal classroom, Robert Dudley.

King Henry, who had not taken a long summer progress in years due to his ulcerated legs, decided he would progress as far north as York and in May 1541, he set off with Queen Katheryn and Princess Mary with a large train. The towns they passed did not put on great displays or occasions for the king's passing through, though the north still harboured a love for their Catholic princess, so for Mary to go north would have been an important occasion. Most of the royal court joined them, including Ambassador Chapuys, and Ambassador Marillac of France, with Mary riding behind the king and queen, with the ladies of the court and mighty archers at her back. They journeyed through Peterborough, Stamford, Gainsborough, Lincoln, Hull and Pontefract towards York, stopping at Grimsthorpe Castle in Lincolnshire in August, home to the Duke of Suffolk.[39]

With foreign ambassadors on the trip, the Duke of Norfolk was busy negotiating with Marillac, again suggesting Mary could marry the French prince Charles, now Duke of Orléans. Francis, the dauphin of France, so often touted as a groom for Mary, had died in 1536, leaving his younger brother Henri as heir. As the new dauphin, Henri married Catherine de Medici, but they had no children and it was still possible that children born to younger prince Charles and his future wife could take the French throne. England's succession was safe with Prince Edward, but Mary could still have a kingdom of her own if she and Charles produced France's heir. By the time the royal train reached York on 18 September, negotiations were in full swing, but Mary remained illegitimate, despite being unofficially in the line of succession. King Henry would not legitimise Mary, and France would not take her without said recognition. Ambassadors from both France and Scotland were interested in the move that could see an alliance made between all three countries, and Marillac sent King Francis a report on Mary that gives a full description of the twenty-five-year-old princess. Marillac wrote:

> 'I have taken pains not only to see (Mary) and consider her stature and proportions, but also to inform myself, via a woman who has served in chamber... (the lady) saw the time of her ennui (Mary's illnesses) which she suffered because of her afflictions, and other characteristics from which one hopes (Mary) may bear children.... The said Mary is of medium stature, bigger bones than is consistent with lightness and grace, however she is well enough made. Her face, particularly

her mouth, is like her father's, as is her laugh and her voice, although she has a more masculine voice for a woman... as for her hair, that receded somewhat as did the queen's, her mother's...Her skin is smooth and fresh and she does not look more than eighteen or twenty... her beauty moderate... as for her walk and bearing, one can assume she is not delicate. Above everything she likes early morning exercise and when the weather is good, she enjoys walking two or three miles in the park and one seldom sees her sitting down when indoors.[40]

Marillac's long letter went on to call Mary intelligent with excellent French and Latin and had read the most complex works of the period including More and Erasmus, noting she found these books comforting in the days of being sidelined in Princess Elizabeth's household. Marillac said Mary spoke well, was universally respected by all and was an excellent musician. Mary's illnesses had eased off, and despite having a Spanish doctor and apothecary, Mary was not being prescribed anything unusual or for a serious medical problem, suggesting children would be present in her future. Marillac noted he could get a portrait painted, but no painter would take the job without the king's permission, which would arouse suspicions about negotiations. By 1541, Henry was not a liked king, though probably did not realise how much loathing he incited in his people. If Prince Edward grew to be as disliked as Henry, Mary marrying a French duke could be seen as a viable option for her seizing the throne. Mary's prospects were entirely hindered by her father.

While Marillac was working hard to secure Mary for the French royal family, Ambassador Chapuys' spies were leaking the information to Emperor Charles, who wanted Mary to marry into his brother's family in Hungary.[41] But news within the English court would again bring everything to a halt. While the summer progress was ongoing, Prince Edward fell ill at Hampton Court Palace, suffering from quartan fever.[42] While quartan fever is one of the milder forms of malaria, Edward would have suffered fevers raging over 40C in three-day intervals. Marillac reported to King Francis:

'The King, on his return from the North to Hampton Court, was surprised to hear that the Prince of Wales, his only son, was sick of a quartan fever, an unusual malady for a child of three to four years, who is not of a melancholic complexion. (Henry) summoned all the physicians of the country to advise, and, after long consultation, they agreed, as one of them secretly told me, that the fever would put (Edward) in danger. My informant added that, apart from this accident, the prince is so gross (fat) and unhealthy that I could not believe, judging from what I could see now, that (Edward) would live long.'[43]

Prince Edward hovered on the brink of death for ten days, and even the now-obese King Henry, who would spend all his time eating, drinking, and often lamenting on the 'loss' of Lord Cromwell,[44] would not rest as he worried for his son. Dr William Butts was in charge of Edward's care, forcing the boy to eat nothing but soups and broths to recover and hydrate, while the four-year-old prince demanded meat. Butts finally relented to Edward's constant harassment, who called the doctor a knave and fool and ejected Butts from his company.[45] Fortunately, Butts took this rejection as a sign the boy was recovering, but reports all mentioned that Edward would not live a long life.

For now, Edward was well and able to continue his happy life at Hunsdon, Havering and Ashridge manors, where he had children his age to play with, as well as his sisters. Edward had struck up a close friendship with Lady Jane Dormer, the granddaughter of Sir William Sidney, Edward's chamberlain. They spent several years in each other's company, playing, dancing, chatting, reading and on one occasion when Lady Jane lost a game of cards to Edward, he told her, 'Now, Jane, your king is gone, I shall be good enough for you'.[46] Edward would regularly refer to her as 'my Jane', and Jane later wrote of Edward that his 'inclination and natural disposition was of a great towardness to all virtuous parts and princely qualities, a marvellous sweet child, of very mild and generous condition'.[47]

In autumn, Prince Edward moved to Hertford Castle and soon he had Princess Mary for company, moving her household, which now included Queen Katheryn's ladies. They needed a new mistress, as Katheryn was arrested for an alleged relationship with Francis Dereham before marriage, and then another with Thomas Culpepper after marriage. Whether Katheryn was the whore portrayed, a victim of her naivety, or preyed upon by men, remains conjecture, though there was little doubt she was to some degree 'familiar' with these men, by choice or force. Katheryn was sent to Syon Abbey with her sister Isabel Lady Baynton as company. Princess Mary had nothing to do with the scandal, not questioned, likewise her household. Katheryn and Mary had exchanged gifts in the past, though whether they had ever liked one another is not proven by these generic gestures. Mary was horrified, Princess Elizabeth too, and their father was devastated, as he had been infatuated with the teenager for upwards of eighteen months.

Queen Katheryn and her lady-in-waiting Jane Boleyn, Lady Rochford were beheaded on 13 February 1542 for the crimes of adultery and assisting with said adultery, respectively.[48] It is little wonder the negotiations to get Mary into France slowed; the English king had just beheaded yet another wife. Mary was now a decade older than she could have expected to leave England and head a royal household, and she knew her father would not allow her to marry, mentioning so to her ladies. Both the French and the Imperial ambassadors needed Mary legitimate so she could marry, but in March 1542, Mary again fell drastically ill. Stress certainly made Mary's stomach illness much worse, and on 22 April, Chapuys wrote to Queen Mary of the Netherlands, telling her that Princess Mary had suffered a fever for a month, suffered over of the happenings of England and 'sometime lay as one dead'.[49] Chapuys feared Mary would die, and she lay ill for two months before she could sit up and write to Chapuys again for his support.

Despite all ongoing, the royal children were in their father's favour over the summer of 1542, moving and sharing households through a surprisingly quiet period. On 17 September, Mary and Elizabeth returned to court to dine with their father, who had also spent time with his thriving five-year-old son. Henry lavished gifts and jewels on his daughters, and Chapuys noted Emperor Charles' suggestion that England ally with the Empire and invade France, and the possibility of England invading Scotland, cheered the king.[50] But Henry's sister Margaret, Dowager Queen of Scotland died in October 1542, though her daughter Lady Margaret Douglas remained with Mary in England. Henry and Margaret had never been close, but it was still the loss of the king's final sibling (though Anna of Cleves remained trapped in England, labelled the king's beloved sister, and had struck up a genuine friendship with Henry, Mary and Elizabeth). The other major loss was Margaret's son, King James V of Scotland just after the Battle of Solway Moss in November 1542. James' daughter Mary was only six days old at the time of her father's death and was now the sole heir to the Scottish throne. Infant Mary, Queen of Scots was soon be suggested as a wife to Prince Edward, uniting their two countries. But King Henry's invasion of Scotland, which had resulted in the death of the King James, meant even those neutral to such a match were bitterly opposed. The coming battles between England and Scotland would dominate the lives of Henry and his children, particularly Prince Edward's, for years to come.

Chapter 13

The Education of Heirs and Leaders

While King Henry was in a good mood, life was positive for his children. By the festive season of early 1543, the family gathered at Hampton Court Palace, Henry sending workmen to labour tirelessly to completely refurbish Mary's Hampton Court accommodation so the princesses could stay near their brother. Mary rode through London to Hampton Court, greeted like a queen herself by the people, and all the men of the court rode out to bring Mary to her father. In the absence of a queen, Mary was again the highest-ranked woman in England, even if she had no official title. Instead of the usual New Year at Greenwich, the siblings gathered at Hampton Court to exchange gifts. The king gave Mary a gilt standing cup and a gold tablet, and Mary gifted him a book lined with gold. Princess Elizabeth gave Mary a chain and golden silk hose.[1] Henry was especially generous, giving Mary two gold girdles, a rosary made of lapis lazuli, and several other bejewelled rosaries, a mirror sounded by diamonds and rubies, pictures in golden frames, and several loose rubies and silver plate.[2] Mary was treated supremely by the court; they saw her value as the king's daughter. Everyone from her close allies like Lady Margaret Douglas, down to the Boleyn sisters Lady Calthorpe and Lady Shelton, sent gifts. Mary's accounts show payments for musicians of all kinds, the king's juggler, Welsh minstrels, and even a harp player. Gifts of all sizes, from apples to golden sleeves arrived, and Mary kept up with potential French suitors and Imperial alliances alike.

The royal households soon parted ways, Edward and Elizabeth likely to Hunsdon and Hatfield, while Mary went to Whitehall in London, into new lodgings specially built for her. Mary had her own courtyard and a long gallery along the river's edge, with oriel windows up on the second floor. King Henry soon moved to Whitehall too and was reported to see Mary two or three times every day, as he seemed especially lonely. Henry was still busy; the French still wanted Princess Mary as a bride, while discussions continued over the new Treaty of Greenwich, marrying Prince Edward to Mary, Queen of Scots, and Princess Elizabeth to James Hamilton, the Regent of Scotland's young son, though in truth neither side was happy with any arrangement, no matter what ambassador Sir Ralph Sadler tried to organise.[3]

Mary stayed with her father at Whitehall, and this is possibly where King Henry met Kateryn Parr, Lady Latimer. It is unlikely Lady Kateryn was one of Mary's ladies as she had no husband at court and may have gone to visit her sister Anne Herbert living in Mary's household. On 16 February, a note stating a gift of French, Italian, and Venetian gowns, Venetian and French hoods, along with cotton, linen and tippets were given to Lady Kateryn Parr from King Henry, so Lady Kateryn made gowns suitable for herself and her stepdaughter Margaret Neville.[4] Henry was a generous man when it suited, and had given gowns and fabrics as gifts to ladies at court many times, though this was a large gift by anyone's standards.

Easter came with Princess Mary still at court and Elizabeth and Edward in the country. Mary was unwell and was bled by her physicians, as were all of her women, and one of Mary's chamber men bought her a gift of a spaniel to cheer her.[5] By May, Mary was well, though marriage alliances were a mess. But an unexpected guest arrived, Philip, Duke of Bavaria, back years after making his suit to marry Mary, but all Philip received was a gift of 2,000 crowns (about £1,500,000 today) to leave the country. In June, Mary moved to Carew Manor in Beddington, while Elizabeth remained at Hatfield and Edward moved to Havering.[6] After a quick visit by Mary to see Anna of Cleves at her home at Richmond Palace, by late June, Princesses Mary and Elizabeth reunited at Greenwich. Also, there with Mary's ladies was the newly admitted Kateryn Parr, as her husband Lord Latimer had died in March, leaving Kateryn free to attend the princess. By 12 July, King Henry had made another impulsive move, and he married Lady Kateryn at Hampton Court Palace.[7] It was a good marriage for Henry; Kateryn was very well-read and educated (and had already been pushed into marriage twice before, so was unlikely to be shocked by the reality of a third) and had a friendship with Princess Mary. Kateryn's mother Maud Parr had served Queen Katherine of Aragon, and Kateryn was goddaughter to the late queen. The fact Kateryn had just married her godmother's husband was likely not mentioned at the ceremony. Soon, many of the great ladies of England were summoned into Queen Kateryn's household, all friends of Mary's, making the transition much simpler. Given that Kateryn had been twice married without children suggested she would not have any children with the king, nor was much expected to be produced by the marriage. This also would have left Mary, Elizabeth and Edward, at least privately, relieved. Queen Kateryn had mentioned she did not want to marry the king, but her opinion went unheard.

The marriage did not mean slowing down for the king; he signed the Treaty of Greenwich to marry Prince Edward to Mary, Queen of Scots, and, while Princess Mary lay ill through September, Henry planned to invade France with Emperor Charles. The princesses were able to join the summer progress and have private stays at various manors, visiting Oatlands, Guildford, Windsor, Hanworth, The More, Ampthill, Dunstable, Grafton and Woodstock. Mary and likely Elizabeth travelled with the king and queen to visit Prince Edward at Ashridge, before moving on to Missenden and Bisham, before rejoining the king at Oatlands and onto Hampton Court. At the same time, Henry moved Edward to have their households' live side-by-side, and parliament opened to ensure that all three children were included in the Act of Succession, which was formally completed a few months into 1544.[8] Prince Edward remained the heir-apparent, with Mary succeeding her brother if he died childless. Princess Elizabeth would take the throne if Mary died childless, though neither princess became legitimate. Queen Kateryn is often credited with reuniting the royal family and bringing this change to pass, however, nothing suggests her assistance, as Henry had already developed better relationships with all his children before the marriage. Christmas and New Year were again held at Hampton Court Palace, with all three royal children present.

With a queen back at court, Mary and Elizabeth were able to spend considerable time close to their father and stepmother. Elizabeth was now ten years old, and fiercely intelligent, so an intelligent queen holding court would be a comfort to the girl. Once again it was a generous festive season, though Mary's gift to her father was a large chair decorated with a panel of embroidery, as he was increasingly unable to walk with his massive weight and leg ulcers.[9] Prince Edward received a clock from his eldest sister and gave her a standing cup. Queen Kateryn gave Mary a silk nightgown costing 25l (£10,000 today), roughly the same value as King Henry's new embroidered chair, while Mary gave the queen jewels. Princess Elizabeth gifted her sister a wrought iron braiser. The court was generous to the royal family, especially Sir Edward Seymour, Earl of Hertford, always mindful to keep his place close to the king.

In February 1544, the court relocated to Whitehall, as they were to receive a visit from Juan Esteban Manrique de Lara, 3rd Duke of Najera, to discuss the coming Anglo-Imperial invasion of France. After meeting Henry, Najera met with Queen Kateryn in her chamber with Princess Mary and her ladies, though not Princess Elizabeth. The group danced for hours before Mary kissed the duke on the lips as a sign of amity between their nations. Najera later described Mary as attractive and good at hiding her accomplishments through her prudence and added:

'it is said of her that she's endowed with very great goodness and discretion, and among other praises I have heard... This princess is so much beloved throughout the kingdom, that she is almost adored. The dress she wore was a petticoat of cloth-of-gold, and gown of violet-coloured, three-pilled velvet, with a headdress of many rich stones'.[10]

Spain was happy to have Princess Mary's confidence, with Emperor Charles' son Prince Philip and his new wife Maria Manuela of Portugal asking after Henry and Mary specifically, and Infanta Maria of Spain sent Mary a gift of Spanish gloves.[11] Things were not so comfortable with French King Francis, who sent Henry a large jewelled ring for Princess Mary, not Queen Kateryn, but it was no use looking for peace now; Henry was going to personally ride into battle with his army at Boulogne, and leave England in Kateryn's hands.

Mary spent time ill after meeting the Spanish delegation, but by 26 June, she was well enough to join Princess Elizabeth and Prince Edward at the wedding of their cousin Lady Margaret Douglas to Matthew Stewart, Earl of Lennox, one of the Scottish hostages in London, held after the countries' various skirmishes. The siblings gave their cousin a gift of a large ruby surrounded by diamonds and pearls and enjoyed a five-course dinner, wine, dessert and dancing. King Henry attended the festivities, sitting at the table with all three of his children before it was time to head to war.[12]

As soon as King Henry landed in France, it became obvious England and the Empire were not equals. Fearful, King Francis negotiated peace with Emperor Charles. With the help of the Emperor's sister, French Queen Eleanor, the men signed the Treaty of Crépy, but King Henry invaded France on his own. The war was as half-hearted as Henry's first plan to invade France in 1513, and while the English captured Boulogne on 14 September,[13] the French returned as soon as Henry left the country, leaving the English army to repel a second wave of fighting in October. As with Henry's 'victories' in Tournai decades earlier, the capture of French land led to headaches and eventually concession.

King Henry sent letters to each of his children and niece Margaret while away, and upon return, had his children's portraits painted. The first portrait created was by 'Master John', likely Joannes Corvus, though could have been created by Susanna Horenbout. Susanna was a lady-in-waiting to queens Jane Seymour, Anna of Cleves, and Kateryn Parr, and the first known female artist in Tudor England. 'John' could have been Susanna's husband John Gilman. 'Master John' painted Mary richly dressed in red velvet, her French hood back enough to show her red hair, which was naturally wavy.

Her blue eyes and fair eyebrows dominated her round face with a small mouth but did not indicate Mary's character. A later portrait of Elizabeth by William Scrots shows her exquisite beauty, her red hair also under French hood, her gown of crimson silk and cloth of silver with gold tissue detailed in a pomegranate design. Elizabeth holds a book, likely the New Testament, in her fair hands while the Old Testament sits in the background. Her black eyes, reminiscent of her mother, show one clear difference compared to the portrait of her older sister. Prince Edward's portrait, also painted by William Scrots around the same time as Elizabeth's grand creation, shows Edward as a miniature Henry, copying the stance and dress of his father to perfection. Edward, approximately nine years old in the portrait, still the Prince of Wales, had a jewel around his neck showing the coronet and feathers of the title. Edward wore a crimson russet satin gown with hanging sleeves trimmed with velvet, all embroidered with gold thread and lined with lynx fur. While his hair had the red tinge of his father, Edward was more like his mother with strawberry blonde hair and blue eyes. An updated version of the portrait, done one year later, shows the boy again emulating his father, and portrait x-rays in the 1980s show several attempts to make his stance identical to King Henry's in the Holbein portrait.

At the same time, the large mural painting of the family was underway at Hampton Court. Henry and Edward are in the centre, with Queen Jane beside her son, her miniature Henry. Mary and Elizabeth both feature, but standing back from their father's throne, not given a cloth of estate. By the time the portrait was completed in 1545, Mary was only slightly taller than Elizabeth. Queen Kateryn probably decided to say nothing about the inclusion of Jane Seymour, but not herself.

While King Henry had been in France, and Edward Seymour had been running a muddy and pointless war against Scotland, Prince Edward had been making changes too. He was now old enough to have a formal household established and his education properly begin. No longer living among the women, it was time for Edward to have an all-male household, headed by what Edward wrote as, 'well-learned men, who sought to bring (him) up in learning of tongues, or the scripture, of philosophy, and all liberal sciences'.[14] The finest scholars of the kingdom were available for such tasks; they had been friends with the late Thomas Lord Cromwell, and with Thomas Cranmer (who while still archbishop, was struggling without his partner in reforming England), the two men who had overseen the new scripture in England. Richard Cox became Edward's almoner and tutor, considered the finest schoolmaster of his time, and with a reputation for discipline. His deputy was John Cheke, the professor of Greek at Cambridge, and the university did not wish to lose him. But only Cheke could educate Edward in a manner worthy of a prince. The task was described as 'to be master of princes on earth, is to have the office of gods that be in heaven, because they have, among their hands, him afterward ought to govern all the world'. Prince Edward would have the opposite childhood of his father, who was cloistered away by a king wanting to hold his only son close; Edward would receive training to be the finest king England had ever seen.

Edward would not learn alone, as Mary had done, but given friends and classmates about his age, to foster good relationships with noble families. Edward's classmates were his cousins Charles and Henry Brandon, and Henry and Edward Seymour, as well as the heirs to the earldoms of Shrewsbury, Arundel, Derby, Bath and Ormond. But Edward struck up his closest friendship with Barnaby Fitzpatrick, son of the Irish 1st Baron of Upper Ossory, who history later painted as Edward's whipping boy, so the future king (and his noble classmates) was spared the cane, though this is a myth. Prince Edward was whipped as a student on only one occasion, with Dr Cox despairing at Edward refusing to do his work. Cox had created an elaborate classroom for the boys, making learning like the sieges their fathers faced in France. While their fathers dispatched French soldiers, the boys were to destroy captains of ignorance by learning. But haughty young Prince Edward, well aware of his station in life, refused to work, Cox proclaimed that 'Captain Will', the nickname for ignorance in the classroom, needed to be 'vanquished' from Edward. The young prince received a whipping from Cox's cane. Edward was a fast learner, and never misbehaved for Cox again.[15] The prince soon became proficient at Latin and moved into Greek classics, with Cox soon proclaiming Edward was 'a vessel most apt to receive all goodness and learning, witty, sharp and pleasant'.

Prince Edward, with his classes taking place at Hampton Court Palace, had no shortage of supplies. The Royal Library was stocked to perfection, the king digging through Thomas Cromwell's library after the Vicegerent's execution. Edward had his own desk, complete with a black velvet cover embroidered with an E, and a cabinet containing his compass, knives, a chess set, along with weights, scales, and papers. A separate desk covered in green velvet held writing tools and his reading glasses, as Edward's eyesight was notoriously poor, which Princess Mary also suffered. The room hosted globes, hourglasses, and ambassadors' gifts such as elephant teeth. Also kept nearby were items Edward owned belonging to his mother; a little hair comb shaped like a horse carrying a rider, 'sorcery tools' or items to play magic tricks, books, and a puppet. The room held a grand depiction of Christ's passion and a staff made of unicorn (narwhal) horn, two 'spatelles' (silver and white mixing sticks for sorcery), likely trinkets kept for fun. Edward also had a box of crimson satin where he kept extra shirts, herbs and songbooks.[16]

Prince Edward did all the leisure activities expected of a prince; hawking, fencing, riding, fishing, kept greyhounds and was painted with a pet monkey, likely borrowed for the portrait. But Edward also had Thomas Sternhold, a music and singing teacher, and Edward immediately thrived, just as his father had as a boy. Edward enjoyed learning the lute so much he wrote to the king to thank him for sending Sternhold to his household.[17] Edward had also taken to writing to Queen Kateryn for her help, and her quiet reformist nature had slipped into the appointments of the teachers given to Edward and Elizabeth. Edward wrote to his godfather Thomas Cranmer in Latin, playing down his skills, as he did to multiple English scholars.[18] Among the letters is one of sadness, as Edward had hesitated to write to King Henry in France, fearful of being a burden. But when Henry returned home in late September 1544, Edward wrote, 'I have heard that I am to visit your majesty... My first wish was that your kingdom might have peace and secondly, that I might see you. These done, I shall be happy'.[19] Henry did not reply to his affection-starved son. Expensive gifts were routinely shipped to Edward, and the young prince took these as signs of affection writing, 'if you did not love me, you would not give me these fine gifts of jewellery'. The boy knew no other fatherly affection and hopefully found solace in these gifts.[20] Edward had a dire need to impress his father, as evidenced in his letters concerning his education, and even as a young boy, he was desperate to be the best king possible.

Edward also wrote to his sister Princess Mary, adding, 'for in the same manner as I put on my best garments very seldom, yet these I like better than others; even so I write to you very rarely, yet I love you most'.[21] The letter was soon followed up by a letter to the queen, asking her to look after Mary. Another person writing to Queen Kateryn frequently was Princess Elizabeth. Since the wedding of Henry and Kateryn, Elizabeth had spent almost no time in her father's company at court like Mary, due to her age. But by the time Henry was to go to France and Edward start his learning, Elizabeth returned to the court's affections, as Kateryn wanted to spend more time with the intensely intelligent young princess. On 31 July 1544, Elizabeth wrote to Kateryn in Italian (despite knowing the queen did not understand the language), lamenting that they had not met when Elizabeth went to court for the dinner and party held by Henry before the French battle. The households and schedules of Kateryn and Elizabeth kept them apart, with Elizabeth keen for her father to win in France so she could spend more time with the king and queen.[22] While Mary remained at court, and Edward set up his new life at Hampton Court, Elizabeth was left living at St James' Palace near Whitehall, though as St James' was routinely safe from the plague of the summer, it is more likely she was there for her safety rather than any attempt to separate the royal children. But Elizabeth was able to be with Kateryn and Mary to visit Hampton Court throughout August and stay with the royal household for the limited summer progress, travelling to Woking, Nonsuch, Beddington, Eltham and Otford, before they all travelled to visit Leeds Castle once the king returned home on 3 October. Much of the trip was simply Kateryn, Mary and Elizabeth, as Edward had to return to his household. At this time, Queen Kateryn was Queen Regent in control of the country while the king was away, a role not bestowed to anyone since Katharine of Aragon. Kateryn was in control of all legal and financial affairs of the kingdom, as well as ensuring the troops abroad were suitably financed, fed and armed. Queen Kateryn was only four years older than Princess Mary, and yet was wielding full power over the country and Privy Council without hesitation, and Mary and Elizabeth were there to witness the possibilities of their futures. The Privy Council split between London, the French frontline and north in Scotland as the border wars raged. Women were left in charge at such a pivotal time, and Elizabeth was there to embrace that transformation. She had celebrated her eleventh birthday and was already proving to be a remarkable intellectual with limitless potential.

By 1544, Elizabeth needed new tutors. She had already surpassed the knowledge of Kat Champernowne and had been getting lessons from Richard Cox who was concentrating on Prince Edward by 1544. William Grindal was hired as a new tutor for Elizabeth to work alongside her Italian tutor Giovanni Battista Castiglione. Grindal was a master of Greek, Latin and classics, allowing Elizabeth to expand her language and reading, as she had already learned Italian, Spanish, and French. Elizabeth was already writing in Italian by this time, and needed expert tutors nearby, such as Grindal and Cox, alongside their contemporaries Roger Ascham and John Cheke. Cheke personally developed a way of learning through phonetics to help his young students. As Elizabeth was welcome back at court, she could access Edward's teachers when required, and with these men, all with strong reformist leanings like the queen, Elizabeth immersed herself in evangelical teachings and thoughts as much as Prince Edward. These tutors continued to encompass Elizabeth and Edward for several years, and a biography of Cheke later expressed that he:

> 'not only sowed the seeds of that Doctrine in the heart of Prince Edward, which afterwards grew up into a general Reformation when he came to be King, but by (Cheke's) means the same saving truth was gently instilled into the Lady Elizabeth'.[23]

While Cox, Cheke, and Ascham concentrated on Edward, Elizabeth was more than safe in Grindal's hands. Like her sister Mary before her, Princess Elizabeth was immensely intelligent and had no trouble learning anything put to her. Elizabeth soon translated *The Mirror of a Sinful Soul* from French to English, Queen Kateryn's English work *Prayers or Meditation* into Latin, French and Italian, and then later translated *The Dialogue of Faith* from Latin into French. By 1547, Elizabeth could write in secretary script, and also Italic script taught by Castiglione. She translated *Institution ode la Vie Chrestienne* into English for Queen Kateryn from its original French, a deeply reformist book loved by Kateryn, whose deep reformist views became ever more obvious as the years passed. By the time King Henry became concerned over Kateryn's religious views, those same reformist ideals were already instilled in Elizabeth, and her conviction to never marry, if not already deeply entrenched, was only reconfirmed in 1546, when Henry no longer tolerated Kateryn's private opinions.

Princess Elizabeth was sometimes considered similar to her mother Anne Boleyn, witty, flirtatious, intelligent, and prone to anger and outbursts. Queen Kateryn Parr was remarkably different. Kateryn had not wanted to be queen, but for an unknown reason, had wanted to marry Sir Thomas Seymour, Prince Edward's uncle. Stuck with the king on account of being unable to say no, Kateryn made the best of her position, and in 1544 anonymously published *Psalms or Prayers*, an English version of Bishop John Fisher's Latin work of the same name. A year later, she published *Prayers or Meditation* under her own name, a version of Thomas à Kempis' *The Imitation of Christ*, updated to the reformist doctrine. Both books were immensely popular and would have needed permission for printing by King Henry and Archbishop Cranmer. Elizabeth did the triple translation of *The Imitation of Christ* to give to her father as a Christmas gift. But by 1546, Henry's tolerance of reformist views, combined with meddling by Catholics Bishop Stephen Gardiner and Lord Chancellor Thomas Wriothesley, almost resulted in Henry arresting Queen Kateryn for being a secret Protestant. Kateryn excelled where others failed; throwing herself at her husband's feet to beg for mercy as a 'mere woman in need of correction', and Henry abated at the last minute. Young Elizabeth could see first-hand just how women needed to appease powerful men, and quietly continued her personal beliefs in private. This was a plan previous queens, notably her mother, had failed to master.

Through 1545 and 1546, the royal children spent little time together, though with the youngest two being close in age they did have the chance to forge a sibling relationship. Prince Edward wrote to Elizabeth on one occasion:

> 'change of place did not vex me so much, dearest sister, as your going from me. Now there can be nothing pleasanter than a letter from you. It is some comfort in my grief that my chamberlain tells me I may hope to visit you soon.'[24]

As Elizabeth and Edward's quiet lives between Hampton Court, Ashridge, Hunsdon and Hatfield continued, Mary's life as a princess at the royal court continued along the lines it had most of her life. She was considered an important part of English royal life by those abroad who constantly brought her name into international alliances. After the war in France, England was not on good terms with King Francis, who was at peace with the Emperor. This meant marriages into the Empire or France were closed for Mary, no matter what ambassadors tried to whisper. Ambassador Eustace Chapuys had been in England for sixteen years by July 1545, an endless advocate of Princess Mary and her mother. But health was no longer on Chapuys' side, with gout afflicting him for years, and his successor François van der Delft was sent to England.[25] Chapuys was the vital link between Mary and her Spanish connections, but by this time, Mary knew as well as anyone that the chances of her making a marriage and alliance was impossible. Chapuys retired to Leuven in the Low Countries but continued to advise Emperor Charles, never faltering in his belief in Mary.

Princess Mary had been assisting Queen Kateryn with her attempt to translate the Gospel into English for those who could not speak Latin, with Henry's permission. Archbishop Thomas Cranmer had been reforming England's religion as gently as possible without Thomas Lord Cromwell's protection and King Henry had allowed it, but mass remained unaffected. Mary had accepted her father's still-messy religious leanings and agreed to help with a new translation of the bible, though suggestions Mary feigned illness to excuse herself seems without merit. Mary's illness meant she did little of anything in the summer of 1545, and other translators helped Queen

Kateryn to finish the work. Due to the wide range of men Kateryn had working on the translation means that Mary's contribution can be hard to identify, but she gained credit as part of the wider project.

Marital alliances continued while Princess Mary was sick and Henry and Kateryn were at Portsmouth, preparing for an attack by sea from France. Charles, Duke of Orléans, so long touted as a husband for Mary, died after being dared to roll in bedsheets in a house once inhabited by a family who died of the plague.[26] That meant Mary's troubles of being married into France finally ended, though the idea of Emperor Charles' widowed son Philip marrying either Princess Mary or Elizabeth resurfaced. King Henry was more interested in finding a bride for Prince Edward, possibly Philip's sister Infanta Maria of Spain. As with all negotiations, all marriage suggestions were again dead by February 1546. But by the same time, an ambassador was sent from Poland, looking to talk alliances with Henry and Kateryn, who both met the ambassador at Greenwich after spending time at Hampton Court with Edward. But rumours laced with gossip suggested King Henry was interested in finding another wife for himself; Catherine Willoughby, Duchess of Suffolk was now a widow, as her much older husband Charles Brandon, the Duke of Suffolk, was finally dead. Queen Kateryn was annoyed by such rumours about her friend; Lady Catherine was mortified at the thought. Henry had not been able to take a mistress in many years, so at least women at court were finally safe.

Poland was not the only country sending ambassadors, as German embassies were also in alliance discussions in March 1546, and then again in September. The Landgrave of Hesse and Elector of Saxony were both sending men to England and vice versa. Soon, a familiar face arrived, Philip, Duke of Bavaria, who had tried to gain Mary's hand in 1539 and 1540. Philip arrived in late March 1546, and while Mary was still illegitimate, she was in the line of succession and even more valuable than when Philip first became enamoured with her. On 12 April, it was time for Philip of Bavaria to leave England, but first, he met with Mary, at Whitehall, where they sat and spoke for an hour.[27] The Duke Palatine was a staunch Lutheran and claimed he had never heard mass spoken, instantly angering the conservative men of court close to Henry's ear. Mary knew her father would never let her marry, and so likely gave little credence to this offer.[28] It was this meeting that inspired Prince Edward's letter to his older sister advising her against marriage and various other 'merriments'.[29]

In May 1546, both Mary and Elizabeth were part of Queen Kateryn's household and given items from the Great Wardrobe to use for Whitsuntide. King Henry's ulcers and obesity continued to see his well-being decline, and his advisors remained desperate for his favour, while also undermining evangelical Queen Kateryn. Kateryn may have been outsmarting the men at court to stay in favour, but Mary did not need to do the same. There is little explanation for Henry's huge gift of jewels sent to Princess Mary in July 1546, which made her feel and appear deep in her father's affections.[30] Mary received twenty large diamonds, ten large rubies, over sixty pearls and an emerald brooch. Another selection of gifts showed a diamond and pearl girdle, and diamond-encrusted brooches showing the History of Solomon's temples, the History of the Old Testament, the History of Abraham, and one showing the story of Pyramus and Thisbe, the ill-fated lovers of Babylon. She would have looked fine indeed when Philip of Bavaria arrived back in September 1546, though with Henry ill, he could not send away his daughter to a man who could return with her backed by a foreign army. Yet Henry's relationship with Mary seemed secure, sending away for a consignment of hunting equipment, along with a horse for Mary, suggesting they did spend time together as Henry continued to decline. But Mary was unwell through the latter part of 1546, with the king's physicians prescribing Mary lozenges and enemas.

While Mary tried to recover her health, the Privy Council around the king rallied to their own causes as Henry slowly declined. The Catholics were not in favour and the reformers looked to capitalise on that. On 2 December, Henry Howard, Earl of Surrey, the once-endless companion of Henry Fitzroy, was arrested for looking to usurp the king.[31] Surrey felt entitled and was against the 'reformist newcomers' at court for some time, thinking the Howards had as much claim to the crown as the Tudors, even quartering his coat of arms with those of Edward the Confessor. Surrey's sister, Mary Howard, widow of Henry Fitzroy, was happy to speak against her brother, as were his close friends, who had heard Surrey say his father, the Duke of Norfolk, was the man most appropriate to rule over Prince Edward. Surrey had asked his sister to seduce King Henry to control him, despite having married Henry's son over a decade earlier.[32] Within ten days of Surrey's arrest, he and his father were in the Tower. Surrey was convicted of treason and beheaded on 20 January, while his father was also convicted but given a short stay of execution. King Henry spent much time during his final weeks angered at the potential coup, personally going through the papers on the conspiracy. Henry believed himself still in power and even able to be in control after death, despite the powerful reformist factions at court ready to pounce. Thomas Lord Cromwell's 1536 Act of Succession meant Henry could appoint a council of guardians to aid Prince Edward if he ruled England as a minor, and this remained in the 1544 update of the law.

Henry checked the list of councillors appointed, last updated in 1544, and decided to exclude most conservative Catholics. The most notable removal was Bishop Stephen Gardiner, finally ousted from a position of power after years of working for himself at the expense of the king. The council leaned towards Edward Seymour and his supporters, along with William Paget, the current Master Secretary. Queen Kateryn was removed as Regent to rule over Edward, but she was not informed, and sixteen men were put in place to rule with the young king. Henry looked to ensure his son would not be marred by the conspiracies and corruption of the court. Councillors were allowed to appoint themselves titles and lands, given so much power it is often doubted if Henry ever wrote or signed these papers, or if a dry stamp of Henry's signature was used. Whether King Henry signed this clause, dated 30 December 1546, when he was still lucid, or right before his death is a matter of eternal contention.

Queen Kateryn and Princess Mary remained together for Christmas and New Year at Greenwich, but Henry would not see anyone, staying with his council at Whitehall. Gifts were sent and received between the royal family members, and Kateryn sent Prince Edward portraits of herself and the king to look upon while they were all separated for New Year 1547. Among the royal family correspondence, through Henry's dark time, Edward remained appreciative of Kateryn, the pair unaware she would not be his Regent, and Edward wrote to Mary, thanking her for a fine New Year gift.[33] But neither the queen nor his children could see the king, locked away at Whitehall, with Edward Seymour and William Paget controlling everything in Prince Edward's favour. Henry did meet with French and Imperial ambassadors on 17 January, which sucked any remaining life from him and he banned all visitors. As it had ever been, friends and enemies were lurking in every corner.

When Henry's time was close, he called in those he wished to see one more time, none being his children. Seymour and Paget sat with the king for hours. Paget took the chance to look at Henry's desk while alone with the king and found papers about Queen Jane Seymour. While a painting of Henry's final days, handing over the throne to Edward and vanquishing the Pope is entirely imagined, Henry was surrounded by his visiting privy councillors on his final night. Queen Kateryn could not gain access to her husband; she had tried to get her rooms prepared on 11 January so she could visit, without luck, and then sent another sixteen letters to her brother-in-law William Herbert in the privy chamber, to find out what was happening with the king. She even travelled by barge from Greenwich on 23 January to see her husband, and Henry would not admit her.[34] One person was admitted,

Sir Thomas Seymour, the same man Kateryn had wanted to marry. Also included was Seymour's friend Henry Grey, Marquess of Dorset, father of Ladies Jane, Katherine, and Mary Grey, cousins to the royal children. Most council men were reformers or (at least publicly) neutral, while only overtly Catholic Bishop Cuthbert Tunstall stood opposed to the new religion. Most of the major players in King Henry's life had passed away in preceding years, though the Duke of Norfolk was surprisingly still alive in the Tower, saved from execution as Henry died before he sign the execution paperwork.

Prince Edward was living at Hertford Castle, twenty-five miles north of London when King Henry VIII took his final breath, Archbishop Cranmer in attendance during the early hours of 28 January 1547. His children were suddenly free of him and yet imprisoned by what life would hold. Edward Seymour rode north to Hertford Castle to his nephew at once, not telling the boy the news, preparing him for an instant trip to London under the guise of being officially bestowed the title of Prince of Wales. The party stopped thirteen miles outside London at Enfield House (also called Elsyng Palace at the time) where Princess Elizabeth and her household were staying. The siblings had spent the festive season separated, and Elizabeth was equally surprised as Edward by the unannounced visit on 29 January. Once Seymour had two of the royal children secure, he told them the news, and the siblings cried in one another's arms.[35] Edward was a king at nine years old, a boy desperate for his father's approval, and yet left without parental care. Elizabeth was thirteen and would realise her precarious situation now she was a vulnerable illegitimate sister, no longer a safe daughter to a mighty king.

The scheming the royal children did not know about was well underway by the evening of 29 January. No one knew of the king's death; Ambassador van der Delft heard whisperings in London that Henry was dead, and watched the royal dinner taken to the royal bedroom despite knowing no sovereign lived to eat it, but London was closed and no news could travel.[36] Edward Seymour was already being addressed as the leader of the Regency Council that Henry had set up without a head. Seymour's scheming to get himself named Lord Protector over his nephew the young king had worked, and all on the council were prepared to accept Seymour's reign. Edward Seymour, Earl of Hertford was the logical choice; Prince Edward now had no parents, Queen Kateryn held no power, and Sir Thomas Seymour was not as well respected. King Henry only had deceased sisters, who only had surviving daughters and granddaughters by 1547. Edward Seymour was the most logical choice to rule England for his nephew, if not considered a dull man with a snobbish wife.

On 31 January 1547, Seymour received the official title of Lord Protector of the realm from the new council sitting at the Tower. Prince Edward moved to London to await his ascension, with Princess Elizabeth left behind at Enfield. Who told Princess Mary the news of her father's death, while staying with Queen Kateryn at Greenwich, goes unrecorded, as does her reaction. Kateryn was already receiving romantic overtures from Thomas Seymour as early as 29 January while receiving the news of Henry's death. King Henry's will and succession were assured, and there was no panic to ensure Mary was watched. But Mary was the opposite of her little brother, an adult, a staunch Catholic and beloved as a potential monarch at home and abroad. Yet Edward was male, the only thing that mattered. Princess Mary was stunned by the freedom she suddenly had; she knew she had lost her best years of finding a martial alliance and creating her own royal family, but now she had options, albeit at her brother's whims. Queen Kateryn was suddenly free from a marriage she had clearly stated was against her will. For Mary, in particular, her grief at losing her father mixed with great relief, as her own life could begin, her oppressive childhood under her father's eye had extended for too long; she was about to celebrate her thirty-first birthday, despite being prepared as a ruler and treated as an adult since she was only a baby. Life as a queen or empress dangled before Mary her entire life, and then pulled away, leaving her sitting in various manor homes with her books and her entertainments, endless waiting for a true adulthood that never came. Only now could there be a future for all three of Henry's surviving children, and their households were broken up in preparation for a new world.

Chapter 14

A Tudor Born to Rule

Lord Chancellor Wriothesley cried when he announced the news of King Henry's death in parliament; tears more likely for himself than the king.[1] Wriothesley only received his position because everyone more important than him was away fighting France or Scotland when the role became vacant in 1544. Despite being a conservative, he lacked any great understanding of either side of religion. He grew up under Cardinal Wolsey's tutelage and served the ousted Stephen Gardiner before being welcomed into Thomas Cromwell's household. After betraying Cromwell with lies and seeing his master beheaded, Wriothesley had waited in the wings for power, a priggish man with no allies. It was little wonder that newly ennobled royal uncle Thomas Seymour considered seeing Wriothesley tossed in the Tower in February, alongside Princess Mary, King Edward's strongest Catholic opposition.[2] Wriothesley received an earldom to shut him up, while Edward Seymour became Duke of Somerset, claiming King Henry had granted it in a likely-forged document no one could access. John Dudley became Earl of Warwick and William Parr, Queen Kateryn's brother, became Marquess of Northampton. Thomas Seymour became Baron of Sudeley but was privately angling for more power. He soon took Lady Jane Grey into his new household, promising her father that she might one day marry King Edward and be queen.[3] Meanwhile, Thomas Seymour lobbied his brother for a bride of his own, asking for Princess Mary's hand. Mary laughed at the notion.[4] Sir Thomas bargained instead for Princess Elizabeth almost immediately, while enjoying romantic visits with Dowager Queen Kateryn.[5] Power in England had already made a total shift away from everything the royal children knew.

The day Wriothesley cried false tears in parliament, King Edward arrived in London to great fanfare, cheering crowds and guns firing from the Thames. The boy stayed at the Tower, customary before a coronation, a cloth of estate and gold arras hung about him. He wrote to Queen Kateryn to console her, 'although nature prompts us to grieve and shed tears for the departure of him now gone from our eyes, yet Scripture and wisdom prompt us to moderate those feelings'.[6] To his sister Mary, Edward wrote, 'we ought not to mourn in our father's death, since it is His will, who works all thing for good… I will be to you a dearest brother and overflowing with kindness'.

Carpenters and plumbers built a lead coffin around King Henry's body, while those embalming the body were shocked to find clogged arteries, adding there was 'hardly half a pint of pure blood in his whole body'.[7] Stephen Gardiner oversaw the funeral on 15 February, and as Henry was lowered into the vault beside Queen Jane Seymour, surrounded by sixteen yeomen of the guard, the officers' staves were snapped and thrown down. King Edward recorded these moments in his journal, the boy sensing it strange. Mary and Elizabeth did not attend their father's funeral, as was expected and customary, Elizabeth left at Enfield and Mary at Greenwich, wondering what the world would now hold.

Edward left the Tower of London on 19 February, dressed in vivid white velvet embroidered with silver and diamonds, rubies and pearls shaped into lovers' knots, with a gold gown and sable cape,[8] for a four-hour parade through the city and its people, before the coronation the following day. Archbishop Cranmer oversaw the coronation, cutting down the Liber Regalis ceremony, in use since 1375, so the boy did not get tired; it was to be a twelve-hour ceremony cut to seven hours. Cranmer's biggest change to the oath was that a king would serve his people, rather than simply rule them.[9] The boy was then coronated using St Edward's crown, along with another specially made crown for his small head, as the imperial crown was far too big. King Edward VI did manage to hold the orb alone but needed the Earl of Shrewsbury to help him hold the spectre. The only Tudor monarch ever born to rule was officially in power. Edward was a typical child; he simply noted down in his autobiography he received a crown and sat with his uncle Seymour and godfather Cranmer during a celebration. Foreign ambassadors found the entire event ill-planned and confusing.[10]

Ill-defined and without precedent was to be the theme of King Edward's reign. His uncle Edward Seymour held total power but without legal backing, so all was beset by roadblocks if the Privy Council did not bow to his desires. Thomas Seymour seemed intent, by accident or design, on causing endless problems for his older brother, seeking to undermine the Protectorate. John Dudley backed his friend, Thomas Seymour, leading to a lack of trust or support for Edward Seymour. Thomas Wriothesley was dismissed as Lord Chancellor and Keeper of the Great Seal soon after the coronation and was left to die in disgrace when he would not support the new Lord Protector. King Edward's childhood ended the moment his father died, and while his sisters remained in a permanently uncertain position, the new king was expected to either be an adult ruling a realm, or a mere puppet for Edward Seymour.

Kateryn Parr, Dowager Queen of England, married Thomas Seymour just weeks after the death of King Henry, not securing the Lord Protector's permission. The relationship remained secret for four months, and even then, caused widespread disharmony through its illegality.[11] Kateryn had both Princess Elizabeth and Lady Jane Grey in her household, which would give rise to rumours of molestation and harassment that would eventually do long-term harm to the reputations of all involved.

A grand story about King Edward was recorded in early 1549, claiming to tell of events of the young boy on the night of 16 January. A report said Thomas Seymour, after gaining a key, let himself and accomplices into the king's chambers in the night, only to disturb Edward's little dog, who barked and alerted the king and his cousin Michael Stanhope. Stanhope rushed out to find the dog dead, tales moving between the dog being either shot or stabbed.[12] The captors claimed they were checking to see if the king was properly guarded and fled. At once, Thomas Seymour was suspected by all, looking to kidnap the king from the Protector's almost claustrophobic court, and flee north to Holt or Bewdley Castle, taking Princess Elizabeth along the way. King Edward was unhappy in the Lord Protector's care but had the plot been true, he may not have liked this option any better. Thomas Seymour went to the Tower the following evening and was beheaded not long after. The Lord Protector had finally rid himself of his challenging brother.

As Lord Protector, Edward Seymour looked to do all he could for his nephew but enjoyed total power and authority more than he should have. His fighting in France and Scotland proved his capability for his position, and he won the Battle of Pinkie in Scotland in September 1547. But rebellions and riots at home caused enough problems for King Edward and his uncle, making parliamentary and religious changes limited. Commissioners sent out by the Lord Protector through 1549 did more harm than good, angering landlords and tenants alike, and enflaming religious grievances.

By October 1549, King Edward and the Lord Protector were holed up at Windsor Castle away from the council, and even Edward wrote in his diary he felt like he was imprisoned. Seymour had never secured legal authority, and a coup d'état within the Privy Council ordered Lord Protector Seymour arrested and imprisoned. John Dudley, Earl of Warwick took over as leader of the council, a group that was never meant to have a leader, but two years of Seymour's rule had proved the Council to be ineffective. The council majority still ruled over Dudley, and King Edward eventually had his uncle released from the Tower. Edward Seymour returned his nephew's kindness by launching a counterattack against Dudley, forcing King Edward to behead another Seymour uncle in 1552. As young Edward noted about the affair, 'the bible said, Woe to thee, O land, when thy king is a child, and thy princes eat in the morning'.[13]

John Dudley, elevated to the Duke of Northumberland in 1551, did not make the same mistakes as Seymour, relying on council power and letting the young king appear in charge. King Edward had his secretaries William Cecil and William Petre close by and hoped to make religious changes, while Dudley and the Council concerned themselves with secular matters in parliament. Political life calmed; a claim that King Edward pulled all the feathers from a falcon and tore it apart as a threat to his councillors in 1551 seems to only be French gossip. Dudley oversaw major changes to improve England's disastrous economic situation, betrothed King Edward to Elisabeth of Valois (daughter of new French King Henri), created alliances, ended the wars with France and Scotland, and ensured laws which implemented Thomas Cranmer's religious changes. Despite bouts of smallpox and measles in 1552, and continuously losing his sight and hearing,[14] things looked to be taking a brighter turn for the teenage king.

Princess Mary visited her brother in February 1553; the siblings had only reunited twice since his ascension to the throne, including when they met at court in 1550, where Mary and Edward both reduced to public tears over a fight about Mary's continuing Catholic practices.[15] By the time Mary visited in 1553, Edward had fallen ill, suffering from breathing problems. He was described as struggling with, 'difficulty in drawing his breath, which is due to the compression of the organs on the right side', and had recurring fevers.[16] By April, King Edward moved from Westminster to Greenwich for the fresh air, and after difficulties, was well enough to sit at a window by mid-May. But the reality was not so rosy; an attendant reported, 'the matter he ejects from his mouth is sometimes coloured a greenish yellow and black, sometimes pink, like the colour of blood'.[17] By 1 July, Edward appeared on a balcony to see well-wishers, but was a skeleton of his former self, and would never be seen in public again. His childhood tutor John Cheke remained at Edward's side, but Edward confessed he was pleased death would take him.

Throughout everything in his short life, Edward cared most about continuing his father's religious reforms and was desperate to ensure Princess Mary did not take the throne and restore Catholicism. King Edward made several drafts of his will and looked to void his father's Act of Succession and remove his sisters' chance to rule. Edward looked to his aunt Queen Mary Tudor's granddaughters, considering future sons born to Jane, Katherine or Mary Grey as heirs, only to revise and state the three sisters (daughters of Edward's cousin Frances Brandon and her husband Henry Grey, Marquess of Dorset) as heirs who could take the throne in their own right. This put Council leader Dudley in a prime position; his son Guildford Dudley was recently married Lady Jane Grey. It was at Greenwich Palace, the site of many of his father's happiest moments, that King Edward died at eight o'clock on the evening of 6 July 1553, his final words, 'I am faint; Lord have mercy upon me and take my spirit'.[18]

Despite unsubstantiated rumours of poisoning, surgeons found Edward's lungs the reason for his death, possibly consumption, or tuberculosis. But Edward also could have suffered suppurating pulmonary infection, just as his half-brother Henry Fitzroy suffered in 1536. These lung abscesses would have caused lung collapse and blood poisoning, and eventually organ failure. King Edward was only fifteen years old, and died without a single family member around him, a sad end for a boy so longed for, and born out of one of England's greatest struggles.

Chapter 15

The Reputation of a Royal Sister

There would be no glittering court life for Princess Elizabeth when her father died. No parliament to oversee, no relatives jockeying to increase her power and relevance. Elizabeth felt as if she did not have a friend in the world while her brother sat on the throne. The life she had led under her father, quietly tucked away in nursery-like environments likely felt like a dream. Elizabeth would come to live a stunted existence; too close to the throne to be embraced with support, too far from her family to receive the care she still needed. Her life would be stifled by her brother, just as her father had done, but without the wrath of Henry VIII to incur, courtiers could hurt Elizabeth without fear of punishment.

As soon as Edward was spirited away from thirteen-year-old Elizabeth at Enfield, she moved to Greenwich where Queen Kateryn and Princess Mary remained, equally isolated and lost. But Greenwich would have felt like a relief, for Kateryn could remain the mother Elizabeth lacked. But within a week of her father's burial and brother's coronation, a vulture perched nearby: Thomas Seymour. He wrote Elizabeth a letter, stating how he wished to marry her, just thirteen years old, while he was a man of forty. Seymour wrote, 'I dare not tell you of the fire which consumes me, and the impatience with which I yearn to show my devotion'.[1] Seymour wanted to marry the new king's sister, despite already having a plum role as the king's uncle. Elizabeth confided in her governess Kat Ashley (formerly Champernowne), and then quietly told Seymour to leave her alone, as she looked to mourn and remain single and virginal for another two years.[2] Seymour had already tried to gain Princess Mary as a bride, and now the little sister was not interested either. Elizabeth did what many women do when faced with a distasteful overture; she meekly and quietly declined, without harsh words or threats, to appease the male ego. Affidavits in later years showed Seymour could not take this hint, and he was busy with multiple schemes. Seymour had convinced Henry Grey, Marquess of Dorset to allow his eldest daughter Lady Jane Grey to be a ward in the Seymour household, part of a plan to surround himself with the influential.

Seymour married Lady Kateryn Parr thirty-four days after King Henry's death.[3] Their wedding on 3 March 1547 was a strict secret, coming only a week after Seymour tried to woo Kateryn's stepdaughter. Kateryn and Princesses Mary and Elizabeth remained in London, though 'grieving widow' Kateryn soon moved her household to Chelsea. Princess Mary prepared to leave for Beaulieu, just one of the many immense estates she inherited from her father, and was now able to make an independent income as an adult. Lady Kateryn, Princess Elizabeth, and Lady Jane Grey began a new life in their huge, triple household in Chelsea, with Seymour sneaking in and out for visits. The secret spread: first Kateryn's sister Anne Herbert and her husband knew of the marriage, then Catherine Willoughby, Duchess of Suffolk heard it directly from the dowager queen. Princess Elizabeth's governess bumped into Seymour, who confessed to the marriage.[4] Elizabeth spent months being shuffled between Chelsea and St James' Palace in London, and she could not see King Edward, at the Lord Protector's insistence. It was June 1547 before Thomas Seymour managed to squeeze into King Edward's rooms and ask permission to marry Kateryn, to which the king agreed. This allowed the marriage to become public knowledge, though spoken of as if it had only happened after the king's acceptance.[5]

Princess Mary was furious and considered Kateryn's household no longer suitable for Elizabeth. Mary's new household was one still firmly in mourning, but Elizabeth politely rebuffed her sister's invitation to move to Beaulieu.[6] Kateryn remained at court dressed and acting like a queen, while others gossiped about her foolish marriage.[7] The Seymour brothers were at loggerheads and Anne Stanhope, Edward Seymour's wife, bitterly hated Kateryn. All this played out while Princess Elizabeth and her cousin Lady Jane Grey sat in the background, seeing the futility of the adults at court.

By the end of the summer, Elizabeth was living full-time at Chelsea after a stay at Hanworth, fortunately with many of her old household staff, including tutor William Grindal. Elizabeth could read, study, and simply feel safe with Grindal and they were joined by fellow scholar and tutor Roger Ascham. Most of Elizabeth's household had been there her entire life alongside Kat Ashley (having married one of Elizabeth's attendants and distant relatives, John Astley/Ashley). Blanche Parry remained a gentlewoman, as did Mary Hill, Elizabeth Cavendish, and Mary Norris. Ralph Taylor remained her chaplain, William Russell remained a groom of her chamber, and Russell's servant, named only Charles, made Elizabeth's corsets to perfection. Even the laundry woman had served all of Elizabeth's thirteen years. Elizabeth's life had been harmonious for the past several years, and she had been surrounded by intelligent men and women. When

Lady Kateryn published her last work, *Lamentations of a Sinner* in 1547, Elizabeth felt safe to revisit her own translations of reformist ideals. She was not as safe as she thought, unaware of Lord Protector Seymour's overtures for a Scottish husband for the young princess.

By this time, Princess Elizabeth's chief ladies, Kat Ashley and Lady Blanche Parry were fighting over who was the number one lady in the household. Due to an argument over who would sleep on the pallet bed at the foot of Elizabeth's bed, it was removed from her room entirely, leaving her strangely unchaperoned at night.[8] Later, eyewitness accounts from the duplicitous Kat Ashley showed this was an opening to a situation that stained Elizabeth's reputation. As soon as Thomas Seymour moved into the Chelsea household with his new wife, his early morning visits to Elizabeth's bedroom began. Seymour had a key to Princess Elizabeth's room, surprising her while she slept in just a nightgown and summer bedsheets. For him, only partly dressed, being in her bedroom was exceedingly inappropriate under any circumstances. Elizabeth was unable to do anything but dress in a hurry and pretend he never visited. Seymour took it further on his next visit; Elizabeth was already out of bed and tried to get away from him, and he touched her inappropriately as she turned away, the pair equally in a state of undress. Elizabeth ran into the next room to see her ladies, Seymour following her, playing off the whole situation as a fun joke for everyone to share.[9] The household now suffered a strong imbalance of power. There could be no innocent explanation for why a half-dressed man was sneaking into a child's bedroom. Kat Ashley was Elizabeth's governess and chaperone, but she welcomed Seymour's over-familiar visits with Elizabeth, whether she was in bed, studying, or spending time outdoors. Lady Kateryn, as wife to Seymour, had no rights whatsoever, with him syphoning massive sums of money from her accounts and starting fights with her without cause.[10] If King Henry and his rotation of wives had not already put Elizabeth off marriage, this new arrangement certainly would.

Kat Ashley provided no support for Princess Elizabeth when they visited Hanworth, standing silent as Seymour climbed under the princess' bedcovers, only speaking when Seymour went to kiss Elizabeth, who tried to hide her body under the sheets.[11] Seymour had won the hearts of all the women in the household and none would dare speak against him, but he was known to fly into rages with Lady Kateryn. Kat Ashley knew what Seymour wanted from her young charge, and suggested Elizabeth should have been Seymour's bride. Another morning visit from Seymour found Elizabeth hiding behind the bed curtains surrounded by maids she had ready for the ambush, her discomfort of his lechery obvious.[12] Only then did Kat Ashley dare to confront Seymour to stop his behaviour; she ensured Elizabeth was up and dressed when he came in every morning. Seymour had no interest in games when Elizabeth was dressed.[13] But still, Elizabeth slept alone at night, and Lady Kateryn was often away from Chelsea, or Hanworth where they often moved the household for country visits. Elizabeth was a child being tempted by a man, with little understanding of reality, and soon people began to wonder if Elizabeth enjoyed Seymour's attention. Even if she did, only one of them was a married adult.[14] Even Kat Ashley did not defend her mistress, as she was enamoured by Seymour. Ashley freely admitted that she knew Seymour, 'had won a queen and wished to also be homely with a princess'.[15]

The infamous altercation between Princess Elizabeth, Seymour and Lady Kateryn came at Hanworth soon after. Elizabeth routinely enjoyed walks in the gardens and was walking with Kateryn when Seymour approached them with his dagger.[16] Elizabeth turned to Kateryn, clutching at her stepmother, as Seymour, without explanation, sliced at Elizabeth's heavy dress. Whether it came to one hundred pieces or that was a later exaggeration, Elizabeth fled indoors, chastised by Kat Ashley for being undressed in public. Elizabeth shared the tale but Ashley hushed up the story. This story is often told as one where Kateryn held Elizabeth down as Seymour could slice at the girl, though the sole recollection of events does not suggest this. Lady Kateryn summoned Kat Ashley to explain why Elizabeth's conduct in the household was inappropriate, as Seymour had told tales of Princess Elizabeth embracing men in his sight. All the ladies backed Elizabeth's story, and there were never any men around the princess, as Elizabeth swore. Kat Ashley feared it was Kateryn making up the lies herself.[17] Kateryn knew of Seymour's morning visits to Elizabeth's rooms and had joined him on a few occasions to play on the bed with Elizabeth, as if to watch or defuse the situation. Elizabeth's household was soon left behind at Hanworth, safe away from her stepparents. Lady Jane Grey was not able to stay at Hanworth, though fortunately Seymour had never acted inappropriately with Jane, nor had any of her ladies left her unguarded.

Princess Elizabeth spent most of the winter in early 1548 at Hanworth without the spectre of Lady Kateryn and Seymour. It was a bitingly cold season in which her beloved tutor William Grindal caught the plague and suddenly died. Grindal had a remarkably close friendship with equally brilliant scholar Roger Ascham, who soon lobbied for Grindal's job, with Elizabeth interviewing him personally behind Kateryn and Seymour's backs. After a good reference from King Edward's tutor John Cheke, Elizabeth's education was soon safe once again, but soon she needed to travel back to London to rejoin her stepmother's household. With war on the horizon, Thomas Seymour as Lord Admiral was busy, embroiled in problems at court or becoming the number one pirate off English shores rather than defending England. Princess Elizabeth seemed buoyed by life with Seymour away, as studies with Roger Ascham were going very well, working on the Greek New Testament each morning, followed by classics in the afternoons, along with Philip Melanchthon's *Commonplaces of Theology*, a heavy Lutheran text. Ascham, a noted scholar, considered Elizabeth's Latin, Greek and English composition excellent, and the fervent reformist John Bale himself read Princess Elizabeth's translation of *Mirror of a Christian Soul*.[18] Bale was one to inspire and teach other reformers, and yet Elizabeth was doing the same to Bale, who aided her to publish her works, renamed *A Godly Meditation of the Christian Soul* in April 1548. Lady Jane Grey was likewise a brilliant scholar, the girls quietly becoming two of England's most educated women when given the chance to live in peace.

Sadly, the household soon moved to Seymour Place in London, putting Princess Elizabeth back within her abuser's reach. The early morning visits, with Seymour only partly clothed in a nightgown soon resumed, but Elizabeth was now prepared and up, dressed, and reading when he snuck into her bedroom. He persisted every morning until Kat Ashley eventually snapped at him.[19] Not only had his advances failed, but her ladies also no longer believed Seymour's innocence during the visits.

After the Christmas and New Year celebrations at court, Lady Kateryn announced she was finally pregnant to Thomas Seymour and was showing by the time her household relocated back to Hanworth in April 1548. The huge triple household at Hanworth then prepared a move to Sudeley Castle in Gloucestershire so Kateryn could give birth in the area of Seymour's barony. Servants in the household believed there to be 'goodwill between the Lord Admiral and (Elizabeth)' at the time of the move,[20] and she and Lady Jane Grey were leading cheerful, quiet lives. But when Princess Elizabeth sent a note to Seymour in London on behalf of Lady Kateryn on 9 June, she added her own note on the back, 'thou, touch me not', before crossing it out and adding, 'let him not touch me'.[21] Kateryn was no fool and was noted as 'suspecting the often access of the Admiral to the Lady Elizabeth's Grace',[22] and it was noted within the household that Seymour loved Elizabeth 'too well'.

Seymour arrived back at Hanworth on 11 June to escort the household one hundred miles north and pulled Elizabeth aside to talk.[23] Lady Kateryn soon found the pair in a room together, Seymour embracing the girl. Kateryn was white hot with rage; Kateryn also screamed at Kat Ashley for not watching Elizabeth closely enough, and banished Elizabeth to live with Kat Ashley's sister Joan and her husband, Sir Anthony Denny. Lady Kateryn was unwell with her pregnancy, but she and Elizabeth spoke before Elizabeth's household began their move, just one day after the incident. The pair parted on 'good' terms, but no one knew why Elizabeth was suddenly leaving. Seymour accompanied Elizabeth's household part of the way to Cheshunt where the Dennys lived, not arousing any suspicion, but Kat Ashley watched his every move. A safer home would have been Hever Castle, the former home of the Boleyns where Anna of Cleves now lived. Lady Anna had been close to Henry VIII after their divorce and remained close to Elizabeth and Mary, but old allies and relationships were increasingly frozen during Edward's reign.

But rumours of Seymour's behaviour had already spread, just as Princess Elizabeth fell seriously ill for the first time in her life, with migraines, stomach problems, jaundice and menstrual issues, similar to what plagued Princess Mary in times of stress.[24] But the fact Elizabeth suddenly moved from Kateryn's care and then took to her bed flew the rumour mill into action. Edward Seymour sent Thomas Bille, the royal physician, to Cheshunt who ensured Elizabeth was back to full health by September 1548. No diagnosis was given or mentioned. Rumours of a hidden pregnancy abounded, made stronger decades later by a midwife who gave a deathbed confession of aiding a high-ranked girl wearing a mask to give birth, only for the baby's father to throw the boy on a fire. Through the centuries the tale has been levelled at Elizabeth and many others as the woman involved.[25] A poem written fifty years later suggested Elizabeth had defended her honour by pulling a dagger on Seymour,[26] but one can only hope the man never got that close to her, or worse still, had an opportunity to get Elizabeth pregnant.

Princess Elizabeth still wanted Lady Kateryn's love and affection, and through a series of letters, the pair soon rekindled their fondness for each other. By the time Kateryn prepared to take to her confinement in the style of a royal woman, she and Elizabeth were on good terms and Elizabeth had even written to Seymour to ensure her good wishes reached Kateryn. Lady Kateryn gave birth to a daughter, named after her godmother Princess Mary, on 30 August, and for a moment, all seemed well. But by 3 September, Kateryn had been overcome by puerperal fever, and was delirious, but not so far gone that she could not tell Seymour how angry she was at him for denying her treatment from the physician on the day of infant Mary's birth.[27] Seymour had rushed the doctor from Kateryn's room so he could see his new daughter, leaving Kateryn to feel she was denied care. Kateryn claimed Seymour laughed at her grief, that he wished her pain, and all said within earshot of Elizabeth Tyrwhitt, one of Kateryn's dearest friends.[28] By 5 September, Lady Kateryn was dead, slipping away while praying with Seymour and Lady Jane Grey.[29] Young Jane also stood in as chief mourner two days later, while Elizabeth was given the news of Kateryn's death by Kat Ashley. Ashley also reminded Elizabeth she could now have the husband that 'should have been hers' eighteen months earlier.[30] Elizabeth did not want to comfort Seymour with letters, but Kat Ashley did behind Elizabeth's back.

Lady Kateryn's death inspired Princess Elizabeth into action; she was fifteen and old enough to have her own household and live as an adult. Anthony Denny suggested Hatfield where Elizabeth spent much of her childhood, and Elizabeth, who had an income of 3,000l a year (£830,000 today) from her father's will, set up a household with between 120 to 140 people to serve her. Her movements were being watched by Thomas Seymour, who had his nephew John Seymour help Elizabeth's move to Hatfield.[31] John Seymour quietly asked Kat Ashley as they prepared a horse if Elizabeth's 'great buttocks were grown any less or no'. His uncle needed to know.[32] Meanwhile, Lady Jane Grey's parents pulled her from Seymour's household, only to change their minds once Seymour offered money and a story of how Seymour himself would become the powerful uncle by the king's side. Seymour started enquiring about gaining money to form an army; to marry Elizabeth, Seymour would have to defy his brother, the Lord Protector, and King Edward.

In the shadow of what was the Seymour brothers' feud coming to a head, Kat Ashley lied and travelled to London to discuss Elizabeth's potential marriage to Thomas Seymour, speaking with Lord Protector Edward Seymour and his wife Anne. Lady Anne was the highest-ranked woman in England after the princesses, and while Anne was gravely disliked, she was right to speak harshly to Ashley.[33] Lady Anne made it plain that it was an improper marriage for a princess, that Elizabeth was not suitable after the rumours of her behaviour, and that Ashley was a terrible governess for allowing such things to occur in Elizabeth's young life. This rebuke only made Kat Ashley speak even better of Thomas Seymour when she returned home.

With parliament in session in London, Princess Elizabeth wrote to Seymour in the hopes of dealing with a few business issues. Her cofferer Thomas Parry went to London with the letters, only to be sweet-talked by Seymour into revealing secrets about Elizabeth's household. Kat Ashley betrayed Elizabeth again, faking an injury to go to London for care, only to go to Seymour in hopes of arranging a marriage.[34] Elizabeth wrote to

Seymour, refuting marriage claims and refusing him a visit to Hatfield. Rumours had already started about how Seymour had kept Lady Kateryn's household together in preparation for a new bride.

Rumours, gossip, and suggestions of scandal lurked all over London. Seymour offered Elizabeth a stay at his Seymour Place home in London for Christmas. She refused and took to her sickbed at Hatfield instead,[35] and said she would not accept any marriage to anyone without council permission, as was law, but Seymour took that as a challenge to gain support. Before long, Seymour was arrested on a raft of charges including embezzlement, counterfeiting, wanting to secretly marry Elizabeth, and wanting control over King Edward. The feud between the Seymour brothers had grown so great one had to topple. Thomas Seymour had been acting strangely for weeks, so to suggest he was planning things such as kidnapping the king was not hard to believe. A botched break-in at the king's apartments on 16 January 1549 pointed straight at Seymour.[36] The fact a scrap of papers outlining parliamentary charges against Seymour was found at court before the event went ignored.[37] Lord Protector Seymour had won over his younger brother.

By 21 January 1549, Princess Elizabeth was questioned about her part in Seymour's attempted kidnapping of King Edward, as Seymour had planned to stop at Hatfield to pick up Elizabeth as his fiancé and ride north to 'safety'. Elizabeth and her servants looked like potential accomplices to the plan. Kat Ashley and Thomas Parry were arrested and later taken to the Tower. Elizabeth was placed under the watchful eye of those loyal to the Lord Protector and the late Lady Kateryn. Princess Elizabeth was repeatedly questioned and shown false evidence of wrongdoing, but she was too smart to fall for tricks, sitting on a throne that once belonged to her father to answer questions, and did not buckle under pressure. The Lord Protector wanted his brother convicted of treason and needed Elizabeth's proof of an upcoming marriage to seal the deal. She would not assist and wrote to Edward Seymour herself claiming her innocence.[38] More than a week of interrogation continued, with Robert Tyrwhitt, her chief interrogator, lying to her that Londoners believed Elizabeth was pregnant with Thomas Seymour's baby.

Thomas Parry cracked first in the Tower and admitted discussing marriage behind Elizabeth's back with Seymour, of how Seymour had been sneaking into Elizabeth's bedroom, and all the tales within the household over the years.[39] Kat Ashley folded a few days later, corroborating Parry's accounts of Seymour's attentions and desires for Elizabeth, and Ashley admitted she personally liked Thomas Seymour.[40] Parry and Ashley both knew Elizabeth would not marry Seymour unless the royal council instructed it, and the princess was forced to recall Seymour's outlandish behaviour toward her for the past several years, which formed the basis of the thirty-three charges against him. But Elizabeth, in her confessions and depositions would not condemn Seymour, Ashley, or Parry, and other witnesses never mentioned any collusion between the group. Seymour was condemned to death by attainder for treason, the charges a mixture of fact and hatred from his brother and beheaded on 20 March 1549. A tenuous source claimed Elizabeth replied to the news with, 'this day died a man of much wit and very little judgement'. Given all that occurred, Elizabeth would not have been far wrong.

Princess Elizabeth received Kat Ashley and Thomas Parry back into her household after their six months in the Tower, in time for Elizabeth's sixteenth birthday at Hatfield. Not long after, Lord Protector Edward Seymour was also deposed and imprisoned. By Christmas, Elizabeth was back at court with her little brother, greeted with the finest respect and triumph. The younger royal siblings reunited and both Seymour brothers were gone from court. Lady Jane Grey had also come through the difficult period unscathed and was reunited with her family.

Elizabeth recovered at Hatfield over the next few years of her brother's reign, mistress of her household and lifestyle, while King Edward quietly ruled without much interference, backed by John Dudley, Duke of Northumberland. Princess Elizabeth was considered 'an assured young woman' noted for her intelligence, and in August 1551, an Italian Duke wanted her hand, and soon after, a German prince, though her refusal to marry made all negotiations impossible. But her brother's illnesses through 1552 would have raised sincere concern, and when he caught yet another illness in January 1553, a lung infection, there had to be pause for thought. Elizabeth was not permitted to see her little brother as he slowly succumbed to illness and changed the Succession Act to give the crown to Lady Jane Grey. The powerful Dudley family, which Lady Jane had just married into, were all on Jane's side, including Elizabeth's friend and one-time classmate Robert Dudley, who rallied men to Lady Jane's cause. Elizabeth needed to be especially careful about who she supported as England finally received its first Queen Regnant.

Conclusion

Triumph of the True Queens

A lifestyle with happy sisters had beckoned for Mary and Elizabeth after the death of their father. In her father's will, Princess Mary was well provided for, with Beaulieu in Essex, Kenninghall in Norfolk, Hunsdon in Hertfordshire, and the stronghold of Tattershall in Lincolnshire. She made a yearly income of 3,4891 (£960,000 today) from her lands and was finally free to live life as an adult running her households. Her brother King Edward was carefully guarded by Edward Seymour, and the entire council around the boy king was determined to ensure the Reformation moved decisively through England, leaving Mary isolated as a Catholic. Princess Mary spent all of 1547 living quietly at Beaulieu, before returning to court for Christmas to see Edward and Elizabeth together.

Princess Mary suffered from grief after her father's death, regularly falling ill, and moved quietly between her huge estates in relative peace, unaware of her little sister's troubles with Lady Kateryn and Thomas Seymour. Mary stood as proxy godmother to Kateryn's baby daughter, who soon found herself an orphan after the death of her mother, and her father beheaded seven months later. The child was named after Princess Mary, yet Mary took no part in raising the girl, who died around the age of two.[1] Without it being stated, the princesses were kept apart, Elizabeth watched due to the Thomas Seymour affair, and Mary was considered suspicious as a Catholic. Her younger siblings celebrated Christmas together without Mary in December 1549, but in 1550, religious matters came to a head. Mary would not conform to the new religion despite heavy warnings from her little brother, yet the 1549 Act of Uniformity meant everyone in England had to submit to the new religion. Thomas Cranmer's new *Book of Common Prayer* was compulsory for prayer and worship. Princess Mary had written from Kenninghall to King Edward's council in July 1549 on the matter of religion, and rumoured treaties for Mary to marry Luís of Portugal soon began, so she could leave England. All came to nothing, and in early 1550, Emperor Charles was sought on the matter of Mary marrying Albert, Marquess of Brandenburg, another fruitless endeavour. Mary appealed to her cousin Emperor Charles to assist her in matters of religion, and a plan was formed for her to escape England, though it proved impossible.[2] Mary remained at Beaulieu in 1550 after being denied a request to see her brother at Windsor or Oaking. But Mary attended the New Year court festivities with her brother and sister, with Edward and Mary having a blazing argument over religion, leaving them both in tears.[3] A few months later, Edward and Mary met alone to discuss religion as Mary still refused to recant her Catholic faith. As time passed, Mary remained at Beaulieu, hearing her Catholic masses more discreetly, and things calmed between the king and his eldest sister.

In 1552, King Edward's health declined with smallpox and measles, and Mary travelled to visit her brother at Greenwich in June 1552, just before his summer progress. Letters between the pair remained cordial, and Mary visited again in January 1553 at Westminster, just as Edward again fell ill. Many of the nobles at court looked to Princess Mary as the 'rising sun' rather than the old spinster hidden away on big estates. Mary remained at Beaulieu, thirty-seven miles from London, while her brother suffered from his lung infection, and wrote to Edward in May after hearing of his recovery, the final happy conversation between the pair. Edward soon went into a sharp decline and Mary moved to her home at Hunsdon close to London where word came her brother passed away on 6 July 1553.

Finally, the moment Mary's extended childhood, stunted adulthood, and all her struggles had waited for; she was Queen of England. But to discover her brother had renounced their father's Succession Act and given the throne to their cousin Lady Jane Grey would have been a stab to Mary's heart. She fled Hunsdon for her stronghold at Kenninghall in Norfolk, and soon an army of 30,000 rallied to her cause.[4] It was only a week before the weak men of the court began to crumble in the face of Princess Mary and her supporters, and on 19 July, Mary was publicly proclaimed queen.[5] Mary rode into London on 3 August 1553 with her sister Princess Elizabeth and Duchess Anna of Cleves, 800 nobles and 10,000 horsemen at their backs, with the country ready to accept Henry VIII and Queen Katharine of Aragon's daughter as their ruler at last.

It would have been a fine ending for the tale, that after decades of striving for a son, the daughter who was raised to be a queen and treated, respected, educated, and prepared as a ruler, defied the odds and took the throne as the first successful female leader of England. If only it had been that simple. England was not a country desperate for Catholic reform; while King Edward had been fanatical as a Protestant, and the population had eased into his reforms after decades of Henry VIII's whimsical leanings, there was no desperation to now wind back the clock. That was what Mary wanted, a

Catholic world like her mother had ruled over, to restore the monasteries, the masses, the clergy, and the idolatry of her parents' early reign. This resulted in men and women of all ranks exiling themselves to Europe for their safety, while leading reformist leaders, including Archbishop Thomas Cranmer were locked away. Royal councillors initially supported Lady Jane Grey as queen, so Mary released Bishop Stephen Gardiner and Thomas Howard, Duke of Norfolk from the Tower after spending King Edward's entire reign locked away, to be at her side. Crowned on 1 October by Gardiner, Queen Mary had much work to do. She wanted to re-establish links with Spain, like the good old days of her mother's reign, and within a year of Edward's death, Mary married the much younger Prince Philip of Spain, the son of Mary's long-time betrothed, and cousin, Emperor Charles. Even the Catholics at court and in parliament hated the marriage. Thomas Wyatt the Younger led a rebellion to topple Queen Mary and put Elizabeth on the throne, leading to executions when Mary defeated them all. Though innocent, Princess Elizabeth remained in the Tower for months as she was the inspiration for the rebellion. The Dudley family, who had tried to put Lady Jane Grey on the throne, were also executed or imprisoned the same year. Princess Elizabeth was able to reconnect with Robert Dudley, who was in the Tower at the same time as her imprisonment. He was almost the sole survivor of his family and the Protestant faction at court. Catholic Anna of Cleves was even considered suspicious as a highly ranked noblewoman, with a Lutheran brother, and a friendship with Princess Elizabeth. Mary and Anna's long-term friendship would never recover. Elizabeth was later banished to Woodstock Palace under house arrest, but the relationship between the sisters had completely broken down. They had been made rivals from their birth thanks to the behaviour of their father, and years of trying to reconcile were destroyed again by the men of the royal court. By this time, both the women were adults and had very little in common.

In September 1554, Queen Mary thought she was finally pregnant at thirty-eight, the same age her mother, aunts and grandmother had all entered early menopause. Princess Elizabeth reunited with her sister in time for the birth in May 1555. But no baby ever came, Mary was sick but never pregnant, an embarrassing situation not unlike her mother's first pregnancy. At home and abroad, England looked weak; after Princess Elizabeth, the next heir to the throne was Mary, Queen of Scots, who was betrothed to the new dauphin of France. Horrific burnings continued around the country as Queen Mary had 284 scholars, tutors, intellectuals, clergy and ordinary men and women killed for reformist heresy, including Thomas Cranmer, Hugh Latimer, Nicholas Ridley, John Rogers and John Bradford. The reformers who had caused so much heartache for Katharine of Aragon when her marriage was annulled had to pay the price under Queen Mary's reign. At Queen Mary's side, she had the most fervent Catholics, her Archbishop of Canterbury was Cardinal Reginald Pole, son of Mary's executed governess Lady Margaret Pole, Countess of Salisbury. She also had Bishop Edmund Bonner, the man who happily organised burnings, and scholar John Foxe wrote of him, 'this cannibal in three years space three hundred martyrs' slew, they were his food, he loved so blood, he spared none he knew.'

For the everyday people in Queen Mary's England, her religious changes were largely well accepted, and people were happy to have her as their leader. But successive years of wet weather destroyed crops and led to a widespread struggle. Trade with the Low Countries was suffering, and the powerful Italian merchants of London were gone, chased out by King Edward's Reformation. England's currency was debased under Edward and Mary, leaving people under pressure. But Mary's marriage to a Spaniard did not help her cause. Queen Mary remained separated from her husband as he managed his own countries while she tended to hers. King Philip made a Spanish treaty with France, and while Spain benefitted from their destruction of the Americas, England had nothing. A coup against Queen Mary in France was put down, but hardship remained. When King Philip returned to Mary in 1557 to consider a war against France, Mary thought herself pregnant at last. The baby, due March 1558, to be born in a confinement given to many Tudor queens before her, never came, another phantom pregnancy, all part of Mary's desperation to give England a Catholic male heir. Like her mother before her, Queen Mary could not produce a male heir.

England had been at war during Mary's pregnancy after rebels in France backed Yorkist cousin Thomas Stafford's weak claim to the English crown. As a result, Mary sent forces into France, hurting her alliance with the Pope, one she had strived to repair and maintain. As a result of the fighting, England lost Calais, England's last European city. Queen Mary's final months were laced with grief, loss, and humiliation, her people hungry, and filled with anti-Catholic and anti-Spanish sentiment. She died on 17 November 1558 at St James' Palace, aged only forty-two, but had finally accepted Princess Elizabeth as her heir-apparent. It was only after her death that stories of Mary's cruelty began to surface, and decades before the expression 'Bloody Mary' began to be used. Misogyny has stained Mary's reign as one of cruelty, and she undoubtedly treated reformers harshly, but the idea of the country darkened by fear for five years is the stuff of historians who could not handle a Queen Regnant.

Princess Elizabeth was born only as a consequence of her father's greed and desire, only to be put quietly aside, never considered for any such key role, as if she only served to be forgotten. This extreme lack of foresight led Princess Elizabeth to struggle for recognition under her father, her brother, and her sister. King Edward was the only Tudor monarch born to rule, even his father did not have that claim. Yet greedy men slid in and controlled the motherless boy, a child only loved as a symbol, never a person. The boy was never loved by his father, and never truly close to anyone in his lifetime. Lives were lost before and after Edward rested in Henry VIII's indulgent nursery, only for the child to never really live. The wounds of the royal children inflicted by their father could never truly heal.

But Princess Elizabeth had maintained a level of quiet popularity among reformers through her sister's reign, and King Philip, Mary's husband, saw the value in Elizabeth as her heir. Elizabeth began preparing to be queen at Hatfield after Queen Mary's second false pregnancy, and international ambassadors already looked to her. Philip himself offered to marry Elizabeth after Mary died, yet another foolish suggestion. The Duke of Savoy had been suggested as a husband for Elizabeth under Mary's reign, while Mary's advisors battled each other over whether Elizabeth needed to be put on trial for rebellion and being a reformer. It was at Hatfield that Elizabeth learned of her sister's death on 17 November 1558. By then, she was ready to meet with the men who would serve her in London, among them Robert Dudley, who had worked for Mary's husband Philip for several years. Queen Elizabeth was only twenty-five when she ascended to the throne at Westminster Abbey, but her years growing up in the households of King Henry, and life under Edward and Mary, would have felt like a trial by combat. Queen Elizabeth was more prepared to rule than any Tudor who came before her. She would love, hate, give and receive loyalty, be entertained and flattered, and she considered many suitors, but above all, she ruled for almost forty years. No husband, no scandal, no religion, no one man could overshadow England's greatest age.

Epilogue

The Illegitimate Children of Henry VIII

While battling for legitimate heirs, it is possible King Henry VIII had a volley of illegitimate children. Most men and many women had at least one child born out of wedlock; it was simply a reality of the age. Some men rumoured to be the king's sons made outlandish claims, while some simply never made any claim whatsoever. Bessie Blount's daughter Elizabeth Tailboys never claimed to be the king's daughter, despite the fact her brother Henry Fitzroy certainly was of royal blood, and there was no clear alternative as Elizabeth's father. She lived a life deeply favoured by Queen Elizabeth, without complaint or demand. King Henry VIII may have had too many wives, and probably too many mistresses, but he was clear; love and legitimate children were the only things he desperately craved.

Catherine and Henry Carey

Of the handful of illegitimate children ascribed to King Henry's name, Catherine Carey holds the greatest claim. Yet even then, the story of her parentage is as flimsy as the evidence for King Henry's involvement with Catherine's mother.

Mary Boleyn is well-known as a mistress to the king; a tale so often told it gives rise to its own common myths and tropes. But had Henry never taken a shine to Anne Boleyn, the affair between the monarch and the eldest Boleyn sister would be unknown. Mary Boleyn's early life was like her sister's; sent abroad and came of age in France working in a queen's chamber, only to be recalled to England when her father found a suitable husband for his girl. In Mary's case, she was married to William Carey in February 1520. Carey was a similar rank to the Boleyns; well-placed but not exactly important and had a claim to greatness by being related to Edward III, like everyone in the royal court. Carey and Mary attended the Field of Cloth of Gold, another 'achievement' claimed by everyone in royal service in the period, and only once ever again were Mary Boleyn and King Henry recorded in the same place.

In a tale which has all the makings of a dreamy and unbelievable love story, Mary Boleyn possibly played the role of Kindness in a pageant named The Assault on the Castle of Virtue.[1] Henry was among the men who stormed the 'castle' of virtuous women, offering 'fruits made for pleasure'. The theory states while Henry fluttered his eyelashes at Mary Boleyn, Anne Boleyn was busy fluttering hers at Henry Percy, despite books and films suggesting different options.

While the pageant was real, whether Henry began an affair with Mary Boleyn at all has zero basis in fact, save for one comment made by Henry a decade later when accused of sleeping with Mary Boleyn and her mother Elizabeth. Henry refused the idea of sleeping with Elizabeth Boleyn, and Thomas Cromwell stepped in and denied an affair between Henry and Mary Boleyn.[2] Interestingly, an affinity between the Boleyn sisters could have been used as evidence King Henry could not marry Anne Boleyn. Henry did ask for dispensations in the matter of his annulment, but Mary Boleyn was not mentioned. Katherine of Aragon never argued Henry's affair with Mary Boleyn was why he could not marry Anne Boleyn. These facts alone place doubt on any meaningful affair between the two.

It is entirely possible Henry saw young Mary Boleyn in the years before this soap-like pageant and had an encounter with her, as he had been forced to relinquish Bessie Blount after she gave birth to the king's confirmed son and unconfirmed daughter. Many theories on how Henry and Mary met up for their trysts are based entirely on hearsay and fiction, with no evidence ever discovered. William Carey was rewarded with lands and titles in the summer of 1522, and Sir Thomas Boleyn was also promoted to Treasurer of the Household, a sign of the affair in full swing. However, Boleyn had been at court for years and deserved such elevations, and Carey was given gifts worthy of any man of the privy chamber. Nothing is certain.

What is certain was by early 1524, Mary Boleyn gave birth to Catherine, named after the queen, who could have been her godmother. By this time, Mary was in her mid-twenties, beautiful and possibly capable of making Henry happy, at least on an occasional basis. But she was married, and naturally, baby Catherine was attributed to William Carey, and despite later slander, no one at the time suspected auburn-haired Catherine to be the king's daughter. Catherine Carey's birth came at a time when King Henry was increasingly anxious about the royal succession, and the birth of auburn-haired Henry Carey, likely in early 1526, only made things more complicated.

Catherine and her brother Henry likely lived with their parents during their early years; William Carey was granted the borough of Buckingham in February 1526, in a specific entail that stipulated the land could only be inherited by all 'lawfully begotten' heirs. By this time, Mary and King Henry had likely given up any potential relationship. Life for young Catherine Carey was like any of the period, until the sweating sickness outbreak, when William Carey suddenly died on 22 June 1528.[3] Carey had not done as well as a man sharing his wife with a king could expect, leaving a string of debts. Catherine probably stayed with her mother Mary after Carey's death, while Henry Carey went to live in Anne Boleyn's care, now she was the Boleyn in the king's affections.

Despite the Boleyn family's standing, Catherine Carey's early life is a mystery. Young when her aunt was queen, her movements and life go unrecorded, though when her mother Mary married William Stafford and fell pregnant in 1534, Catherine likely lived either in Calais, where soldier Stafford was stationed or at the various estates in Staffordshire owned by Stafford's noble father. Mary and her new husband were quiet during the execution of Anne Boleyn, but in late 1539, Thomas Cromwell, who was mindful Mary Boleyn had now lost her whole family to either illness or execution, invited her and young Catherine to court to meet Anna of Cleves.[4] Husband William Stafford went into royal service as gentleman-pensioner of the Spears. Mary Boleyn did not stay long at court; Henry did not need reminders of his past close by, but Catherine was given a place in Anna of Cleves' household at court, as short-lived as it would be. Catherine used the time wisely; by 26 April 1540, sixteen-year-old Catherine married Francis Knollys, who had also been drafted into the gentlemen-pensioners. Marrying Catherine, the first cousin to Princess Elizabeth, and possibly her half-sister, was a coup for a man with only minor estates who had followed his knighted father into royal service.

Staying at court, Catherine transferred to new Queen Katheryn Howard's household in late 1540, only to leave and embark on a family Henry VIII could have only dreamed of – sixteen children born over twenty-two years. After the marriage, an act of parliament ensured Francis Knollys' lands were jointly in Catherine's name, and soon after, Mary Knollys was born. A year later came Henry Knollys, likely named after the king, the same year Francis Knollys entered the House of Commons. Mary Boleyn sadly died in obscurity in 1543, with any Stafford-born children also lost. But Catherine's husband and her stepfather Stafford remained in Henry VIII's service until he died in early 1547. By this time, Catherine had also given birth to Lettice, William, and Edward, and lived between their estates at Rotherfield Greys in Oxfordshire and Reading in Berkshire when not in London.[5]

Being married to a staunch Protestant, Catherine was well-placed when Edward VI took the throne, even if he had no interest in suggestions the Boleyn daughter may have been his half-sister. Francis Knollys did well, being knighted in 1547 for his work against Scotland, aided William Cecil in religious changes, and by the time King Edward died in 1553, was already well-endowed with lands and estates. These came in useful, as Robert, Richard, Elizabeth, Maud, Thomas, and Francis the younger had been born to Catherine, many with the rich auburn hair of the Tudors. But darker times soon befell Catherine as her alleged half-sister Queen Mary took the throne, leaving Protestants like herself at Mary's mercy. Would Queen Mary have known the rumours of Catherine's parentage? Almost certainly, as rumours of her existence, and that of her brother had been used to slander the Boleyn family. Princess Elizabeth, who had always maintained good relationships with her Boleyn relatives, stood in an ever-more dangerous situation and wrote to Catherine just before she, Francis and their children left England for the safety of Germany. Elizabeth wrote to Catherine:

> 'The length of time, and distance of place, separate not the love of friends, nor deprives not the show of goodwill ... I am driven by a need to write farewell, it is which in the sense one way I wish, the other way I grieve. Your loving cousin and ready friend, Cor Rotto (broken heart)'[6]

Catherine and Francis Knollys needed to relocate to Frankfurt, despite trying to see out their time in England. This period of instability gave Catherine a break from childbirth; she had given birth every year since she had married, so unless unfortunate miscarriages occurred, she was likely apart from her husband at times, before giving birth to Anne in 1555. Catherine then joined Francis in Germany, taking only five of her children, forced to leave the rest behind, probably at Rotherfield Greys.

Catherine's husband Francis did well among the Protestants in Germany, and they relocated to Strasbourg in 1557, before returning to England on the death of Queen Mary in November 1558. The following month, Catherine moved into Queen Elizabeth's household as Chief Lady of the Bedchamber, Elizabeth's most senior lady-in-waiting.[7] Catherine was in the shadow of power in England, and yet neither she nor her husband ever suggested Catherine was any more than Elizabeth's cousin. Francis was soon admitted to the Privy Council as Queen Elizabeth took power, reuniting the enormous Knollys family in England at last.

As soon as Catherine was safe back in England with her husband at court, the yearly pregnancies returned, with daughters born in successive years, Catherine, Cecily, Margaret, and then Dudley Knollys, though Dudley did not survive long after birth. Thankfully, Catherine was never again recorded as pregnant, though her remaining surviving portrait shows her pregnant, likely with Dudley. Flemish painter Steven van der Meulen, favoured at court by Queen Elizabeth, painted both Catherine and her brother during this period, as they enjoyed wide approval from their cousin Elizabeth. Their comfortable and favoured lives continued in relative peace throughout the 1560s with Catherine as head of Elizabeth's chamber, but she fell ill and died on 15 January 1569 at Hampton Court Palace.

But Catherine was certainly not forgotten. All her sons entered parliament, married into the nobility and were wealthy with lands around England and in Flanders. Catherine had sadly lost four daughters by the time of her demise, but her other five daughters all married in noble houses, and three moved into the privy chamber of Queen Elizabeth, all strikingly beautiful women with flaming Tudor hair. Elizabeth Knollys married Puritan Sir Thomas Leighton, though spent her time working in the Queen's bedchamber. Anne Knollys married Sir Thomas West, Baron de la Warr, and despite working at court, managed to have fourteen children. But it was Catherine's daughter Lettice who would be most remembered, eclipsing even her mother, despite Catherine being the daughter of a Boleyn and possibly the king. Lettice was only fifteen when Elizabeth took the throne, a decade younger than the queen, and the resemblance between the two women is irrefutable. Lettice was soon married off to Walter Devereux, who would later become Earl of Essex. Two children followed, and when Lettice visited her cousin, Queen Elizabeth, in 1565, visibly pregnant for the third time, she was seen flirting with Robert Dudley, Queen Elizabeth's favourite.[8] The romance between Lettice and Dudley had sparked, and furious Elizabeth sent Lettice away. All was fine for several years, until Lettice saw her husband leave on a two-year mission to Ireland, and embarked on an affair with Dudley, with rumours of bastard children to add to the six she had with Devereaux.[9] Within two years of Deveraux's death in Ireland, Lettice Knollys and Robert Dudley were married in secret; he had famously refused marriage for over a decade in the hope of Queen Elizabeth changed her mind about him, but then married the younger, prettier version of the queen.[10] Queen Elizabeth never forgave Lettice for her marriage, and when Lettice's child to Dudley passed away, Elizabeth cared none. Robert Dudley died in 1588 with his wife grieving at his side, and Elizabeth grieving in private.[11] Lettice quickly married one of Dudley's servants and did not see Elizabeth until 1599, their feud not quelled by time. In 1601, Queen Elizabeth executed Lettice's third husband Christopher Blount, and her son Robert Devereux, Earl of Essex (who had been the new favourite of the queen), when they attempted a coup.[12] Lettice spent the rest of her life, another thirty-three years, largely alone, but the family continued, with the blood of Catherine Carey, Mary Boleyn, and possibly Henry VIII, remaining in noble power.

Henry Carey, born on 4 March 1526, had a similarly obscure upbringing as his sister Catherine. He likely lived with his family until his father's death in 1528 and became a ward of Anne Boleyn, who placed him in a Cistercian monastery to be educated. He did benefit from the tutoring of French scholar Nicholas Bourbon in 1535, but other than that, his life goes unrecorded.[13] As all monasteries were closed by 1540, Henry Carey could have been placed in any number of households, possibly even Princess Elizabeth's. He was not forgotten; his sister was a noblewoman, and in 1545, he married Anne Morgan, granddaughter of Blanche Milbourne, Lady Troy, one of Princess Elizabeth's early governesses. His wife's aunt, Blanche Parry, also spent time serving Princess Elizabeth. Jane Calthorpe and Anne Shelton were both sisters to Thomas Boleyn, and Henry Carey being in the same household as Princess Elizabeth and her aunts is not an unreasonable suggestion. Despite the pedigree the Carey household had through their Beaufort/Spencer lineage (William Carey's aunt was Countess of Northumberland), it seems as if the Carey family quickly forgot Henry and his sister Catherine after William Carey's death. These details only fuel speculation about their true parentage.

Henry Carey was selected for parliament in 1547 under King Edward and again in 1554-5 under Queen Mary, suggesting he had moderate religious views and obeyed the constantly changing religious rules. As soon as Elizabeth became queen in November 1558, she knighted her cousin Henry Carey and made him a baron after her coronation a few months later.[14] Elizabeth gave Carey her manor at Hunsdon, which had been a home belonging to Queen Mary only months earlier, and where Elizabeth (and possibly Henry Carey himself) spent much time growing up. Carey also gained lands in multiple locations, a pension, a court role, and became a Knight of the Garter. They clearly knew each other very well. Whether Elizabeth thought him her cousin or her brother mattered none; as a Boleyn, he was as favoured as his sister. Decade after decade, Carey served his queen, including facing off against rebellions and possible invasions of England. His wife Anne gave him thirteen children, with illegitimate children also born to Carey through the years, including in 1587, when his mistress, fifty years his junior, gave him a son named Henry, and the Italian mistress was married off to a cousin. By this time, Carey was Queen Elizabeth's Lord Chamberlain and started a group called the Lord Chamberlain's men, who included William Shakespeare. But Henry Carey fell ill in July 1596 and died at Somerset House on The Strand in London, which had once belonged to the Seymours, the great rivals for Henry VIII's affections against the Boleyns. Queen Elizabeth offered Henry Carey the earldom of Ormond on his deathbed, a title once belonging to their shared grandfather Thomas Boleyn, but Carey declined.

The families of Catherine and Henry Carey ensured the family line with dozens of children. Whether they secretly carried on Henry VIII's bloodline, while his legitimate children could not, is entirely a matter of conjecture. Even if the rumours were untrue, the Carey children and grandchildren had strikingly similar looks to Queen Elizabeth, so perhaps it was the Boleyn genes that prevailed over the Tudors. After all, it is not a descendant of Henry VIII who sits on the English throne today, but a descendant of Mary Boleyn, in King Charles III.

Etheldreda Malte

Among the women King Henry VIII is thought to have bedded, few stand out; but of those thought to have become pregnant, one was listed as a royal laundress. What did persist was the suggestion that Henry fathered a daughter named Etheldreda Malte. King Henry had his pick of women at court and had no reason to keep his indiscretions and choices a secret. So why did Etheldreda's mother's name get lost among the bevvy of women unfortunately remembered as royal mistresses? A daughter born to a laundress would have been forgotten, and yet the baby of this rumoured affair instead lived her life in the orbit of her supposed half-sister Queen Elizabeth.

The window between 1525-1535 is littered with supposed affairs between King Henry and 'forgettable' women, among them Joan (or Jane or Joanna) Dingley alias Dobson. Dingley was a common name at court among the lesser-ranked members right through to those working in the privy chamber. Sir John Moore, from the merchant hub of Dunclent (also spelt Dunkelyn, Douklin or Dobson) in Worcestershire,[15] had a daughter named Joan (or Jane), who married James Dingley at a young age in the mid-1520s, but James died soon after.[16] Later rumours claimed Joan 'met' King Henry, and Etheldreda (or Audrey) was born in the late 1520s, and the Moore and Dingley families remained working quietly at court.

Joan Dingley remarried to Michael Ashfield in the 1530s and they lived at Farmington Manor, within the grounds of Gloucester Abbey prior to its dissolution, and Ashfield's death, in 1539.[17] Etheldreda likely lived with her mother during these years, and Joan's third husband, Thomas Parker of Northleach Manor, also at Gloucester Abbey, left Etheldreda land in his will in 1546.[18] Joan had several young sons with Parker before 1546, but Etheldreda was unusually given land and holdings of her own accord. The land was possibly dissolved monastery lands Joan gained in 1539, no small task for a widow.

A man of a similar social standing as Joan Dingley was John Malte, the king's tailor. By 1530, Malte was doing well in the king's household, and by the mid-1540s had been lavished with manors and lands far beyond what a servant could expect, earning thousands from the leases granted to him while he designed, created, and finished King Henry's attire. But in January 1547, as Henry was aware of his failing health, he finalised a 1,312l 12d (over £550,000 today) gift of lands, manors, and livestock to 'John and Etheldred Malte, alias Dyngley, bastard daughter of the said John Malte and Joan Dyngley alias Dobson'.[19] Someone had finally claimed the parentage of Etheldreda. The fine lands and grants were for Etheldreda and her heirs, not for Malte's sons. Malte also created his own will, bestowing lands in Berkshire, Hertfordshire, and Somerset on 'Audrey, bastard daughter of Joan Dingley, wife of Dobson', making her an heiress worthy of a good husband. King Henry had ordered Malte to ensure Etheldreda's education, and she was also betrothed to Sir Richard Southwell, but she soon married Sir John Harington of Stepney, an attendant of Sir Thomas Seymour.

Harington, a notable poet and a Gentleman of the King's Chapel under Henry VIII, told his son of the days he sang directly for King Henry in his youth and lived in Thomas Seymour's household as early as 1546.[20] Etheldreda was likely beautiful like the other girls rumoured to be Henry's illegitimate daughters, and being well-married to an heiress was a triumph for the poet Harington. But the couple spent much of their lives apart, with Harington in Seymour's household, though his wife Etheldreda was possibly already living in Princess Elizabeth and Lady Jane Grey's households. Harington was imprisoned in the Tower with Seymour in 1549, and refused all notion of Seymour's wrongdoing, despite being able to return home if he gave up Seymour's secrets. After Seymour's execution, Harington was set free, drafting a poem, the last line reading, '(Seymour's) blood was split, guiltless, and without just cause'.

After being released from the Tower, Harington worked for the Grey family while Etheldreda continued serving Princess Elizabeth. The couple had a daughter named Hester (or Esther) in 1553, but the relationship had soured by this time.[21] Harington had already fallen for Isabella Markham, who worked alongside Etheldreda as one of Princess Elizabeth's ladies. Harington was imprisoned again in 1553 for conspiring with his new master Sir John Grey, and again in 1554 during Wyatt's Rebellion. Princess Elizabeth was kept in the Tower at the same time, and Etheldreda was one of the six ladies supporting her supposed half-sister in prison.[22] This shows that Etheldreda was one of Elizabeth's closest and most trusted ladies. Despite their long associations with noble families, neither Etheldreda nor her husband ever supported anyone except Princess Elizabeth, not even Lady Jane Grey.

If Etheldreda was a child of Henry VIII, Queen Mary had no interest in maintaining relationships; Etheldreda's name was barely mentioned again, aside from notes on leases across her vast landholdings in the 1550s. Etheldreda survived the rest of Mary's reign unscathed, and attended Queen Elizabeth's coronation in early 1559, only to die only a few months later.[23] Harington waited just two months before marrying Isabella Markham, and through a series of messy legal changes, Etheldreda's daughter Hester Harington inherited nothing of her mother's vast estates, except for Watchfield Manor in then-Berkshire. Hester's much younger half-brother, also named Sir John Harington (born to Isabella Markham), inherited everything from his father and was one of Queen Elizabeth's loyal godsons. Harington the younger remained popular with Elizabeth, despite constantly falling out with many over his 'risqué' poetry and went on to invent the flush toilet. Hester married William Stubbs MP, a lawyer in Sir Francis Walsingham's office. They likely married in the early 1570s, and Hester lived until 1639 aged almost ninety, giving birth to at least six children, with three daughters living into adulthood.

Etheldreda never had any early connections to bring her into royal circles, and had John Malte been her real father, she would have come to nothing. The Harington family believed Etheldreda an illegitimate child of the king, and never made any attempt to hide her connections. Portraits of Etheldreda and Hester were sold at Sotheby's in 1942, but there are no public descriptions of their likeness. While they were listed as Holbein portraits, this is unlikely given the dates. Holbein possibly painted Etheldreda, in a three-quarter length portrait in her youth, and an artist following Holbein's style painted Hester, wearing a brown dress and holding a book, in later decades. At the time of her death, Etheldreda's main residence was St Catherine's Court, which had been part of Bath Abbey before the Dissolution of the Monasteries. Records in St Catherine's Church next to the priory reads that it was seized by King Henry VIII who 'granted it to a servant John Mawlt, taylor, and his bastard daughter Etheldred alias Dingley.' While it seems farfetched that King Henry took prime real estate and gave it to his servant's illegitimate daughter, there will also never be any further evidence Henry quietly supported his daughter.

John Perrot

Many men claimed to be illegitimate sons of Henry VIII, for assorted reasons. As with claims made by others through the centuries, the information is impossible to verify, just assertions made by bold men in return for favour or protection. One such case is John Perrot.

Perrot was born in the second week of November 1528, likely at Haroldston manor in Pembrokeshire, Wales.[24] Perrot's mother was Mary Berkeley of Thornbury, Gloucestershire, daughter of Thomas Berkeley and Susan FitzAlan. Mary Berkeley lived as a ward with her uncle Maurice Baron Berkeley, alongside another ward Thomas Perrot, son of Sir Thomas Perrot and Lady Katherine Poyntz. Because Mary Berkeley is often mistaken as Maurice Berkeley's daughter or granddaughter, the waters are instantly muddied as to the lineage of her children. Fellow wards John and Mary married at a noticeably young age and lived in Pembrokeshire, with their daughters Jane and Elizabeth when baby John was born in 1528. Assertions have been made that Mary Berkeley was a lady-in-waiting to Katherine of Aragon, yet there is no evidence to prove this. The Berkeley/FitzAlan families were prestigious and well-connected families in England and Ireland, while the Perrot men fought at the Battle of Flodden and were wealthy Welsh landowners. It is not impossible to suggest young Mary Berkeley, only around fifteen when she had her first child in 1526, could have been at the royal court. But without evidence, it cannot be taken as fact.

John Perrot was educated at St David's in Pembrokeshire, the burial place of Edmund Tudor, King Henry VII's father, and at sixteen, joined the household of William Paulet, 1st Marquess of Winchester's household in approximately 1544. In Henry VIII's final years, Paulet was Lord Chamberlain and Lord Steward of the Household, so Perrot would have been at court, perhaps able to meet the king. Perrot was found brawling with two Yeoman of the Guard at one of King Henry's palaces, but rather than being punished, the tall, athletic, auburn-haired young man went free.[25] Just one month after Edward VI took the throne, John Perrot received a knighthood and a placement at court. Sir John Perrot soon married Anne Cheyney, daughter of Sir Thomas and Lady Frideswide Cheyney, and soon had a son, Thomas.[26] As the sole male heir of Thomas Perrot, John inherited lands and power in Pembrokeshire, Wales, being elected High Sherriff of the area in 1551, and soon moved into William Parr, Marquess of Northampton's retinue as an ambassador to France. French King Henri was impressed with Perrot's hunting abilities during an embassy in 1551 and paid Perrot handsomely when he returned to England. He needed the money; John was upwards of 8,000l in debt (more than £2,000,000 today), from which King Edward pledged to save him, but Edward's death combined with losing his wife saw Perrot withdraw from court life.[27]

There was no room for rumoured illegitimate children during Queen Mary's reign. John Perrot remained on his estates in Wales, hiding 'heretics' from Catholic enforcers, but was denounced and sentenced to time in Fleet Prison for his crimes.[28] One of his hidden reformers was his uncle Robert Perrot, who had once been a Greek tutor for Edward VI. Perrot's stay at Fleet was brief, given a reprieve and offered a position hunting out other heretics in Wales, but he instead exiled himself to France and joined the Welsh Earl of Pembroke in the battle of Saint-Quentin in 1557 when Queen Mary's men faced off against French agitators. Saint-Quentin was one of the few English victories on the continent.

At the rise of Queen Elizabeth, John Perrot was one of only four men selected to carry Elizabeth's canopy of estate at the coronation, an incredible honour for a man with no noble pedigree. Perrot then received Carew Castle and the lordship of the sea and navy defence of south Wales, followed by being an MP for various regions over the next three decades. If Queen Elizabeth did suspect him of being an illegitimate royal son, she was wise to keep him close and compliant. Perrot soon remarried to Jane Prust, and they quickly had three children, William, Anne, and Lettice.[29] While rumours of John Perrot's parentage were 'widely known', whether that was true during his lifetime is without basis.

Sir John Perrot was known for his short temper, and that was put to the test when he was ordered to take up the post of Lord President of Munster in 1569, to bring the Irish region under English control. In response to the Desmond rebellions, Perrot arrived in Ireland in 1571 to face off against the powerful Geraldine dynasty. In one fight, Perrot hacked off the head of a slain Irishmen and put it on display at Kilmallock.[30] Perrot was foolish, expecting to win the rebellion by personal hand-to-hand combat against Geraldine dynasty leaders, and was ambushed in 1572, only to avoid death during a lucky escape. He resigned from his post in 1573 without permission and returned to Wales, soon becoming very unpopular with his erratic and greedy behaviour. Queen Elizabeth persisted with Perrot, naming him Lord Admiral of the Welsh waters, where he spent his time battling piracy between Wales, Ireland and occasionally the Low Countries, and he and his eldest son Thomas were faced with death on more than one occasion with their foolish endeavours chasing Spanish ships. Young Thomas Perrot was knighted in Ireland for his bravery but then thrown in Fleet Prison for his behaviour aboard captured ships. Once released, John Perrot had his son Thomas joust before Queen Elizabeth, where relationships were restored, only for the family to fall into disrepute again when Thomas Perrot secretly married Dorothy Devereaux. Dorothy was the stepdaughter of Robert Dudley, who had just secretly married Lettice Knollys and Thomas Perrot was briefly put back in Fleet Prison.[31] Sir John Perrot himself, by this time, had lost his second wife Jane but had his three other legitimate children and at least four illegitimate children to preside over.[32] Sir Thomas Perrot was released to fight in the Low Countries in 1586.

John Perrot, undeterred by his constant problems, convinced his supposed half-sister Elizabeth to give him another chance. The queen made him Lord Deputy of Ireland in 1584, resulting in four years of fighting, wins and losses, ill-thought campaigns, moderate submissions and truces, and delayed plantation and colonisation plans. After getting into drunken brawls with his own men, Queen Elizabeth recalled Perrot in January 1588, as she need to deal with the Spanish Armada.[33] Perrot removed himself to Wales but maintained links with Ireland, and once Elizabeth defeated the Spanish, Perrot was accused of treason in Ireland. Perrot was quoted as saying, 'God's death, will the Queen suffer her brother to be offered up as a sacrifice to the envy of his frisking adversaries?' The quote is tenuous, as Owen Hopton, who recorded the words, was not at the Tower at the time of Perrot's arrest.[34]

The treason case was flimsy, and Sir John Perrot was not sent to the Tower until 1592, where he rallied against his queen and alleged sister, saying, 'God's wounds, this it is to serve a base bastard pissing kitchen woman, if I had served any prince in Christendom I would have not been so dealt withal'. Perrot was found guilty and left in the Tower where he suddenly died in September 1592, where poisoning was suspected.[35] His son Sir Thomas Perrot died just two years later after a short illness, and it was Thomas' daughter Penelope and her husband Robert Naunton, who later recorded John Perrot's supposed claims of being Henry VIII's son. Other than their journals on the matter, no evidence exists. Despite all the drama of Perrot's life, all his children did surprisingly well for themselves, including his illegitimate son Sir James Perrot, who went on to become an MP and control much of Pembrokeshire, publish religious works, and become independently wealthy. While playing down the royal connections, Sir James Perrot's book on his father is still available today. Had John Perrot been a son of Henry VIII, he certainly inherited the bad temper and none of the wise counsel.

Thomas Stuckeley

In the mid-1520s King Henry VIII's affections were on the move. Despite the rumours of the king and the Boleyn sisters, many others were put forward as possible lovers of the king, one such lady being Jane Pollard. By 1525, Jane had married Sir Hugh Stukeley and was almost thirty years of age. Sir Hugh and Lady Jane had ten children, five sons and five daughters, however, with sketchy details, the birth order of the children is hard to judge. Their marriage went ahead around 1512, with their youngest son born in 1529. Thomas Stuckeley was roughly the middle child of this surprisingly healthy large family, with all ten children living until adulthood.[36] Jane Pollard herself was one of eleven children and had married well into a high-ranking family. Hugh Stukeley's father Sir Thomas was the eldest of seven, had been Knight of the Body to King Henry in 1516, and had inherited the vast glamourous estate of Affeton in Devonshire.[37] Sir Hugh and Lady Jane certainly had the family connections to move in royal circles, and Affeton was a home fine enough to host the king and many nobles, including the respected and beloved Courtenays. But how Jane could have come into contact with the king, even casually, is entirely unknown. Only rumours remain.

Jane's son Thomas Stuckeley entered the household of Charles Brandon, Duke of Suffolk in approximately 1543, at the age of eighteen, making Stuckeley's birth around 1525. He already had two uncles in Suffolk's household by this time, and Stukeley travelled with Suffolk to the French Battle of Boulogne in 1544. When Suffolk died in 1545, Stukeley spent time in the household of King Henry's advisor the Bishop of Exeter, and in 1547 on the death of King Henry, Stukeley was given the role of standard bearer for Boulogne, a role he held for three years. Boulogne was handed back to the French in 1550, and Stuckeley travelled home with Lord Protector Edward Seymour and remained in his household.[38] But he did not remain long, as in April 1551, Stuckeley travelled as part of an embassy to see King Henri in France, to discuss marriage between King Edward and

Henri's daughter Elisabeth of Valois. Stukeley is recorded at the French court, being 'made much of,' and another in the group was his alleged half-brother, John Perrot.[39] Stukeley soon returned home with the group, but when Edward Seymour fell into disgrace, Stukeley fled to France, fearing he would be pulled down in the scandal. But he returned a year later with a letter from King Henri to King Edward, saying 'most high and mighty prince, we most affectionately and heartily recommend you our good and dear friend Thomas Stukeley, an English gentleman, who during these wars had ever behaved himself well and valiantly in our service'.[40] King Henri went on to ask that Stukeley not be punished for leaving for France without permission.

But John Dudley, head of the royal court under King Edward, called on Stuckeley to answer accusations of spying as soon as he arrived. Stukeley claimed he came home to double-cross France on England's behalf, to give King Edward the news of a potential French invasion at Falmouth. Dudley and his secretary William Cecil did not buy the tale, and investigations found Stukeley had spent no time in France with King Henri. He was quickly thrown into the Tower, though suspicions about the French remained. King Edward had Stuckeley released in 1553, and Stukeley soon went to get a letter of recommendation from the newly crowned Queen Mary. Granted this letter, he headed to see the Duke of Savoy and then Emperor Charles in Brussels as part of the English embassy. Stuckeley remained in the Low Countries at the Emperor's court to avoid paying his debts in England, missing Wyatt's rebellion against Queen Mary. He then wrote to Mary again with lies, telling her that King Edward had promised to pay Stukeley's debts, as a favour. Mary believed Stukeley and gave him a pardon to return to England, with a six-month window to settle debts and not be arrested. Soon enough, Stukeley was back in trouble for using counterfeit money but had also married Anne Curtis, the sole heiress to her grandfather's wealthy merchant estate. Stuckeley ran up debts of up to 100l per day (£27,500 today) and then fled abroad to join the Duke of Savoy again. In 1557, they took part in the Battle of San-Quentin, Stukeley again alongside his alleged half-brother John Perrot. Despite the win in France, Stukeley returned to England to face piracy charges, though Queen Mary again had him pardoned.[41] Just as Queen Elizabeth took power, Stuckeley's wife finally inherited her father's estate, settling his money worries. He ingratiated himself with Elizabeth's favourite Robert Dudley, and lived in wealth and comfort, becoming the Captain of Berwick in the north in 1561 but spent winters in London. In 1562, Stukeley met with Queen Elizabeth and told her he would one day be a prince. Elizabeth played along, suggesting

Stuckeley write to her once he had his own principality. Elizabeth asked what language they would speak in once he had his success, and Stukeley replied, 'In the style of princes, our dearest sister'.[42]

Thomas Stukeley already had five small ships and wanted to create a colony in Florida, and Queen Elizabeth offered him a one-hundred-ton ship with one hundred men for the endeavour. After parading down the Thames and out to sea, Stuckeley spent time engaged in piracy against Flemish, French and Spanish ships off the Irish coast. Elizabeth was furious and he was arrested in Ireland, though his loyal friendships saved him from harsh punishment.[43] Stuckeley was put to work for the English rulers in Ireland for the next five years but was then imprisoned in 1569 for plotting with rebels and speaking harshly of Elizabeth, who had blocked his advancement several times. After release from prison in October 1569, rumours of him aiding the new Holy Roman Emperor Philip (husband of the late Queen Mary) in Ireland swirled, and he fled Ireland on a ship claiming to be heading to London but sailed for Lisbon. Emperor Philip invited Stuckeley to live in comfort in Madrid, styled as the Duke of Ireland.[44] A Spanish invasion of Ireland was to distract Queen Elizabeth from a potential Spanish invasion of England, and also to aid the Ridolfi plot, a plan to assassinate Elizabeth and replace her with Mary, Queen of Scots. Plans soon fell apart and Elizabeth defeated her former brother-in-law Emperor Philip and demanded Stuckeley leave Spain.

Without support, Stuckeley travelled to Rome and allied with Pope Pius, who gave him three ships to fight in the Battle of Lepaento, in which the Holy League defeated the Ottoman Empire. Stuckeley was welcomed back to Spain in 1572, living in Seville with a fleet of ships ready to dethrone Elizabeth, but delays beset the project. Stuckeley left Spain after enjoying 27,000 ducats from Emperor Philip and joined the new Pope Gregory in 1575, who planned to install his son as King of Ireland. Years of plans, infightings, spying and intrigue passed, and it was not until 1578 that Stuckeley left Rome with 4,000 men, stopping in Cadiz to gather more men and sailing onto Lisbon. But the King of Portugal stopped Stuckeley and invited him to commandeer the Portuguese and German armies who were gathered to fight in Morocco. Stuckeley abandoned all his plans. The mercenaries and Irishmen in Stukeley's retinue carried on, but the plan to take Ireland soon collapsed. Stukeley set sail for Morocco, arguing with the Portuguese soldiers at every opportunity. The Battle of Alcácer Quibir commenced, and on 4 August 1578, Stuckeley was killed when his legs were torn off by a cannonball.[45] But within this wild pirate's tale which sometimes bordered on insanity, his dramatic death may have been exaggerated and Stuckeley was likely murdered by his own Portuguese troops who hated him.

Stuckeley certainly lived a life of a man who felt he was invincible, but if he was Queen Elizabeth's half-brother, the likelihood of her bailing him out of endless crazy endeavours never materialised. Stuckeley's crazy life inspired George Peele's play *The Battle of Alcazar with the Death of Captain Stuckeley*, printed in 1594, and *The Famous History of the Life and Death of Captain Thomas Stuckeley,* a play printed for Thomas Pavier in 1605. Some of the finest actors of the period hosted the productions, but the tales have muddied the waters of the truth about Stuckeley's life. There were also several ballads written, and a biography written in 1878 was based on the information collected for the 1605 play. Whether Thomas Stuckeley was the son of a king or not, he lived a big life and died a big death.

Richard Edwardes

Several other rumoured sons are attributed to Henry VIII, labelled so by family histories with no plausible explanation. The first is Richard Edwardes. Edwardes was born in North Petherton, Somerset in 1525, to William Edwardes and his wife Agnes Blewitt.[46] The legends say King Henry visited hunting grounds and met Agnes, who cannot have been more than fifteen in 1525, and fathered her child. The trouble with the theory is that King Henry did not travel on progress anywhere near Somerset in the 1523-1525 window in which Agnes gave birth. Agnes was not a lady at the royal court. A tale that King Henry paid Agnes a stipend for her baby's education is similarly nothing but theory. The theories grow wild through amateur sleuthing (what one historian has called 'wikipedia genealogy'); that Henry married Agnes(!) and they had a son, that Agnes received 'Edwards Hall' in Wales (no such place exists) or that Agnes Edwardes had the Tudor rose added to her coat of arms, which does not exist. There is simply no evidence tying King Henry to Agnes Edwardes.

Richard Edwardes grew up with brothers, whose suggested birthdates are without basis, in North Petherton, before attending Oxford in 1540. A poor family sending a son to Corpus Christi College at Oxford was not entirely impossible; Richard's uncle had also attended before him, and other relatives were similarly well-educated. Starting in May 1540, Edwardes studied under George Etheridge, becoming a fellow in 1544 and joining Christ Church College Oxford in 1546. Records also show Edwardes joined

Lincoln Inn to study law but seemingly stayed with the church instead, living at St. Helen's in Worcester, reaching the role of Rector before resigning in 1555, having lived a quiet life.

But Edwardes' talents lay in composing, poetry, and writing plays, and joined the Chapel Royal in 1557, a group that would move with the royal court. The chapel usually had twenty to thirty adults and ten children at any one time. Edwardes received seven yards of black cloth in 1558 when Queen Mary died, so he would have been mourning and performed for her funeral, and then soon after received four yards of scarlet to attend Queen Elizabeth's coronation. He remained quiet in the chapel, acting as Deputy Master of the Children in the Royal Chapel in 1560, and was promoted to Master in 1561.

The role in the chapel meant performing for Queen Elizabeth and preparing the children of the chapel to sing and perform for the queen. Edwardes married Margaret Babb in April 1560 and their son William was born in November 1561, but Margaret did not survive. Edwardes immediately remarried Helene Griffith to care for his son, and their children Marie, Gwyn, Elizabeth, John, and Richard were born in successive years.

Five songs attributed to Richard Edwardes remain, the most well-known *'In Going to my Naked Bed', 'O the silly man,' 'When gripping grieves,' 'Awake ye woeful nights'* from *Damon and Pithias*, and a setting of *the Lord's Prayer* from 1563. Part pieces composed to be played on a keyboard still exist, his compositions following the Franco-Flemish style of the era. Publisher Henry Disle created *Paradise of Dainty Devices*, with ten songs and poems attributed to Edwardes, but it was Edwardes' plays which garnered the most attention. He wrote classical plays set in the (then) modern world, English tragedies, and comedies with a classic Latin feel. Edwardes was one of the first to place light-hearted comedy into tragedies. He wrote, and probably performed *The excellent Comedie of two the moste faithfullest Freendes, Damon and Pithias*, which was finally published in 1571,[47] and in 1566, performed his *Damon and Pithias* at Oxford when the queen came to visit. The actors were students at the university, the play based on Chaucer's *Knight's Tale* was performed over 2 - 4 September 1566. The main character was Emilia, a virgin with the highest purity like Queen Elizabeth, alongside her friend Hippolyta overcoming adversaries. It was so popular that during the performance, the weight of the crowd caused a wall and a flight of stairs to collapse, killing three and injuring five. The play continued, and the final scene when Emilia marries received thunderous applause.[48] Queen Elizabeth paid eight angels to Emilia and Hippolyta; she had loved the performance, story, singing, and promised to reward Richard Edwardes with a gift. Shakespeare would go on to use this play as the basis for his final work, *Two Noble Kinsmen*. So many viewed Edwardes' play that it is well recorded, despite the loss of the original work.

Edwardes was not to get his reward from Queen Elizabeth, as he fell ill and died on 31 October 1566, aged approximately fifty-one. His wife Helene gave birth to their son, named Richard, one month later. If Edwardes was a half-sibling to Queen Elizabeth, it was certainly never suggested in their lifetimes, and only rekindled as a theory in the late twentieth century.[49] Sadly, none of the claims provides any proof. Richard Edwardes was a remarkable man, considered a writer of Shakespeare's quality, and needed no royal connection, real or imaginary, to enhance his standing.

Henry Lee

One of the more unusual claims to illegitimacy was yet another son named Henry, this child born in 1533-1534. This child was born at a time when King Henry was married to Anne Boleyn and their daughter Princess Elizabeth had just been born. Baby Henry's father, Sir Anthony Lee was an attendant to Thomas Cromwell, who married Lady Margaret Wyatt, daughter of Cromwell's dear friend Sir Henry Wyatt. The pair likely met as Margaret Wyatt was close to Thomas Cromwell, and she spent time with him and his wife before her marriage, and again in later years when her husband was in prison. Margaret had nine children in total with Anthony Lee, naming one son Cromwell in honour of the great man. Anthony Lee was the son of Sir Robert Lee and Joan Cope and was born at their estate in Quarrendon in Buckinghamshire. Lady Margaret Wyatt grew up at Allington Castle in Maidstone, Kent, daughter of Anne Skinner and Sir Henry Wyatt, Master of the Jewels and Treasurer to Henry VII and Henry VIII. The beloved courtier had two surviving children, Thomas and Margaret, Thomas Wyatt famously being the poet and disappointing ambassador at Henry VIII's court. Despite much being made of the lives of Thomas and Margaret Wyatt being close to Anne Boleyn when young, there is little to point to anything that suggests they spent much time together in their youth, apart from their family homes being close together.

But Margaret Wyatt, Margaret Lee after marrying in 1532, was a lady-in-awaiting for Anne Boleyn, albeit a quiet woman. Margaret would have spent much time at court, well within King Henry's sights. Henry famously had an unknown mistress in 1534, one who was supportive of Princess Mary behind Anne Boleyn's back, and the Wyatts had been faithful followers of

Katharine of Aragon for years, making it likely Margaret had a soft spot for Mary. But Henry Lee's birth is dated as 1533, though could have been early 1534, but dated as 1533 on the Julian calendar. Margaret possibly was a mistress while Anne Boleyn was pregnant with Princess Elizabeth, but the entire theory comes a line said after Henry Lee's death.

A tale of John Aubrey's *Brief Lives*, written in that late 17th century, reads 'Old Sir Harry Lee, knight of the Garter, and was supposed brother of Queen Elizabeth. He ordered all his family be christened Harry's'.[50] Aubrey gave no evidence of such a claim, or where he heard such a thing. He also got many details wrong about Sir Henry Lee's life.

Henry Lee lived a reasonably quiet life among his educated circle of family and friends as he worked in parliament, and rose to become Queen Elizabeth's Champion in 1570, at the age of fifty-seven. Lee rode into court, threw down a gauntlet at the door, in the middle of the gallery, and again at the Queen's throne, daring anyone to challenge the queen's right to rule, by beating Lee in combat. The role had been largely ceremonial, but after Lee's display, he was awarded the title of the Queen's Champion. This was an official office at court, and Lee was in charge of arranging the tiltyard activities and celebrations on 17 November each year, a role he held for twenty years. Lee wrote impressive speeches for those wishing to lay down the gauntlet each year, prepared excellent entertainment, and also took on the role of Master of the Royal Armories in 1580. Lee received a lavish retirement party in 1590, with songs and performances dedicated in his honour.[51]

Lee had married Anne Paget in 1554, but they had lost two sons and a daughter by the time Anne died in 1590.[52] Lee took a mistress, Anne Vavasour, one of Queen Elizabeth's ladies, after Vavasour was exiled for having an illegitimate child with Edward de Vere. Lee and Vavasour had a son named Thomas, and Queen Elizabeth visited the pair at their home in Ditchley, Oxfordshire in 1592, where Lee presented the queen with a portrait of her created by Marcus Gheeraerts. At no stage was there ever any rumour that Henry Lee was Elizabeth's sibling, only that their mothers had been friends. A single line written eighty years after Henry Lee died at the age of eighty-eight, is all that links him to Henry VIII.

The tales of King Henry VIII's illegitimate children are stories made from precious few recorded clues, plus memory, slander, gossip, and conjecture. But within the dramatic lives of the Tudor dynasty, almost anything is possible.

Bibliography

Manuscripts

(BL) British Library, London
Additional MSS Charters
Arundel MSS
Cotton MSS
Cotton MSS Appendix
Cotton MSS Cleopatra
Cotton MSS Galba
Cotton MSS Nero
Cotton MSS Othello
Cotton MSS Titus
Cotton MSS Vespasian
Cotton MSS Vitellius
Royal MSS

State Papers published under the authority of His Majesty's Commission, King Henry VIII (11vols., London 1830 – 52) numbered by volume from the original print, and letter number

SP I – TNA SP with volume and folio number for domestic Henry VIII, or, SPO https://www.gale.com /uk/primary-sources/state-papers-online

(TNA) THE NATIONAL ARCHIVES, Public Record Office, Kew with call number included
Berrington Collection, Little Malvern Court 705:24, Worcestershire
Belvoir Castle private archive 2527, Grantham, Leicestershire
Longleat House Library 2238 private archive, Longleat, Warminster, Wiltshire
Close Rolls C 54
Masters MS
Records of the Court of Augmentations, division E

Primary Sources

Anstis, J. (ed.), *The register of the most noble Order of the Garter... usually called the Black Book...* 2vols (J Barber, London, 1724)

Arévalo, R. S., *Compendiosa historia Hispanica, Hunterian* (Ulrich Hahn, Rome, 1470

Brewer, J. S. et al, *Letters and Papers, Foreign and Domestic of the reign of Henry VIII 1509-47*

Burnet G., *The History of the Reformation* 2vols (London, 1679)

Cheke, J., Laingbaine, G., *The true subject to the rebell, or, The hurt of sedition, how grievous it is to a common-wealth written by Sir John Cheke ...; whereunto is newly added by way of preface a briefed discourse of those times, as they may relate to the present, with the author's life* (Leonard Lichfield, Oxford, 1641)

Cox, J. E. (ed.), *Cranmer's Works* 2 vol (Parker Society, Cambridge, 1884-1846)

Everett Wood, A., *Letters of royal, and illustrious ladies of Great Britain, from the commencement of the twelfeth century to the close of the reign of Queen Mary* (Henry Colburn, London, 1846)

Giustiniani, S., Brown, R. (ed)., *Four Years at the Court of Henry VIII* vol 1 (Cambridge University Press, 1854)

Granvelle, Cardinal A. P., *Papiers d'Etat* (Imprimerie Nationale, Paris, 1850)

Grouse, F. (ed), *The Antiquarian Repertory* 4 vols (London, 1807-1809)

Guillim, J., Kent, S., *The Banner Display'd: or, An Abridgment of Guillim: Being a Compleat System of Heraldry, in all its Parts ...* Vol. I. (Thomas Cox, London, 1726)

Hall, E., Whibley, C. (ed), *The Triumphant Reigne of Kyng Henry the VIII*, 2 vols (London, 1904)

Harington, J., *Nugae Antiquae* (1779)

Haynes, A. (ed), *Collection of State Papers relating to affairs of the reign of King Henry VIII King Edvard VI Queen Mary and Queen Elizabeth from the year 1542 to 1570, transcribed from the original letters and other authentick memorials left by William Cecil* (London, 1740)

Huth, H., *The Huth library: A catalogue of the printed books, manuscripts, autograph letters, and engravings, collected by Henry Huth, with collations and bibliographical descriptions.* vol 5 (Ellis & White, London, 1880)

Kaulek, J. (ed.), *Corrrespondance Politique de Mm. De Castillon et de Marillac* (Paris, 1885)

Kaulek, J., *Corrrespondance Politique de Mm. De Castillon et de Marillac* (Alcan, Paris, 1885)

Bibliography

Kingsford, C. L., *Chronicle of London* (Clarendon Press, London, 1905)
Kipling, G., *The Receyt of the Ladie Katheyne* (Oxford University Press, Oxford, 1900)
Leland, J., *Joannis Lelandi Antiquarii de Rebus Britannicis Collectanea* (Impensis Gul. & Jo. Richardson, 1770)
Leti, G., *Historia overo Vita di Elisabetta, Regina d'Inghilterra* (Henry Desbordes Amsterdam, 1693)
M. Hume (trans and ed.), *Chronicle of King Henry VIII of England* (London, 1889)
Madden, F., *Privy Purse Expenses of the Princess Mary, Daughter of the King Henry VIII afterward Queen Mary* (William Pickering, London, 1831)
Mattingly, G., *Calendar of State Papers, Spain: Further Supplement to Volumes 1 and 2, Documents from Archives in Vienna* (London, 1947)
Merton, C. I., *The women who served Queen Mary and Queen Elizabeth; Ladies, gentleman, and maid of the privy chamber 1553-1603* (unpublished thesis, University of Cambridge)
Narrative of the visit to the Duke of Najera: Archaeologiia or Miscellaneous tracts relating to Antiquity vol 23 (Society of Antiquaries, London, 1831)
P. de Gayangos, G. Mattingly, M. Hume, and R. Tyler (eds.), *Calendar of State Papers, Spanish* (15 vols., London 1862 –1954)
Parker, M., Bruce, J. Thomason Perwne, T. (ed) *The Correspondence of Matthew Parker, D.D., Archbishop of Canterbury comprising Letters Written by and to Him, from A.D. 1535 to His Death, A.D. 1575* (Parker Society, 1853)
Pocock, N., *Records of the Reformation: The Divorce 1527-1533. Mostly Now for the First Time Printed from Mss. in the British Museum, the Public Record Office, the Venetian Archives and Other Libraries.*, I (Clarendon Press, London, 1870)
Rinaldo, F., Stefani, F., Berchet, G., Barozzi, N. (eds), *Marino Sanuto Diarii, 1 January 1496 to June 1533* 58 vols (Venice, 1879)
Robbins, H. (ed), *Original letters relative to the Reformation* vol 2 (Cambridge, 1847)
Stow, J., *A Survey of London. Reprinted From the Text of 1603* vol 5 (Clarendon Press, Oxford, 1908)
Strype, J., *Ecclesiastical Memorials, relating chiefly to Religion ...* 3 vols (London, 1721)
Theiner, A., *Codex dominii temporalis apostolicae sedis* (Imprimerie de Vatican, Rome, 1861-2)

Secondary Sources

Baumgartner, F. J., *Louis XII* (St. Martin's Press, Virginia, 1996)
Berwick, J. M. del P. C. M. SF-J., Duke of Berwick, *Correspondencia de Gutierre Gomez de Fuensalida, embajador en Alemania, Flandes é Inglaterra 1496-1509* (Madrid, 1907)
Bindoff, S. T., *The History of Parliament: The House of Commons 1509–1558 3 vols* (Boydell & Brewer, London, 1982)
Bullen, A. H., *Edwards, Richard. Dictionary of National Biography, 1885-1900,* vol 17 (Elder & Co, London, 1900)
Butler, K., *Music in Elizabethan Court Politics* (Boydell and Brewer, London, 2015)
Clifford H., *The life of Jane Dormer, Duchess of Feria* (EE Estcourt and J Stevenson, London, 1887)
Cadwallader, L. H., *The Career of the Earl of Essex from the Islands Voyage in 1597 to His Execution in 1601* (University of Pennsylvania, Philadelphia, 1923)
Casaday, E., *Henry Howard Earl of Surrey* (The Modern Language Association of America, New York, 1938)
Chambers, E.K., *Sir Henry Lee; An Elizabethan Portrait* (Clarendon Press, Oxford, 1936)
Chisholm, H. (ed), Thomas Linacre, Encyclopædia Britannica vol. 16 11th ed (Cambridge University Press) Cambridge, 1910)
Chisholm, H. (ed), *Perrot, Sir John. Encyclopædia Britannica.* vol. 21, 11 ed. (Cambridge University Press, Cambridge, 1911)
Chisholm, Hugh, ed. (1911), *Stuckeley, Thomas. Encyclopædia Britannica* vol. 25 (Cambridge University Press, Cambridge, 1911)
Clark, A. (ed), *Brief Lives, chiefly of Contemporaries, set down by John Aubrey, between the Years 1669 & 1696* (Clarendon Press, Oxford, 1898)
De Luna, D. N. (ed) *The Queen Declined: an interpretation of the 'Willobie his Avisa' with the rest of the original edition* (Clarendon Press, Oxford, 1970)
Debrett's Peerage, 1968 (Marston Book Services, London, 1968)
Dyce, A., *Works of John Skelton* (Dyce, London, 1843)
Garett Mattingly, G., *Catherine of Aragon* (Jonathan Cape, London 1942)
Gunn, S., Monckton, L., *Arthur Tudor, Prince of Wales: Life, Death, and Commemoration* (Woodbridge: Boydell Press, Woodbridge, 2009)
Ives, E., *Henry VIII* (Oxford University Press, Oxford, 2007)
James, S., *Catherine Parr: Henry's Last Love* (Stroud, Gloucestershire, 2008)
Jenkins, E., *Elizabeth and Leicester* (The Phoenix Press, London, 2002)

Bibliography

Jones, P., *The Other Tudors: Henry VIII's Mistresses and Bastards* (New Holland Publishers, London, 2009)
Jowitt, C., *Voyage Drama and Gender Politics, 1589-1642: Real and Imagined Worlds* (Manchester University Press, Manchester, 2002)
Kendall, P. M., *Richard the Third* (Sphere Books, London, 1973)
Lehmberg, S., *Cheyne, Sir Thomas c.1485–1558* (Oxford University Press, Oxford, 2004)
Licence, A., *Catherine of Aragon* (Amberley Publishing, Gloucestershire, 2016)
Licence, A., *The Six Wives and Many Mistresses of Henry VIII* (Amberley Publishing, Gloucestershire, 2014)
Linnane, F., *The Encyclopaedia of London Crime* (Sutton Publishing, Gloucestershire, 2005)
Loach, J., Bernard G., Williams, P., *Edward VI* (Yale University Press, New Haven, 1999)
Loades D., *Henry VIII* (Bloomsbury Academic, London 2009)
Marcus, S., Mueller, J., Rose, M. B., *Elizabeth, Collected Works* (University of Chicago, Chicago, 2000)
Marshall, R., *Scottish Queens 1034-1714* (John Donald, Edinburgh, 2003)
Miller, Naomi J.; Yavneh, N. (eds), *Sibling Relations and Gender in the Early Modern World: Sisters, Brothers and Others* (Routledge, 2017)
Morgan, K, O., *The Oxford History of Britain* (Oxford University Press, Oxford, 1988)
Murphy, B., *Bastard Prince: Henry VIII's Lost Son* (History Press, Gloucestershire, 2010)
Norton, E., *Bessie Blount* (Amberley Publishing, Gloucestershire, 2013)
Norton, E., *The Temptation of Elizabeth Tudor* (Head of Zeus, London, 2015)
Parker, G., *Impudent King: A New Life of Philip II* (Yale University Press, New Haven, 2014)
Parr. K., Mueller, J. (ed), *Katherine Parr: the complete works and correspondence* (Chicago University Press, Chicago, 2011)
Penn, T.M., *Winter King: Henry VII and the dawn of Tudor England* (Simon & Schuster, New York, 2012)
Perrot, T., Turvey, R. (ed*)*, *A Critical Edition of Sir James Perrot's 'The Life, Deedes and Death of Sir John Perrott, Knight'* (Edwin Mellen, London, 2002)
Perry, M., *The Word of a Prince* (Woodbridge, Suffolk, 1995)
Porter, L., *Mary Tudor: The First Queen* (Hachette, London, 2010)
Prawdin, M., *The Mad Queen of Spain* (HMCo, Boston, 1939)
Russell, G., *Young and Damned and Fair: The Life of Catherine Howard* (William Collins, London, 2017)

Seward, D., *Prince of the Renaissance: The Golden Life of François I* (Macmillan Publishing, New York, 1973)

Simpson, R., 1820-1876: *Edmund Campion: A Biography* (John Hodges, London, 1896)

Skidmore, C., *Edward VI: The Lost King of England* (Orion, Kent, 2007)

Smith, M., *Richard Edwards. The New Grove Dictionary of Music and Musicians* (Macmillan, London, 2001)

Thomas, M., *The King's Pearl* (Amberley Publishing, Gloucestershire, 2017)

Varlow, A., *Sir Francis Knollys' Latin dictionary: new evidence for Katherine Carey, Historical Research, Volume 80, Issue 209* (Oxford University Press, Oxford, 2007)

Vives, J.L.; Fantazzi, C., *The Education of a Christian Woman: A Sixteenth-Century Manual* (University of Chicago Press, Chicago, 2007)

Vivian, Lt.Col. J.L., (ed), *The Visitations of the County of Devon: Comprising the Heralds' Visitations of 1531, 1564 & 1620* (Henry S. Eland, Exeter, 1895)

Waldman, M., *Elizabeth and Leicester* (Houghton Mifflin, Boston, 1945)

Waller, M., *Sovereign Ladies: The Six Reigning Queens of England* (St. Martin's Press, New York, 2006)

Warnicke, R. M., *The Marrying of Anne of Cleves: Royal Protocol in Early Modern England* (University Press, Cambridge, 2000)

Weir A., *Elizabeth of York* (Ballantine, New York, 2014)

Weir, A., *Britain's Royal Families: The Complete Genealogy* (Vintage Books, London 2008)

Weir, A., *The Six Wives of Henry VIII*. Grove, New York, 2007)

Whitelock, A., *Mary Tudor* (Penguin, New York, 2016)

Wilkinson, J., *Mary Boleyn* (Amberley Publishing, Gloucestershire, 2009)

Williams, N., *The Cardinal and the Secretary: Thomas Wolsey and Thomas Cromwell.* (Macmillan, New York, 1976)

Wilson, D., *Sweet Robin: A Biography of Robert Dudley Earl of Leicester 1533–1588* (Hamish Hamilton, London, 1981)

Wright, T., *The History of Ireland v. II* (Oxford University Press, Oxford, 1849)

Illustrations

1. Vaux Passional, Peniarth MS 482D, f. 9r. Unknown scribe, (National Library of Wales, Aberystwyth)
2. Henry VIII, by Meynnart Wewyck (Denver Art Museum, Denver)
3. Katharine of Aragon, by Juan de Flandes (Thyssen-Bornemisza, Madrid, 141 1930.36)
4. Princess Mary, by Lucas Horenbout (National Portrait Gallery, London, NPG 6453)
5. Princess Mary attributed to Master John (National Portrait Gallery, London, NPG 428)
6. Queen Mary, by Hans Eworth (National Portrait Gallery, London, NPG 4861)
7. Queen Mary, by Antonis Mor (Museo del Prado, Madrid, 056)
8. Possibly Bessie Blount, by Hans Holbein the Younger (Collection of Her Majesty The Queen, Windsor Castle, London, RCIN 912253)
9. Henry Fitzroy, by Lucas Horenbout (Royal Collection, Cleveland Museum of Art, Cleveland, RCIN 420019)
10. Possibly Elizabeth Tailboys or Etheldreda Malte, by Hans Eworth (The Fitzwilliam Museum, Cambridge, PD.1-1963)
11. Emperor Charles V, by Juan Pantoja de la Cruz (Museo del Prado, Madrid, P01033)
12. King Francis I of France, by Jean Clouet (Louvre, Paris, INV 3256)
13. Katharine of Aragon, by Joannes Corvus (English Private Collection)
14. Anne Boleyn, by unknown (Hever Castle, Kent)
15. Jane Seymour, by Hans Holbein the Younger (Kunsthistorisches Museum, Vienna, 881)
16. Anna of Cleves, by Hans Holbein the Younger (Louvre, Paris, INV 1348)
17. Possibly Katheryn Howard, by Hans Holbein the Younger (Metropolitan Museum of Art, New York, 49.7.30)
18. Katherine Parr, by unknown (National Portrait Gallery, London, NPG 4618)
19. Thomas Wolsey, by Sampson Strong (Christ Church, Oxford)
20. Thomas Cromwell, National Trust (Frick Museum, New York, 1915.1.76)
21. Beaulieu Palace, by Amaibrown, Public Domain

22. Hatfield Old Palace, by Starlingjon, Public Domain
23. Hunsdon Manor, by John Preston Neale (British Library, London, HMNTS 10362.b.1.)
24. Princess Elizabeth, by William Scrots (Queen's Drawing Room, Windsor Castle, London, RCIN 404444)
25. Queen Elizabeth, artist unknown (National Portrait Gallery, London, NPG 5175)
26. Queen Elizabeth by Nicholas Hilliard (Walker Art Gallery, Liverpool, WAG 2994)
27. Prince Edward by Hans Holbein the Younger (National Gallery of Art, Washington D.C, 1937.1.64)
28. Prince Edward by Hans Holbein the Younger (National Portrait Gallery, London, NPG 1132)
29. Prince Edward by William Scrots (Queen's Drawing Room, Windsor Castle, London, RCIN 404441)
30. King Edward by William Scrots (Haunted Gallery, Hampton Court Palace, London, RCIN 405751)
31. Henry VIII, by Hans Holbein the Younger (Walker Art Gallery, Liverpool, WAG 1350)
32. Edward Seymour, by a follower of François Clouet (Government Art Collection, London, 101.0131)
33. Thomas Seymour, by Nicolas Denisot (National Maritime Museum, London, BHC3021)
34. John Dudley, Dudley National Trust (National Trust Scotland, Edinburgh, 129763)
35. Possibly Lady Jane Grey, The Streatham Portrait (National Portrait Gallery, London, NPG 6804)
36. Catherine Carey, by Steven van Herwijck (Yale Centre of British Art, Connecticut, B1974.3.22), Henry Carey, by Steven van Herwijck (Private Collection), John Perrot, by Valentine Green and Caroline Hall (National Trust, Philipps House, Dinton, 1439043), Thomas Stuckeley, by Antonis Mor (National Gallery of Art, Washington D.C 1937.1.52), Richard Edwardes, by John Dryden (British Library, London HMNTS 991.k.6-9), Henry Lee, by Antonis Mor (National Portrait Gallery, London, NPG 2095)

Cover: The Great Matter/The Courtship of Anne Boleyn by Emanuel Leutze (Smithsonian American Art Museum, Washington D.C, 1980.28)

All artwork is in the Public Domain, via Wikimedia Commons through the listed collection, galleries, and artists. No other copyrights are known.

Endnotes

Chapter 1: Two Tudor Princes

1. Kendall, p156
2. Morgan, p709
3. Gunn, p1
4. Weir 2008, p151
5. CPR 1485-1494, p306
6. Leland 1770, p253-255
7. Gunn, p10
8. Warnicke, p103
9. TNA SP I/54, ff. 20-28
10. Loades 2009, P36
11. CPR, 1485-1494 p.423
12. CPR, 1494-1509, p12
13. MS Cotton Julius B XII f.91
14. Loades 2009, p39
15. ibid
16. Skelton, p129
17. Weir 1999, p152
18. TNA LC2/i/I, f.73
19. Weir 2007, p36
20. Ives, 2007, p1
21. Kingsford 1905, p255
22. LP App. B p342
23. Penn, p95
24. Weir 2014, p453
25. Rotuli Parliamentorum vi p522
26. Leland 1770, p258–264
27. Loades 2009, p45
28. Prawdin, p83
29. Opus Epistolarum v no.241
30. Fuensalida 1907, p449

31. Baumgartner, p146
32. Mattingly, p58
33. Exch. T.R.,Wills (Hen. VII.) April 1509
34. Williams, p26
35. Tib. E. VIII. f. 100b.

Chapter 2: Prince Henry, Duke of Cornwall and the Heirs Lost to Fate

1. Arévalo 1470, Hunterian Bw.2.19
2. Spanish Tr., I., 5, f.59.
3. LP i.40
4. Licence 2018, p213
5. Exch. Accts. 417(3), f.69
6. Licence2018, p216
7. SP Spain, ii.43
8. SP Spain, ii.46
9. Exch. Accts, 417(3) f.83
10. SP Spain supplement p7
11. ibid
12. SP Spain, ii.43
13. Bergenroth, p36
14. S.P. Hen. VIII., 229, f.14
15. Licence 2018, p213
16. Add. MS. 6113, f.79b
17. Add. MS. 6113, f.79b
18. Sanuto Diaries, v. x. p832,834
19. Add. MS. 18,826, f.14
20. Hall 1904
21. ibid
22. Hall 1904
23. S.P. Hen. VIII,229, f.203
24. SP Spain, ii.117
25. Calig. D. VI.92
26. Vesp. F. III.15
27. LP vol i.2268
28. Vitell. C. XVI.243
29. Sanuto Diaries, v. xix. p122
30. Vitell. C. XVI.243
31. Exch. Accts., 418(5), f.43, f.44

32. ibid
33. Sanuto Diaries, v. xix. p246.
34. Byrne, p42
35. Norton 2013, p61
36. Vesp. F. XIII. 202b
37. Giust. Desp. I.74
38. Giust. Desp. I.77

Chapter 3: An English Princess

1. LP Revels 1516, no.9
2. Giust. Desp. I.155
3. LP ii.1382
4. Giust. Desp. I.181
5. ibid
6. Archæol. XXVII.260
7. Harl. 3504. f.232
8. Whitelock, p29
9. BL. Harl. 3504, f.232
10. AR I, 305
11. Giust. Desp. I.182
12. AR I, p306
13. ibid
14. Thomas, p30
15. The king's monthly payments through 1516 and 1517
16. LP ii.2946
17. MS. Harl. 295, f.103
18. Original Letter Book, St. Mark's Library, Letter no. 127
19. Linnane, p88
20. Galba, B. IV.201b
21. Add. MS. 21, 116.f.40
22. Giust. Desp. II.101
23. Thomas, p31
24. Giust. Desp. II.232
25. Vesp. F. III. 34b
26. LP ii.4326
27. Harl. 433. f.293
28. LP ii.4468
29. Vit. B. xx.92
30. Thomas, p35

31. Giust. Desp. II.224
32. Giust. Desp. II.235
33. LP ii.4564
34. Giust. Desp. II.240

Chapter 4: A Son at Last

1. The Receyt of the Ladie Katheyne, p82
2. The Receyt of the Ladie Katheyne p81-87
3. LP i.279, 713, 664
4. Norton 2013, p69
5. Kings Book of Payments 1513, f. 270
6. PRO E36/215 f.25
7. Calig. D. VI.149
8. Hall, vol 1 p143
9. Norton 2013, p123
10. Hall vol p171
11. Giust. Desp. II.240
12. LP ii.73
13. Norton 2013, 136
14. Murphy, p30
15. Murphy, p60
16. Herbert, p270
17. Norton 2013, p139
18. Murphy, p35
19. LP iii.2356.18
20. BL Egerton, MS 2642, f.7
21. Murphy, p38

Chapter 5: Princess Mary: Queen or Empress?

1. Galb. B. V.26
2. Thomas, p40
3. LP iii.580
4. Calig. D. VII. 158
5. Thomas, p42
6. Murphy, p35
7. Calig. D VII fol. 238v
8. Vesp. F. XIII. 129
9. LP iii.853
10. Vesp. C. I.307

Endnotes

11. Calig. D. VII.235
12. Calig. D. VII.231
13. Thomas, p46-47
14. ibid
15. ibid
16. ibid
17. ibid
18. Thomas, p48
19. ibid
20. Chisholm, 1911, p701–702.
21. Vives, De Institutione Feminae Christianae
22. Thomas, 50-51
23. Guy p97
24. Tit. B. I.290
25. LP iii.1491
26. ibid
27. Calig. E. III. 7b
28. Vit. C. XI. 191
29. Thomas p60
30. Mattingly p69-78.
31. ibid
32. Wilkinson, p57-58
33. LP iii.2074.5
34. King's Book of Payment, LP iii,Revels
35. Add. MS. 8715, f. 22 b
36. Rym. XIII. 768, 767
37. Egerton, 763, no.46
38. LP iii.2305
39. Galba, B. VII. 268, 270, 273
40. LP iii.2323
41. Vit. B. VI. 77, 78
42. LP iii.2956
43. Galba, B. VIII. 90
44. Rym. XIV.13
45. Calig. D. VIII. 302
46. Calig. B. I.47
47. Wien. Rep. P. C.Fasc. 223. No.14
48. ibid
49. MS. Cott. Galb. B. viii, f.135
50. Thomas, p70-71

51. LP iv.83
52. LP iv.1453
53. Vesp. C. III.62
54. Vesp. C. III.66
55. LP iv.1391
56. LP iv.1577

Chapter 6: Henry Fitzroy, Ruler of the North

1. Sanuto Diaries, v. xxxix. p. 1095
2. Sanuto Diaries, v. xxxix. p. 1575
3. Murphy, p48
4. Murphy, p49
5. LP iv no.1510
6. Murphy, p61
7. S. B. Rym. XIV.42
8. SPI/39, f.17
9. LP iv.1512
10. LP iv.1512
11. LP iv.1530
12. LP iv.1514
13. SP iv.385
14. ibid
15. SP iv. 392
16. Murphy, p66
17. Murphy, p68
18. Murphy, p70
19. LP iv.4560
20. LP iv.2072
21. Murphy, p80
22. ibid
23. LP iv.3520
24. LP iv.2802
25. LP iv.2878
26. LP iv.2955
27. LP iv.2875
28. LP iv.2974
29. Vit. B. IX. 108
30. Venetian Calendar iv.17
31. Vesp. C. IV.175.

32. LP iv no.3860
33. Calig. B. III.276
34. LP iv no.3405
35. LP iv no.4534
36. SP iv no.515
37. SP iv.515
38. Murphy, p96
39. LP iv no. 4891
40. Murphy, p105

Chapter 7: The Princess of Wales

1. LP iv.1577.3
2. LP iv. 1577.4
3. LP iv.1577.11
4. LP iv.1577.13
5. LP iv.1611
6. Thomas, p80
7. Gunn, p65
8. LP iv.2159
9. Titus, B. I.314
10. Titus, B. 1.305
11. Royal MS.14 B. XXVI
12. Thomas, p85-86
13. Cal. D. IX.268
14. Vesp. C. IV.29
15. Vit. B. IX.42
16. Cal. D. X.349, 354
17. Rym. XIV.234
18. LP iv.2917
19. LP iv.2974
20. Masters' MS. f. 113 French version, Cal. D. X. 39 f.39,40 English version
21. Vit. B. IX.78
22. Thomas, p99
23. Du Mont, IV. pt. 1, 476
24. Thomas p100
25. Vesp. C. IV.100
26. Vit. B. IX. 108, initial account of the Sack of Roma
27. LP iv.3140

28. SP I/1897
29. Pocock's Records of the Reform., I. 11
30. SP VI./594
31. SP I/235
32. Vit. B. IX.218
33. LP iv.3564
34. Galba, B. IX 97
35. Vit. B. IX.189
36. LP iv.3643 and 3644
37. LP iv.2874
38. LP iv.3913
39. LP iv.4096
40. Vit. B. X.195
41. Harl. 419. f.103
42. LP iv.4803
43. Thomas, p117
44. Cal. B. II.77
45. Vit. B. XIV.18
46. Vit. B. XI.186
47. Theiner, p566
48. Add. MS. 28,580, f.125
49. SP. VII.261
50. LP iv.6748
51. Harl. 296, f.38
52. Thomas p121
53. Ibid

Chapter 8: The Destruction of a Royal Family

1. LP v.10
2. LP v.112
3. LP v.124
4. LP v.1487
5. LP v.171
6. LP v.187
7. LP v.216
8. LP v.238
9. LP v.308
10. LP v.631
11. LP v.375

12. LP v.439
13. LP v.512
14. Stowe's Survey, V. I. p723
15. LP v no.868
16. Add. MS. 28,584, f.177
17. LP v.862
18. Add. MS. 28,585, f.120
19. LP v.1377
20. Thomas, p131
21. MSS Cleo. E. IV. 30, 253
22. LP vi.2123
23. SP Spain iv.ii, 1061
24. SP Spain iv.ii no.1059
25. LP vi.324
26. Add. MS. 28,585, f.264
27. LP vi.391
28. Vesp. F. XIII. 203
29. LP vi.720
30. LP vi.805
31. LP vi.849
32. LP vi.1009

Chapter 9: A Worldly Jewel Lost

1. ibid
2. LP v.278.21
3. LP iv.6083
4. Murphy, p126
5. Murphy, p121
6. Casaday, p44
7. Herbert, p17
8. Casaday, p51
9. ibid
10. Venetian Cal, 1527-1533, no.876
11. Casaday p52-53
12. Casaday, 057
13. Calais Chronicle, p44
14. ibid
15. Add. MS. 4,622, f 298
16. Austis, Order of the Garter, II. 393

17. LP vii. 556
18. LP vii.772
19. LP vii.904
20. LP vii.1013
21. LP vii.1193
22. LP viii. 263
23. LP vii.1466
24. R. MS. 7 F. xiv. f.83
25. LP viii.263
26. Murphy, p154
27. ibid
28. R. MS. 7 F. xiv. f.83
29. Anstis, Order of the Garter. ii. 398
30. Wien, Rep. P. C., Fasc. 230, No.29
31. Wien, Rep. P.C.,Fasc. 230, No.32
32. Murphy, p170
33. Murphy, p 174
34. LP xi.147
35. LP xi.40
36. LP xi.108
37. LP xi.148
38. Murphy, p178-9
39. LP xi. 233
40. Murphy. p180
41. R. MS. 7 F. xiv. f.83
42. LP xi.164 i-iv

Chapter 10: A Reformist Princess

1. Pocock, II.p566
2. LP vi.1018
3. LP vi.1065
4. Harl. MS. 543, f.128
5. LP vi.1125
6. Titus, B. I.493
7. Wien. Rep. P. Fasc.,c, 288, no.55
8. Arund. MS. 151, f. 194
9. Harl. MS. 416, f. 22
10. LP vi.1186
11. LP vi.1164

12. LP vi.1207
13. LP vi.1185
14. Harl. MS. 6,807, f.7
15. LP vi.1252, 1253
16. LP vi.1392
17. LP vi.1528, 1558
18. Otho, C. X. 210
19. LP vii.14
20. Huth Library Catalogue, v.1692
21. Thomas, p148
22. LP vii.229
23. Thomas, p149
24. LP vii.393
25. LP viii.469
26. Thomas, p152
27. LP vii. 690
28. LP vii.810
29. LP x.913
30. LP vii.1129
31. LP vii.1172
32. Wien, Rep. P.C., Fasc. 228, no 61
33. LP vii.1257
34. LP vii.1297
35. Add. MS. 28,587, f.81
36. LP viii.440
37. LP viii.263
38. ibid
39. Thomas, p165
40. LP viii.438
41. LP ix.556
42. LP ix.964
43. LP ix.1036
44. SP I/452
45. LP x.141
46. LP x.199
47. LP x.29
48. LP x.282
49. Add. MS. 28,588, f.23
50. ibid
51. Wien, Rep. P. C., Fasc. 230, 1–4

52. ibid
53. Wien. Rep. P. C., Fasc., 229½, 1-4
54. Bruce, Perowne 1853, p59
55. SP Foreign, Elizabeth, i,1303
56. MSS Otho. C. x.273
57. MSS Otho. C. x.263b
58. LP xi.7
59. Vesp. C. xiv.245
60. LP xi.7
61. LP xi.639
62. LP xi.40
63. Otho, C. x.230
64. Add. MS. 28,589, f.85
65. MS. 19,751. f.194. Bibl. Nat.Paris
66. Vesp. F. III.196
67. Thomas, p216

Chapter 11: Finally, A Male Heir

1. Add MS. 28,589, f.193
2. Add. MS.25,114, f.244
3. LP xii.i.734
4. LP xiv.ii.782, f.82
5. Titus B. I.481
6. LP xii.1297
7. Madden, p82
8. LP xii.ii.22
9. Harl. MS.282, f.203
10. Marshall, p.108
11. MSS Titus, B. I429
12. LP xi.528
13. LP xii.ii.764
14. Nero C. x. 1
15. LP xii.ii.894
16. Harl. 442,f.149
17. Skidmore, p17
18. Bibl. Nat.Paris,Fr. 2997, f.3
19. Heralds' College MS.I. 11,f.37
20. SP viii.368

Chapter 12: Changing Queens, Changing Fortunes

1. Add. MSS.28,590, f.80
2. LP xiv.ii.782,f.117
3. Madden, p66–69
4. Kaulek, 23
5. Wien., Imp. Arch., Rep. P.C. Fasc.231, ff77–82
6. SP. i. 561
7. Murray, p122–3
8. LP xiii.i no.41
9. Skidmore, p27
10. LP xiii.ii no.986
11. Cott. Appx.xxviii. 39.
12. ibid
13. LP xix.ii no.871
14. 6 LP xiv.i no.651
15. LP xiv.i.651
16. MSS Cleo. E. VI., 285
17. Parl. Roll. 31 Hen 8 c 10
18. Parker, p.12
19. Vit. C. XI.,f. 213.
20. Harl. MS. 282, f.143
21. MSS Vit C. XVI. f. 290
22. Otho, C. x.271
23. MSS Otho, C. x.272
24. MSS Otho, C. x. 271
25. Privy Purse Expenses of the Princess Mary, p95
26. ibid, p257
27. ibid, p83
28. ibid p10
29. LP xv no. 283
30. SP viii, 562
31. Thomas p244
32. LP xiv no.380
33. Burnet, vol I, 187-99
34. MSS Vesp. F. xiii.202
35. Hall, ii, p306-7
36. Thomas, p246
37. Thomas, p247

38. ibid
39. ibid
40. Kaulek, 347
41. SP Spain, vi.i no.196
42. Skidmore p27
43. Kaulek, 350
44. Kaulek 274
45. SP I/243, f.292
46. Jane Dormer, Duchess of Feria, p59
47. ibid
48. Russell, Young and Damned and Fair: the Life of Catherine Howard
49. Spanish Calendar, vi.i,no.246
50. Add. MS. 32,647 f. 175.

Chapter 13: The Education of Heirs and Leaders

1. Privy Purse Expenses of the Princess Mary, p97
2. ibid
3. LP xviii.i no.454,455
4. Norton 2015, p13
5. Privy Purse Expenses of the Princess Mary p214
6. ibid, p122
7. LP xviii.i no.873
8. Parl Rolls 35 Hen. 8 c.1
9. Privy Purse Expenses of the Princess Mary, p10
10. Najera 1831
11. Privy Purse Expenses of the Princess Mary, p11
12. Rutland i. 30.
13. Scarisbrick, Henry VIII, 395.
14. Skidmore p31
15. SP I/95 f.261-2
16. BL Harl. MS 1419A f.133-1335
17. BL Harl. MS 5087, f.7
18. BL Harl. MS 5087 f.33
19. Skidmore p35
20. ibid
21. BL Harl. MS 5087, f.11
22. Otho. C. x.231
23. Langbaine, Cheke, 1641.
24. BL Harl. MS 5087 f.11
25. SP Spain viii, no.83

26. Seward, p241
27. Privy Purse Expenses of the Princess Mary, p13
28. SP Spain, viii. no.243
29. LR I p9,31
30. Privy Purse Expenses of the Princess Mary, p186,188
31. LP xxi.ii no.697
32. ibid
33. Harl. MS. 6986 f.13
34. TNA E101/424/12 f. 68, 74,76, 78, 135
35. Hayward 1630 p4,5
36. SP Spain ix p7

Chapter 14: A Tudor Born to Rule

1. BL Add. MS 71009 f.451
2. SP Spain ix p31
3. Ives 2009, p47–49
4. Norton 2015, p38
5. SP Spain ix p57
6. BL Harl. MS 5087 f34
7. Calais Chronicle, p54
8. Skidmore, p56
9. Cox, p126-7
10. SP Spain 1547-49 p48
11. Norton 2015, p42
12. SP Spain letters dated 30,31 Jan, 5,8 Feb 1549
13. Ecclesiastes 10:16
14. BL Add. MS 4724 f104
15. Skidmore, p244
16. ibid
17. Loach, p159
18. Foxe vi p352

Chapter 15: The Reputation of a Royal Sister

1. Leti, p160
2. Leti, p162
3. Norton 2015, p42
4. SP 10/6/57
5. SP10/6/24
6. Letter for Royal and Illustrious Ladies, iii p93

7. James, p276
8. Merton, p85
9. Norton 2015, p85
10. TNA E15/340 f29v. f30, f30v
11. Norton 2015, p92
12. Ashley confession, Haynes 1740, p99
13. ibid
14. Ashley's confessions recall telling her husband of events, who suggested he and other in the households thought Elizabeth liked Seymour's advances
15. Ashley's first deposition, recalled in Elizabeth, Collected Works. p28
16. Ashley disposition SP 10/6/55
17. Ashley confession, Haynes 1740, p99
18. Perry p28
19. Ashley confession, Haynes 1740, p99
20. Parry confession, Haynes 1740, p96
21. Haynes, p17
22. Parry confession, Haynes 1740, p96
23. ibid
24. SP 10/5/8a
25. Clifford 1887, p87
26. De Luna, p49
27. Tyrwhitt Confession, Mueller, p178
28. Tyrwhitt deposition, Mueller, p177
29. Mueller. p619
30. Elizabeth confession, Haynes 1740, p102
31. Norton 2015, p201
32. ibid p202
33. Ashley confession, Haynes 1740, p100
34. Ashley deposition SP10/6/53
35. Perry, p37
36. Robinson 1847, p647
37. Norton 2015, p233
38. Haynes 1740, p89
39. APC ii p262
40. ibid

Conclusion: Triumph of the True Queens

1. James, p299
2. Porter, p169–176

3. ibid, p178
4. Waller, 52
5. ibid, p57

Epilogue: The Illegitimate Children of Henry VIII

1. LP iii Richard Gibson's accounts for Revels held 29 Dec. and 1 Jan. 13 Hen. VIII
2. LP viii no.299
3. LP iv no.4440
4. Harl. MS. 295, f.153b
5. Guillim, Kent, 1726, p255
6. Everett Wood, iii p280
7. Varlow, p315–323
8. Jenkins, p125
9. ibid p212
10. ibid p234
11. Wilson, p302
12. Cadwallader, p83
13. Hart, p105
14. Licence 2014, p164
15. Phillimore et al 1858
16. ibid
17. ibid
18. LP xxi.ii
19. LP xxi.ii no.712.xv
20. Harington 1779, I p14-16
21. Jones, p228
22. ibid p232
23. ibid
24. Turvey 2002
25. Licence 2014, p229
26. Lehmberg, p14
27. ibid
28. Chisholm, p184
29. ibid
30. Turvey 2002
31. ibid
32. Chisholm ,p184
33. ibid

34. Miller et al, p238
35. Miller et al, p238
36. Debrett's Peerage, 1968, p.768
37. Vivian, p721
38. Jowitt, p971-p99
39. ibid
40. Simpson 1878
41. ibid
42. Wright, p461
43. Jowitt, p971-999
44. Chisholm, p105
45. ibid
46. Bullen 1900, vol xvii
47. ibid
48. Waldman, p143.
49. Edwards 1973
50. Richard, p193
51. Butler, p129–142
52. Chambers, p77

Index

Abel, Thomas 115
Adderston, William 11
Albert, Marquess of Brandenburg 36, 169
Aleyn, John, Archbishop of Dublin 90
Andre, Bernard 3
Anna of Cleves, Queen of England 128, 131, 132–134, 139, 141, 165, 170, 176
Anne, Princess of York 14
Anne, Queen of England
   at court 45, 57–60, 69–76, 80, 83, 84, 85, 99, 100, 175, 176, 179
   as queen 80, 89–93, 105, 109, 112, 116, 117, 148, 191, 192
Arthur, Prince of England 1–7, 18, 24, 28, 38, 41, 50, 62, 64, 69, 72, 78, 89
Ascham, Roger 147, 148, 161, 13, 164
Ashley, Kat 118, 121, 126, 132, 147, 160
Astley/Ashley, John 161
Audley, Thomas, Lord Chancellor 80, 125

Badoer, Andrea 14
Baume, Etiennette de la 16
Beaufort, Margaret, Countess of Richmond and Derby 1–3, 6, 7, 10, 12, 15, 20, 35, 54, 64, 101
Berkeley, Maurice Baron Berkeley 183
Berkeley, Thomas 183
Blount, Bessie (Elizabeth) later Tailboys 26, 28–34, 45, 49, 51, 52, 60, 88, 97, 174, 175
Blount, George 55
Blount, Gertrude see Courtenay, Gertrude
Blount, Henry 55
Blount, John 28–30, 33
Blount, Katherine née Pershall 28, 29, 31
Blount, Thomas 28
Blount, William Lord Mountjoy, 21, 28, 29
Boleyn, Anne see Anne, Queen of England
Boleyn, Elizabeth, Countess of Wiltshire and Ormond, née Howard 29, 73, 99, 175
Boleyn, George Lord Rochford 93, 102, 105, 107, 110, 144, 116
Boleyn, Jane Lady Rochford, née Parker 33
Boleyn, Mary, later Carey, Stafford 45, 46, 49, 55, 58, 79, 100, 117, 132, 174–176, 179

Boleyn, Thomas, Earl of Wiltshire and Ormond 20, 31, 36, 37, 43, 45, 46, 49, 69, 81, 99, 102, 107, 108, 125, 175
Bouchier, Henry, Earl of Essex 15, 102, 105, 125
Bourchier, Margaret see Bryan, Margaret
Bradford, John 171
Brandon, Catherine, Duchess of Suffolk, née Willoughby 150, 161
Brandon, Charles 145
Brandon, Charles, Duke of Suffolk 21, 29, 30, 34, 47, 76, 80, 102, 106, 119, 125, 136, 150, 186
Brandon, Eleanor, later Clifford, Countess of Cumberland 42, 117
Brandon, Frances, see Grey, Frances
Brandon, Henry 145
Brandon, Henry, Earl of Lincoln 42, 90
Brereton, Sir William 93, 116
Bright, Anne 22
Brigman, Joan 84
Browne, Anthony 69
Bryan, Elizabeth see Carew, Elizabeth
Bryan, Margaret, Baroness Bryan, née Bourchier 17, 22, 33, 37, 38, 103, 110, 118, 119, 121, 127, 133
Bryce, William 10
Bulmer, William 53
Butts, William 61, 105, 111, 124, 138

Calthorpe, Jane 43, 44, 61, 140, 179
Calthorpe, Philip 43, 44
Campeggio, Lorenzo, Cardinal 25, 36, 59, 71, 72

Carew, Elizabeth née Bryan 17, 29, 30, 110
Carew, Nicholas 17, 30, 93, 110
Carey, Catherine, later Knollys 49, 132, 174–179
Carey, Henry, Baron Hunsdon 175, 176, 179, 180
Carey, William 45, 49, 58, 59, 174–176
Caroz, Luís 12, 14
Carter, William 61
Casali, Gregory di 70
Castelnau, Antoine de, Ambassador of France 113
Cavendish, Elizabeth 161
Cecil, William 158, 177, 187
Chabot, Philippe de, Ambassador of France 91
Chambre, George 124
Champernowne, Katherine see Ashley, Kat
Chapuys, Eustace, Ambassador to the Emperor 72, 73, 75–77, 80, 81, 90, 91–93, 103, 106, 106, 109–118, 121, 127, 128, 131, 135, 136, 139, 149
Charles V, Holy Roman Emperor and King of Spain 38, 39, 41, 46–51, 57, 59, 64–68, 72, 73, 75, 77, 79, 81, 87, 107, 112, 113, 115, 121, 131, 133, 135, 137, 141, 143, 150, 169, 171, 187
Charles, Duke of Angoulême, later Orléans 86, 136, 143, 150
Chaunte, John 11
Cheke, John 144, 145, 147, 158, 163
Cholmeley, William 81
Claude, Queen of France 25, 27, 37, 47, 48, 100
Clerk, John 65, 67, 69

Index

Cleves, Anna see Anna of Cleves, Queen of England
Cleves, Wilhelm, Duke of Jülich-Cleves-Burg 79, 128, 133
Clifford, Henry Baron Clifford 15
Clinton, Thomas Baron Clinton 24
Colet, John 15
Compton, William 12
Corves, Joannes 143
Cotton, George 96
Cotton, Richard 96
Courtenay, Gertrude, Marchioness of Exeter, née Blount 121, 125, 129
Courtenay, Henry, Marquess of Exeter 38, 90, 102, 125, 129
Cousine, Margaret 22
Cox, Richard 144, 145, 147, 148
Cranmer, Thomas, Archbishop of Canterbury 72, 78, 80, 81, 87, 100, 102, 108, 116, 125, 128, 144, 148, 149, 153, 156, 158, 169, 171
Croft, Richard 28
Croke, Richard 55, 56, 59
Cromwell, Gregory 55, 96
Cromwell, Thomas, Vicegerent and Lord Privy Seal, later Earl of Essex 23, 43, 47, 53, 55, 58, 73–75, 78–81, 87–92, 95, 97, 99, 100, 102–138, 144, 145, 149, 151, 155, 175, 176, 191

Dabridgecourt, Cecily 62
Dacre, Thomas Lord 15
Dalby, Thomas 53
Dannett, Mary 62
Darrell, Alice 24, 62
Darrell, Anne 62
Darrell, Edward 29

de Vere, Edward 192
de Vere, John, Earl of Oxford 105
Denny, Anthony 165, 166
Denton, Elizabeth 22
Denton, James 63
Dingley, Joan 180–182
Douglas, Margaret 19, 74, 105–107, 132, 133, 139, 140, 143
Dudley, Edward 63
Dudley, Guildford 159
Dudley, John, later Duke of Northumberland 155, 156, 158, 159, 168, 187
Dudley, Robert, later Earl of Leicester 136, 168, 171, 178, 185, 187
Duwes, Giles 4, 41

Edward IV, King of England 1, 38
Edward VI, Prince later King of England
  birth 124–126
  childhood 127–140
  education 141–154
  as king 155–157
  death 158, 158
Edwardes, Richard 189-191
Elderton, Sir Ralph 123
Elisabeth, Valois Princess of France 158, 187
Elizabeth of York, Queen of England 1 -8, 10, 64, 101
Elizabeth, Princess later Queen of England
  birth 87, 90, 101–103
  childhood before Anne's death 104–116
  under Jane 118–121, 125
  childhood 128, 129, 138, 140, 142, 143, 148, 153, 154

221

under Edward 155, 157,
  160–168
under Mary 169–173
Elizabeth, Princess of England
  (1492-1495) 2, 3
Elmbridge, Anne 62
Elmer, Frances 62
Erasmus, Desiderius 4, 15, 41,
  42, 137

Ferdinand, King of Hungary,
  Croatia and Bohemia 41, 47
Ferdinand, King of Spain (Aragon)
  2, 5, 6, 7, 9, 11, 12, 15–20, 41,
Fetherstone, Richard 41
Fisher, John, Bishop later Cardinal
  15, 109, 113, 148
Fitzroy, Henry, Duke of Richmond
  and Somerset
  birth and early years 32–35, 37,
    42, 49, 50
  in the north 51-61, 67, 80
  at court under Katharine
    83–85
  in France 86, 87
  at court under Anne 88–94
  death 95-98
FitzAlan, Henry, Earl of
  Arundel 125
FitzAlan, Susan 183
FitzAlan, William Lord
  Maltravers 15
Fitzroy, Mary see Howard, Mary
Fitzwalter, Elizabeth 12
Foix, Germaine de 7, 36
Folbury, George 84
Foljambe, Geoffrey 53
Foxe, Edward 106
Foxe, John 172
Foxe, Richard 14

Francis I, King of France 5, 25, 27,
  32, 36, 37, 42, 45, 46, 48, 51,
  57, 64–68, 73, 80, 85–87, 111,
  121, 128, 130, 136–138, 143,
  149
Francis, Dauphin of France 25, 26,
  36, 37, 44, 46, 48, 57, 64, 65,
  70, 73, 80, 86, 111, 112, 136
Franklin, William 53

Gardiner, Stephen, Bishop 55, 72,
  134, 148, 152, 155, 156, 171
George, Margrave of
  Brandenburg 36
Giustinian, Sebastian 18, 20, 21, 26
Greville, Anne née Rede 62
Greville, Giles 62
Grey, Anne 102
Grey, Elizabeth, later Countess of
  Kildare 24
Grey, Frances, Marchioness
  of Dorset, née Brandon 42,
  107, 159
Grey, Henry, 3rd Marquess of
  Dorset 102, 153, 159, 160
Grey, Jane, later disputed Queen
  of England 153, 155, 157, 159,
  160, 161, 163–167, 170, 171,
  181, 182
Grey, John 182
Grey, Katherine 153
Grey, Katherine Lady Maltravers
  61, 105
Grey, Leonard 88
Grey, Margaret, Dowager
  Marchioness of Dorset née
  Wotton 102, 124
Grey, Mary 153
Grey, Thomas, 1st Marquess of
  Dorset 15

Index

Grey, Thomas, 2nd Marquess of Dorset 46, 61, 63
Grindal, William 147, 148, 161, 163
Guildford, Edward 29
Guildford, Henry 29, 30
Guildford, Margaret 30
Guildford, Richard 4

Harington, Esther 182
Harington, John 181, 182
Hastings, Anne 12
Henri, Duke of Orléans, later King of France 32, 57, 64, 66, 68, 70, 73, 86, 87, 136, 158, 184, 186, 187
Henry VII, King of England 1–8, 15, 21, 43, 64, 191
Henry VIII, King of England
   as Prince of York and Wales 2–8
   war in France 15–17, 47, 143, 146
   Mary's childhood 20, 21, 37, 41, 42, 50, 66, 79, 81, 88, 106, 107, 108, 112, 117, 118, 120, 127, 132, 135, 136, 137, 140, 142
   Elizabeth's childhood 102, 106, 107, 128, 132, 140, 142
   negotiations with France 25, 36, 38, 39, 49, 67, 86, 136–138
   negotiations with the Emperor 22, 39, 47, 49, 57, 66, 128, 133, 136, 150
   Katharine of Aragon 9-15, 19, 24, 26, 30, 40, 58, 69, 77, 92
   Bessie Blount 30–34
   Mary Boleyn 45, 46
   Anne Boleyn 75, 76, 85, 87, 92, 100, 107, 112, 114, 115
   relations with Scotland 16, 19, 44, 48, 69, 72, 74, 79, 80, 90, 91, 93, 101, 123, 127, 136, 139, 140, 144, 147
   Fitzroy 52, 53, 56, 83, 84, 86, 90, 93, 96
   Jane Seymour 118, 120–126
   Edward's childhood 124, 125, 128, 137, 138, 140, 142, 145, 146, 150
   Anna of Cleves 128, 131, 132–134, 139, 141, 165, 170, 176
   relationship with Thomas Cromwell 75, 78, 79, 88, 113, 115, 131, 134, 138
   Katheryn Howard 132–139, 146
   Kateryn Parr 142, 143, 146–155
   death 152–154
Henry, Prince of England, Duke of Cornwall 12-15
Herbert, Anne 141, 161
Higden, Brian 53
Hill, Mary 161
Holbein, Hans 129, 144, 182
Horenbout, Gerard 143
Horenbout, Lucas 97, 143
Horenbout, Susanna 143
Howard, Agnes, (Dowager) Duchess of Norfolk, née Tilney 20, 102
Howard, Dorothy 88
Howard, Edmund 15
Howard, Elizabeth see Boleyn, Elizabeth
Howard, Elizabeth, 2nd Duchess of Norfolk, née Stafford 76
Howard, Frances née de Vere 88

223

Howard, Henry, Earl of Surrey 72, 84, 85, 87, 89, 94, 98, 151
Howard, Katherine 88
Howard, Katheryn see Katheryn, Queen of England
Howard, Mary, later Fitzroy, Duchess of Richmond and Somerset 88, 93, 94, 102, 132, 151
Howard, Thomas Lord 94, 102
Howard, Thomas, 2nd Duke of Norfolk 38, 99
Howard, Thomas, 3rd Duke of Norfolk 34, 52, 72, 76, 79, 80, 84, 85, 87–90, 92, 94, 96, 102, 106, 111, 117, 119, 121, 125, 126, 133, 136, 151, 171
Howard, William Lord 102
Hussey John Lord 74, 81, 102, 104, 105
Hutton, Ellen 22

Isabella, Infanta of Portugal 50, 57, 68, 131
Isabella, Queen of Spain (Castile) 2, 6, 9, 40, 41

James IV, King of Scotland 6, 16
James V, King of Scotland 44, 48, 49, 55, 56, 72, 74, 79, 80, 90, 91, 93, 94, 106, 123, 139
Jane, Queen of England 93, 94, 95, 115, 118, 120–125, 144, 152, 156, 177, 123, 144, 157, 156
Johns, Hugh 84
Juana, Infanta of Spain 6, 7, 64, 143
Juana, Princess later Queen of Castile 6, 7, 64

Kateryn, Queen of England 142, 143, 146–155, 160–169
Katharine of Aragon, Queen of England
  as Princess of Wales 2–8, 28
  pregnancies and births 9-20, 25, 26, 30
  as regent 15, 16
  ambassador 15, 18, 23, 37, 38, 46, 47, 48, 65, 66, 68, 69
  Mary's care 18-20, 40, 41, 51, 67, 103–104
  and Fitzroy 32, 51
  divorce 57, 59, 60, 69–81
  exile 100, 103, 104, 106, 108–110, 112, 113
  death – 92, 114, 115
Katherine, Princess of York 20
Katheryn, Queen of England 132–139, 146
Kerne, Edward 131
Kingston, Mary née Scrope 117
Kingston, William 106, 108
Knollys, Catherine Lady Knollys see Carey, Catherine
Knollys, Sir Francis 176, 177
Knyvett, Anne 61
Knyvett, Charles 43

Latimer, Hugh 15, 171
Lawson, George 53
Lee, Edward 70
Lee, Henry 191, 192
Lee, Margaret see Wyatt, Margaret
Linacre, Thomas 41
Lisle, Arthur Plantagenet, Viscount 52, 87, 95
Locke/Luke, Anne 2, 11
Louis XII, King of France 14, 17, 18
Louis, King of Bohemia 36

Index

Magnus, Thomas 55, 58, 59
Malte, Etheldreda 180–182
Malte, John 181, 182
Margaret, Princess, later Queen of Scotland 2, 3, 19, 21, 48, 74, 99
Marguerite of Angoulême, later Queen of Navarre 5, 99
Marguerite, Duchess, later Regent of the Netherlands 14, 38, 39, 73, 99
Maria, Infanta of Portugal, Duchess of Viseu 57, 65, 143
Maria, Infanta of Spain later Holy Roman Empress 143, 150
Marillac, Charles, Ambassador to France 136, 137
Mary, Princess later Queen of England
  birth and infancy 19–26
  early education and alliances 36–50
  Princess of Wales 52, 57, 61–67
  at court 68–78
  exiled from her parents 79–83, 89, 91, 103–118
  under Jane 121, 122, 125
  adulthood under Henry 127, 128, 130, 133–140, 142–147, 149, 15, 152, 154
  under Edward 155, 158, 160, 161, 169, 170
  as queen 170–172
Mary, Princess, later Queen of France and Duchess of Suffolk 3, 7, 17, 21, 24, 37, 55, 68, 74, 75, 100, 159
Mary, Queen, later Regent of the Netherlands 36, 75, 113, 131, 139
Master John 143

Maximilian I, Holy Roman Emperor 6, 16, 17, 23, 25, 36
Medici, Alessandro de, later Duke of Florence 107
Medici, Catherine de, later Queen of France 57, 86, 87
Meulen, Steven van der 178
Milborne, Blanche, Lady Herbert of Troy 126, 152
More, Sir Thomas, Lord Chancellor 15, 23, 35, 41, 42, 55, 108, 113

Neville, George, Baron Bergavenny 15, 47
Neville, Margaret 141
Neville, Sir Edward 129
Norris, Henry 116
Norris, Mary 161

Orio, Lorenzo 51
Owain, Davy ab 20
Owen, George 124

Page, Richard 53
Paget, Anne 192
Paget, William 152
Palsgrave, John 53, 54, 55
Parker, Alice 33
Parker, Arabella 33
Parker, Margery 22, 33, 62, 105
Parker, Matthew 116
Parker, Thomas 181
Parr, Kateryn, Lady Latimer see Kateryn, Queen of England
Parr, Maud 141
Parr, Thomas 20, 55
Parr, William, later Marquess of Northampton 55, 56, 58, 59, 93, 155
Parry, Blanche 126, 132, 161,

225

Parry, Thomas 166, 167, 179, 161–168
Partridge, Anne 55
Pate, Richard 135
Percy, Henry 175
Perrot, John 183–186
Perrot, Thomas 184–186
Philip, Count Palatine and Duke of Bavaria 132, 133, 135, 141, 150, 154
Philip, later King of Spain and Holy Roman Emperor 143, 150, 171–173, 187
Pole, Constance, née Pakenham 61
Pole, Elizabeth 61
Pole, Geoffrey 61
Pole, Henry Lord Montagu 90, 121, 125, 129
Pole, Katherine 22
Pole, Margaret, Countess of Salisbury, née Plantagenet 20, 29, 33, 38, 39, 43, 61, 78, 81, 104–106, 121, 129, 135, 172
Pole, Reginald later Cardinal 121, 129, 131, 172
Pole, Ursula, Baroness Stafford 23
Pope Clement VII, 57, 59, 60, 65, 66, 68, 69, 70, 71, 72, 74–76, 79, 80, 81, 87, 105, 108, 110, 113, 117
Pope IV, 172
Pope Julius II, 9, 12
Pope Leo X, 25
Pope Paul III, 113, 152
Popincourt, Jane 30
Poyntz, Katherine 183

Radcliffe, Robert, Earl of Sussex 15, 105, 125
Richard III, King of England 1, 43, 38, 53, 54

Ridley, Nicholas 171
Rogers, John 171
Rowle, Henry 22
Russell, William 161

Sampson, Richard 63, 105
Sanchez de Arevalo, Rodrigo 9
Saunders, William 55
Savoy, Louise later Duchess 37, 38, 48, 65, 67, 73
Scrots, William 144
Seymour Anne, later Duchess of Somerset, née Stanhope 161, 166
Seymour, Edward the younger 145
Seymour, Edward, later Duke of Somerset 93, 115, 122, 125, 128, 142, 144, 145, 153, 155–158, 161, 165, 167, 169, 186, 187
Seymour, Henry 145
Seymour, Jane see Jane, Queen of England
Seymour, Thomas, later Baron Sudeley 153, 155–157, 160–169
Shelton, Anne 107, 108, 110, 111, 113, 114, 117, 140, 179
Shelton, John 110, 119, 122
Shelton, Margaret (or Mary) 93, 110
Simpson, Thomas 4
Skeffington, Lord William 83, 90
Skelton, John 4
Smeaton, Mark 116, 152
Smyth, Katherine 31
Stafford, Henry Earl of Wiltshire, 15
Stafford, Henry, Baron Stafford 43
Stafford, Henry, Duke of Buckingham, 38

Stafford, William 176
Stanhope, Michael 157
Stanley, Edward, Earl of Derby 102
Stanley, Isabella 29
Stewart, Matthew, Earl of Lennox 143
Stuckeley, Thomas 186–189

Tailboys, Bessie see Blount, Bessie
Tailboys, Elizabeth 32–34, 174
Tailboys, George Lord 85, 96
Tailboys, Gilbert Lord 34, 45, 51, 60
Tailboys, Robert 34
Tait, William 53
Taylor, Ralph 161
Tempest, Thomas 53
Throckmorton, George 71
Tunstall, Cuthbert 41, 153

Vaughan, Stephen 131
Vaux, Nicholas 20
Verney, Eleanor 22
Vesey, John 63

Veyrier, Johan 11, 12
Vives, Juan Luís 41

Warbeck, Perkin 3
Warham, William, Archbishop of Canterbury 14, 69, 70, 79
Weston, Francis 116
Weston, Richard 44
Wicter, Marie 62
Willoughby, Catherine see Brandon, Catherine
Wolsey, Thomas, Cardinal 8, 16, 17, 20, 24–26, 31–34, 39, 42, 44, 45, 47, 52 -63, 65–74, 83–85, 90, 97, 155
Wriothesley, Thomas 131, 132, 134, 148, 155, 156
Wyatt, Henry 53
Wyatt, Margaret later Lee 191, 192
Wyatt, Thomas 122, 191

Zápolya, János of Transylvania, King of Hungary and Croatia 79